HOLY COW

BROADWAY BOOKS
New York

HOLY COW

Sarah Macdonald

BROADWAY

A previous edition of this book was originally published in 2002 by Bantam Books, Transworld Publishers. It is here reprinted by arrangement with Bantam Books, Transworld Publishers.

For information, contact: Bantam Books, Transworld Publishers, a division of Random House Australia Pty Ltd, 20 Alfred Street, Milsons Point, NSW 2061.

PRINTED IN THE UNITED STATES OF AMERICA

Visit our website at www.broadwaybooks.com

First Broadway Books trade paperback edition published 2003

Library of Congress Cataloging-in-Publication Data

Macdonald, Sarah.
Holy Cow : an Indian adventure / Sarah Macdonald.
p. cm.
Originally published: Sydney : Bantam Books, 2002.
ISBN 0-7679-1574-7
1. Macdonald, Sarah—Travel—India—New Delhi.
2. New Delhi (India)—Description and travel.
3. New Delhi (India)—Social life and customs. I. Title.

DS486.D3M215 2004
954'.56052'092—dc21
[B] 2003052456

10 9

To my mum and dad for having me
To Jonathan for taking me
and
To India for making me.

CONTENTS

PREFACE

A GOOD HAND JOB

New Delhi airport 1988

"Madam, pleazzzzzzzzzze."

A high-pitched wheezy whine in my ear.

"For the final time, fuuuuuuuck off."

My low growl through clenched teeth is a shamefully unoriginal, pathetic response, but it's all I'm capable of at two on Christmas morning. For three days my friend Nic and I have been sitting on plastic airport chairs waiting for the stifling, stinky smog to lift. For three nights I've lain on a bed in an airport hotel listening to Nic bounce the sounds of violent double-ender projectile vomits and diarrhea explosions off the bathroom walls.

India is Hotel California: you can check out anytime you like, but you can never leave.

Tonight, in such a lovely place, the voices down my ear corridor belong to the airport toilet cleaner. He has abandoned his post at the urinal to pursue his part-time job as a professional beggar. Shuffling in a stooped circle, he hovers around us as patient and persistent as a vulture waiting for death. He can smell our exhaustion and weakness, and we can smell him—his blue overalls are stained with urine and stink of mothballs; his breath reeks of *paan*, the red chewing tobacco that smells like a mix of overripe fruit and fluoride.

At long last a nasal voice calls our flight. The beggar shuffles forward to make his final swoop.

"Madaaamz, sweet ladies, any spare rupees, please give, please, no wife, many cheeldren, you reesh, me poor, pleeeaze."

His pitiful eyes pierce consciences swollen with Western guilt. His prey surrenders. With her final energy, Nic digs in her pocket and gives the man our last few filthy notes, saved for an emergency toilet supply. The old beggar straightens up, grabs her hand and smiles—his teeth a rainbow of green, yellow and red stains.

"Good money, madamz, so I give you good hand job."

Taking the horrified look on Nic's face to be one of acceptance, he bows his head over her palm, looks up and drones, "Oh madam, very soon marriage, very soon babies, two babies. Oh dear, only girls."

He shakes his head and stifles a tear of sympathy.

"But nice girls, good girls. And madamz, good-bye, never India again, good-bye."

Despite my exhaustion and exasperation, I somehow find the energy to laugh. Nic doesn't believe in marriage, never wants kids and, despite having shed half her body weight down India's toilets, is vowing to return.

The old beggar bugger startles, stiffens and wheels around to face me. He grabs my hand in his claw, smooths its lines with his thick thumb, spits a volley of red *paan* at my feet and perves at my palm. Raising his bloodshot eyes to mine he whispers ominously, "You, you, late marriage, old marriage, very sad. You get great jobbing, happy jobbing, meeting big people jobbing, but late loving."

I yank my hand from his, pick up my backpack and storm toward the plane.

He yells after me, “You, madam, you come back to India, you come for love, you love it, you love us again.”

I break into a run, push onto the plane and sink into my seat. As we take off I give smog-swirled New Delhi the finger.

“Good-bye and good riddance, India, I hate you and I’m never, never, ever coming back.”

1 | Through the Looking Glass

I have a dreadful long-term memory. I only remember two traumatic events of my childhood—my brother's near-death by drowning and my own near-death by humiliation when I was rescued by a lifeguard while attempting my first lap of the butterfly stroke in the local pool. I vaguely remember truth or dare kisses in the back of a bus, aged about twelve, dancing to "My Sharona" at thirteen, behaving like an absolute arsehole in my adolescence and having a hideous hippie phase involving dreadlocks and tie-dye when I was at college.

For my twenty-first birthday my parents gave me a plane ticket and a blessing to leave home and Australia for a year. This middle-class rite of passage had become a family tradition—my mother had hitchhiked around Europe in the fifties and wanted us all to experience the joy of travel before we settled into careers. My trip through Europe, Egypt and Turkey is a bit of a blur and recollections of the two-month tour of India on the way home are vague. I can see myself roadside squatting and peeing with women in wonderful saris, sunset games of beach cricket with a trinity of fat Goan men named Jesus, Joseph and Jude, and the white bright teeth of a child rickshaw driver wearing a T-shirt printed with COME ON AUSSIE COME ON. I recall angst, incredible anger, deep depression and a love-hate relationship with the country, but I can't remember why. I'd filed the soothsayer, his prophecies and my vow never to return under "young stupid rubbish" and let it fall deep into the black hole of my brain.

Until now—a month short of eleven years later.

As I walk into the plane in Singapore, a seed starts to sprout in the blocked sewer of my memory; a seed watered by the essence of stale urine and the whiff of vomit coming from my window seat (where the pink and orange paisley wallpaper artfully camouflages the spew). The high-pitched, highly excited jumble of Indian voices almost germinates a recollection. But after too many going-away parties, involving too much indulgence, I'm too wasted to let the bud bloom. I fall asleep.

Somewhere over Chennai I become aware of an increasingly rhythmic prodding of my inner thigh by something long, thin and hard. I open my eyes to see a brown finger with a long curved nail closing in on my crotch. The digit is attached to a scrawny old Sikh in a turban sitting beside me. He is slobbering and shaking with excitement. I'm too sleepy, shocked and, for some reason, too embarrassed to scream, so I buzz for sisterly assistance.

An air hostess with big hair, long nails and drag-queen makeup slowly strolls over. She looks cranky.

"What?"

"This man is touching me when I sleep," I bleat indignantly.

The hostess rolls her eyes and waggles her finger.

At me.

"Well, stay awake and don't let it happen again, madam."

She wheels on the spot and strides off, swishing her nylon sari.

Months later a friend will tell me that many Indian flight attendants are rich girls whose parents pay a massive bribe to get them a job involving travel and five-star hotels. These brats view passengers as pesky intrusions way beneath their status, and detest doing the job of a high-flying servant. But right now, I'm floored, abandoned and angry.

I stay wide-awake and alert until the hostess with the mostest sprays the cabin with foul-smelling insecticide. She aims an extra jet directly at my head. I can almost hear her thinking, *This should clean the Western whore.*

It's now that I remember that India is like Wonderland. In this other universe everyone seems mad and everything is upside down, back to front and infuriatingly bizarre. I'm Alice: fuzzy with feelings about my previous trip down the rabbit hole, I'm now flying straight back through the looking glass to a place where women are blamed for sleazy men and planes are sprayed when they fly from a clean city to a dirty one. In this world we applaud a dreadful landing that's as fast and steep as a takeoff, we jump up and tackle fellow passengers in a crush at the door while the plane is still moving, and the air hostess gets off first.

I get off last to be embraced by the cold and clammy smog. The cocktail of damp diesel fumes, swirling dust, burning cow dung, toxic chemicals, spicy sweat and sandalwood wraps me in memories. The soothsayer and his prophecies of a decade ago boil to the surface of my brain.

For the old bloke *did* give a good hand job.

My friend Nic got married soon after we came home; she then quickly popped out two gorgeous girls and has never come back to India. I'm still single and at thirty-three, by Indian standards, I'm a spinster to be pitied. I've had good jobbing—only days ago I finished my last *Morning Show* on the Triple J network. I've interviewed famous actors, crazed celebrities and brilliant musicians; I've talked with an audience I admire; and I've enjoyed a lifestyle of traveling, film premieres, theater opening nights, music gigs and festivals. I've left the best job in the world for a country that I now remember hating with a passion. And I've done it for love. My boyfriend, Jonathan, is the Australian Broadcasting Company's South Asia correspondent based in New Delhi, and after a year of yearning, soppy love songs and pathetic phone calls, we've decided we can't live apart. I look to see if the toilet cleaner is here to gloat.

A different tarmac welcoming committee emerges from the mist—five men with massive mustaches, machine guns and moronic stares, each of them clutching his own penis.

I then spend hours inching along an impossibly slow passport queue comprised of harassed foreigners, while Indians move past smiling. It takes half an hour to find my bags in the midst of a screaming and jumping porter mosh pit and another twenty minutes to have my luggage X-rayed again. By the time I am near the exit I'm frantic that I'm late for my most important date. I rush down a long exit ramp that gets steeper and steeper, pulling my trolley deeper and faster into India. I hit the bottom with a bump and fall over. Dazed, disoriented and dusty, I sense a strange sight and sound emerging from the smog. A huge hurricane fence appears to be alive. It's rocking and writhing—fingers, toes and small arms reach through wire gaps; heads poke over the barbed wire, and mouths pressed to the steel groan and moan.

"Taxieeee, taxieee, madam, taxiee, *baksheesh*, money."

Before I can pick myself up, an arm breaks through a hole in the fence, grabs my bags and starts to disappear back into the misty melee. I begin a tug of war with a person I can't see. I start to scream. "Stop. Come back, I'm getting picked up."

"No, no, you are too late, your car not coming, I am taking you," yells a voice from the end of the arm.

Could he be right? Could Jonathan have come and gone? Or been held up on a story? My doubt weakens me and I lose my grip on my bags and fall flat on my back.

Then, through the smog, a tall being with a familiar grin emerges. Jonathan rescues me, grabbing my bags from the invisible man and me to his chest. I'm momentarily comforted, then I pull away and hit him.

"You're late," I wail pathetically. Jonathan recoils like a wounded boy. This is hardly the romantic reunion we'd pictured, and not how I wanted my new life in a new country to begin.

Jonathan bundles me into the Australian Broadcasting Company car with a promise of a stiff drink and a warm new home. We drive slowly through New Delhi's winter streets which seem like hell frozen over, or perhaps purgatory. I can't see beside or beyond the car. Foghorns hail from huge trucks sailing too close for comfort, and every time we stop at a red traffic light, which impossibly instructs us to RELAX in large white uneven letters, a ghostly torso or a gaunt face with an expression straight from *The Scream* rises from the milky depths. Long, skinny Addams family fingers rap on the window—death knocks from beggars. I shrink from the beings as if they're lepers and then realize many actually are. Still freaked from seeing bits of people through the airport fence, I'm now scared by seeing people without bits.

We stop at a huge black gate opened by a very small man with an extraordinarily large mustache and an even bigger smile. It appears he has won a beauty contest of some sort, as he's wearing a white pants suit with a red sash that says WEST END. Beyond Mr. West End looms my new home. I hit Jonathan again: I've left a sunny apartment by the sea in Sydney for a dark, dingy first-floor flat on the intersection of two of New Delhi's busiest roads.

Inside, the flat is large but lifeless; its white walls are stained with diesel fumes and bordered with dark wood; its marble floors are cold, cracked and yellow; its rooms almost empty, bar some ugly, Australian Broadcasting Company–issue pine furniture. Jonathan is a house-proud bloke, but he left most of his things in Australia and has been traveling almost constantly for a year. He quickly promises we will move or renovate. I try not to look too disappointed and he perks me up with champagne and a bedroom strewn with rose petals.

We fall asleep rocked by the reassurance of a love reunion and the traffic vibrations.

• • •

The next morning, after a Sunday sleep-in, we wake wrapped in a noxious cloud of smog and dirty diesel fumes. Marooned inside on the couch we sip *chai*—gorgeous tea made with cinnamon, ginger, boiled milk and a tablespoon of sugar. When the smog lifts we move to the deck to watch a roaring rough sea of traffic wildlife. All around us a furious knot of men and metal constantly unravels and re-forms, ebbing and flowing and going nowhere fast.

Blokes—and a friend or two—perch atop tall, rusty bicycles. Entire families share motorcycles; toddlers stand between dads' knees or clutch his back, and wives sit sidesaddle while snuggling babies. Auto-rickshaws zip around like tin toys. Ambassador cars—half Rolls-Royce and half Soviet tank—cruise with class. Huge tinsel-decorated trucks rumble and groan, filthy lime-green buses fly around like kamikaze cans squeezing out a chunky sauce of arms and legs. Shoes dangle from back bumpers and black demonic faces poke out red tongues from windshields; these are for good luck. But it's probably the holy mantra written on the backs of vehicles that keeps things moving It's not BABY ON BOARD, or JESUS SAVES, or TRIPLE M DOES DELHI. Instead, hand-painted in swirling childish capital letters is: HORN PLEASE.

Everyone seems to drive with one finger on the horn and another shoved high up a nostril. The highway soundtrack is a chaotic symphony of deep blasts, staccato honks, high-pitched beeps, musical notes and a weird duck drone. It's as if Delhi is blind and driving by sound—except it seems many are deaf. Women are curled up on the pavement sound asleep, and a man is stretched out on the median strip, dead to the danger. On the backs of bikes, on the laps of the motorcycle mums, babies are floppy with dreams.

It's clear it would be suicide to drive here and luckily I won't have to. The Australian Broadcasting Company has a driver, Abraham. Abraham's thick curls have crawled off his head like furry caterpillars and they now encircle his ears. He wears a mean pair of black Cuban-heeled cowboy boots and fake Levi's.

But Abe is no cowboy. Small, skinny and incredibly jumpy, he's worked for the Australian Broadcasting Company for twenty-five years but still seems nervous around boss-sahibs. He wrings his hands when Jonathan asks him a question, and whispers answers so quietly we have to lean close to pick them up. This just makes him more nervous and he jumps back as if we are going to hit him. Mild-mannered Abe, however, is Tarzan of the traffic jungle. He knows the strict species pecking order: pedestrians are on the bottom and run out of the way of everything, bicycles make way for cycle-rickshaws, which give way to auto-rickshaws, which stop for cars, which are subservient to trucks. Buses stop for one thing and one thing only. Not customers—they jump on while the buses are still moving. The only thing that can stop a bus is the king of the road, the lord of the jungle and the top dog.

The holy cow.

Eighty-two percent of Indians are Hindus. Hindus revere cows, probably because one of their favorite gods, Krishna, is a cowherd, and Shiva—the Lord of Destruction—has a bull called Nandi.

I've always thought it hilarious that Indian people chose the most boring, domesticated, compliant and stupid animal on earth to adore, but already I'm seeing cows in a whole different light. These animals clearly know they rule and they like to mess with our heads. The humpbacked bovines step off median strips just as cars are approaching, they stare down drivers daring them to charge, they turn their noses up at passing elephants and camels, and hold huddles at the busiest intersections where they seem to chat away like the bulls of Gary Larson cartoons. It's clear they are enjoying themselves.

But for animals powerful enough to stop traffic and holy enough that they'll never become steak, cows are treated dreadfully. Scrawny and sickly, they survive by grazing on garbage that's dumped in plastic bags. The bags collect in their stomachs and strangulate their innards, killing the cows slowly and painfully. Jonathan has already done a story about the urban cowboys of New Delhi who lasso the animals and take them to volunteer vets for operations. Unfortunately the cows are privately owned and once they are restored to health they must be released to eat more plastic.

New Delhi and its cows can wait, though. Jonathan and I need a week's holiday and a catch-up after a year apart.

Before dawn on Monday morning, Abraham drives us through wide avenues, around green traffic circles, past a flower market, and drops us at the New Delhi train station, which doubles as a pavement hotel—rows and rows of bodies stretch across the station—entire families snoring away atop ripped sheets of plastic, filthy rags or just the hard concrete ground.

We negotiate an obstacle course of bodies lying comatose on the concrete as we scamper after a scrawny porter who insists on carrying our backpacks upon his head. The old bloke keeps stumbling and shakes with Parkinson's disease, so Jonathan ends up carrying our bags and very nearly the porter, who looks at our train seats with an obvious longing for a good nap. Feeling sorry for him, I hand him fifty rupees (one dollar). But just before the train lurches from the platform, he's back, yelling at me about "no-good money" and throwing the notes on my lap. I look down and swear—I've accidentally given him fifty American dollars and the poor guy has no idea of its worth. Humiliated more by his mistake than mine, I hand him one hundred rupees to appease us both. He stumbles off singing with delight and a crowd gathers around him in shock. It's way too much. (For the next two years the porters at New Delhi station will recognize me as the Mad Madam who paid two dollars for nothing, and demand a similarly huge sum. Some will even shake to arouse my sympathy.)

Early morning is not an attractive time to travel in India. As we slowly pull out of the city we are hailed with the twenty-one-hundred-bum salute of slum dwellers squatting beside the tracks doing their morning "ablutions." Some smile and wave but most don't even seem to see the train. It's as if Indians, living in a country too crowded for privacy, have developed a remarkable ability to look without seeing. They don't notice the children grabbing their shawls, the beggars pulling at their pants, the filth or the misery, and they seem deaf to the call of the country—a violent guttural growling retch: *crrroooooooooooaaaaaaaaaaaaak*, punctuated by a giant spit of phlegm: *pppppttttttttttttttttttttttttaaaaaaaaaaab*!

It's a sound that punctuates morning, noon and night. Dawn is obviously peak croak time. Inside and outside the carriage a round of throat-clearing begins and crescendos into a symphony of spitting. At about nine it abruptly stops and everyone slurps *chai* and settles back to snore, burp and fart like foghorns. The chorus of bodily functions is loud enough to permeate the music playing through the headphones of my portable CD player.

By nine-thirty the ablution hours have ended and it's safe to look outside the window again. Beyond the gap between the two panes (where a gray mouse is having a great time) we see village after village that looks as if it's been bombed. Concrete bunker homes have roofs of rubble and twisted metal, plastic is piled up on earth huts and the streets of sandy soil are covered in rubbish. Battered buffalo, black-bristled pigs, skittish goats, horribly thin horses and red-arsed mangy monkeys graze the waste. We never lose sight of humanity. Women in bright cotton saris are shopping, sweeping, threshing, planting, weeding, water-collecting, plaiting hair and carrying huge loads of produce on their heads. Children play cricket, fly kites, scrub clean for school and scamper about. Men are mostly sitting on string charpoy beds, drinking small cups of *chai*, playing cards or just squatting on their heels and watching the world go by.

Five hours later we chug into the small town of Derradun where we hire a taxi to take us the two hundred kilometers to Rishikesh. After haggling over the price—which is ten times what it should be, because we aren't Indian—a scrawny, dopey-looking driver who speaks some English promises to be ready in an hour.

"I am Kunti. Kunti will come in one hours," he yells.

We duck into a fly-infested restaurant, where we are pointedly ignored by cheesecloth-clad tourists in trainee dreadlocks who seem determined to believe they are the only travelers to have discovered the delights of Derradun. We eat and wait. And wait. And wait.

After two hours Jonathan waits by the restaurant door while I walk up the long dusty road where we saw Kunti heading earlier. While attempting to avoid a scuzzy dog that has half its brain showing through its scalp, I accidentally walk through a circle of men who gape and giggle hysterically at my arse. I'm wearing hideously baggy pants and vow to buy a sack for future travels. I come across some sort of a taxi rest stop and find our driver lying on a charpoy rope bed holding hands and linking legs with another man. I hate to break up such an intimate scene, but after being ignored for a couple of minutes I walk over to the end of the bed with my hands on my hips and say in my best hey-I-don't-mind-if-you're-gay-but-you've-got-a-job-to-do voice, "You are our taxi man to Rishikesh."

"Yes, madam, I am Kunti." He wobbles his head and doesn't take his eyes off his mate, whose arm he is now stroking.

"You're late."

"No, madam, on time."

He's still not looking at me.

"You were meant to come an hour ago," I sigh (I'm getting really cranky now).

"Yeeeeesss," drawls his friend.

"We've come, we're there," snaps Kunti.

"No, you are here."

"And there."

"So you are here and there?"

"Yes, madam."

They both roll their eyes as if I'm mad.

"So you are in two places at once, are you?"

My eyes are now rolling back in my head.

"Yes."

The driver now moves his eyes to focus on his friend's crotch.

"Can you say no?"

"Yes, madam."

"Say it then."

"Yes, madam."

I stomp back to the restaurant ranting and raving like a lunatic and remembering more and more about why this country drove me mad. Jonathan is sympathetic but more practiced at patience.

"Just think, I have to work here," he laughs, but his eyes betray a rising fear that I'll leave him within a month.

The Tweedledee and Tweedledum of Derradun turn up an hour later pretending it's two hours before and that the previous conversation never happened.

But their Ambassador cab makes up for their shortcomings. It has brown velour seats, an orange roof and a back-window curtain of purple paisley, and it doubles as a mobile temple. The dashboard has a fluorescent Ganesh (the elephant god), an orange toy cow, a snow dome of Sathya Sai Baba (the Afro-haired living god of Bangalore) and a blue plastic Shiva bouncing on a spring. A brown, four-armed Barbie in a sari stands on a lotus and she has an aura of tiny lights that flash when we brake.

"She is Lakshmi, goddess of money," states Tweedledee.

"Our favorite," adds Tweedledum, who is practically sitting on his boyfriend's lap.

"Undoubtedly," laughs Jonathan, clearly amused by the antics of the daft duo.

Below Lakshmi is a faded photo of the driver's parents, a tiny national flag saying "Proud to Be Indian" and a CD spinning on a string. During my last trip to India I was an extreme atheist, contemptuous of all religion. I'd arrogantly ignored the color and spectacle of Hinduism and its acceptance of a multitude of ways to the divine. Now I find myself immediately tickled by the kitsch aesthetic and within half an hour I'm almost a convert—praying to all these gods and more—because Kunti, the most annoying man in the world, drives like the maddest, playing chicken with everything on the road, including the chickens. With one hand on the horn and another on his friend's horn, Kunti steers with his knees and speeds straight toward anything that could kill us, veering just as we are about to crash. I shut my eyes, Jonathan swears and the driver and his friend sing along to a tape featuring the high-pitched wail of a woman obviously being tortured.

Then, of course, after assuring us they know exactly where they are going, we get hopelessly lost.

"You don't know where Rishikesh is, do you?" I say.

"Yes, of course, madam."

"Well, why are you stopping and asking everyone and why do you keep changing directions then?"

They turn the tape up.

Jonathan yells over the top, "Are you lost?"

They ignore us.

Sometime later, on a narrow road where gray stones cascade down a sharp valley, we get out to wee behind some rocks. Just as I'm yanking up my pants a school bus pulls up and all the children get out and run toward us with cameras and autograph books. We bolt like Beatles having a hard day's night, pursued by schoolboys screaming "photo, photo," and girls with long neat plaits giggling "autograph, Auntie, autograph." They trap us beside the car, and we give in.

This is my first photo op this trip, but I'm already on mantelpieces all over India. I now remember that I spent hours on my last journey posing for snaps while holding young babies, hand in hand with shy daughters and with boys trying to put their arm around their easy Western girlfriend. It's again time to abandon shyness, personal space and privacy and to become spectacle as well as spectator. Eleven years ago, as an awkward postadolescent, this annoyed me intensely, but now I see it's a fair exchange for my voyeurism.

Besides, I'm now better at being public property and ready for a change in my public role. Being a broadcaster at Triple J isn't just a job; it's a life. In Australia my identity has been defined through the airwaves. I really enjoy being part of people's lives but I've grown weary of the pitfalls. F-grade celebrities get the sperm-covered letters without the sex, the death threats without the protection and the stalkers without the psychological assistance. A persistent, psychologically troubled bloke had been pestering me for the last year, and while one of my bosses thought it must have been "flattering," it just made me feel scared, vulnerable and violated. Stalkers colonize your mind and I wanted mine back. Leaving my wonderful job was the hardest thing I've ever done but perhaps I didn't do it just for love. A part of me wanted to reclaim myself, to redefine my identity, to grow up professionally, to embrace anonymity and to get rid of the stalker. In some ways I'm already regretting my move away from the good life but right now I'm enjoying the fact that here in India I'm famous for just being white.

In trade for our photo, the school bus driver gives us the first sensible directions to Rishikesh and we head up the Himalayan foothills to stay in a room on the grounds of a handsome old hunting lodge. We tip Tweedledum and Tweedledee handsomely for not killing us and then kiss the ground. Here, a gorgeous garden somehow grows out of crumbling dry dirt: white and pink poppies, yellow chrysanthemums, deep crimson buds, orange star-shaped things and some bizarre cabbage-like vegetables. Steep, jagged cliffs with profiles like steak knives rise above us. Tiny villages perch perilously on top. The buzz of a billion Indians and their noisy cars is so distant I can now hear subtle sounds: the caw of crows, the squawk of mynah birds and the chattering squeak of a tiny squirrel. Yet it's a landscape of tired splendor. The sky is too exhausted to be blue and it sits low on my shoulders; the earth seems drained of its vitality and the trees are limp and dusty. The only thing showing any sparkle is the Ganges—it burbles over small rapids swirling blue-green and broad.

Swimming in India's most holy river is meant to cleanse you of sin, and a sign in front of our hut reads: IF YOU STAND ON ONE LEG IN GANGA WATERS FROM ONE NEW MOON TO THE NEXT—NOT ADVISABLE—IT WILL HEAL YOUR BODY OF ANY PROBLEM IN ANY ORGAN.

Jonathan and I decide to take our host's sensible advice and let our eyes be healed by a quiet look at the holy waters.

But even here, in the middle of nowhere, there's someone. Within twenty seconds two young imps with fishing rods appear and squat beside us to exchange the usual dialogue of the traveler. This involves exchanging "good" names (everyone's names are good in India), admitting we are Australian and agreeing that

Shane Warne is a great cricketer but a naughty man. That's the end of the boys' English but they seem content to stay and stare at us with absolute fascination and intense concentration. We sing them a few verses of "Waltzing Matilda" as if to earn their adoration, but then resolve to shake them by walking through the scrub.

Deep within the faded foliage we're still not alone. Women with long skirts, silver anklets and broad backs unload huge bundles of sticks from their heads as they take time out from their work to laugh at us. We escape by climbing a mountain. Right on the lip, an ancient lady with a weathered, leathery face decorated with tiny tattoos emerges from nowhere and blocks our way. She reaches out, cups my face in her huge, hard hand and babbles in Hindi. I don't understand a word but I'm spellbound. It seems she's telling me something I can't hear but need to know, perhaps that in India solitude is a selfish pursuit and there are rewards for going without.

One day we take a trip into Rishikesh itself, the Ganges holy town where the Beatles came to meet the Maharishi. It's a dirty, dusty strip of clogged streets, ashram yoga centers and mad markets. Spirituality is for sale.

We walk past 3-D photos of Indian gods, plastic key rings of saints, T-shirts saying "Om," vials of holy Ganges water, photos of fat movie stars and even the ratty, dust-clogged dreadlocks of shorn *sadhus*. *Sadhu*s are men who have abandoned their families to travel India's sacred sites and dedicate their lives to worship. They and the shopkeepers seem to worship us as walking dollar signs—we are constantly surrounded, followed, hassled and ordered to give money or buy crap at one hundred times the local price.

We tire of inane chats that always end in "come to my shop," free guided tours that inevitably lead to a beg for funds and offerings of assistance with *puja* (prayers and offerings), which inevitably descend into demands for a huge donation to the nearest

Brahman (a member of the priestly caste). It seems these people are either deaf to the word "no" or they are the biggest optimists in the world—they follow us for miles still trying their sales pitch, their begging plea or their speech about the delights of Rishikesh. One little girl chases me and pulls my shirt for half an hour. I give in and buy her little pots of colored powder for forehead *tikka* spots, but when I open them I realize the gold and silver containers are empty. I return to complain but the imp has gone and in her place is a woman begging.

She hasn't got a face.

Above her neck is a mass of melted flesh like burned candle wax. Two pools of black stare out and stumps of burned flesh wrapped in rags plead up at me. I retch in horror and run. This is my first glimpse of a dowry burning—where a woman is set alight in a "cooking accident" because her husband or mother-in-law wants more dowry money and attempts to kill to get it. If the bride dies, the husband can marry again and collect another dowry; if she lives, she can be shamed into leaving the house as damaged, useless goods. I want to scream with shock, fury and sadness but there're too many people staring at me, following me and grabbing me. There's just no room for rage.

I cross a huge bridge but India is on the other side as well, everywhere there's a mass of begging, pleading, needing, naked wretchedness.

It's Christmas Day and I think I shall go mad here.

In an effort to find some peace on earth, Jonathan pulls me down dark twisting alleyways stretching away from the river. In a street that oozes black mud a man emerges from behind a curtain to hail us warmly. He points to his sign: WEL-CUM ASTROLOGER TO THE STARS.

Jonathan, camera ever by his side, sees an opportunity for a story that the Australian Broadcasting Company will love for the cliché-ridden Christmas silly season—a prediction piece for the new millennium. Our astrologer, Mr. Rakesh, grins at the request and, with a flourish and a bow, pulls aside a curtain to admit us into a tiny room cramped with clumsy, ugly furniture, and adorned with photos of himself and photos of his parents ringed with leis of saffron marigold flowers. Dressed in a stiff white shirt and flared brown hipster pants, Mr. Rakesh orders *chai* from a street urchin, then combs his bright red hennaed hair into a rock-abilly quiff and twirls his mustache in readiness for filming. Dead-pan and directly down the barrel of the camera, he yells at breakneck speed without pausing for breath.

"The year 2000 will be a great year for India, Sonia Gandhi will not become Prime Minister because she is not an Indian, we shall win the cricket because we're the best sportsmen in the world and India will continue to be the most intelligent, most scientific, most spiritual and best country in the universe."

I remark that his predictions sound very pro-India. Mr. Rakesh nods vigorously.

"Yes, you noticed, this is so, but I am telling you, it is usual. We are, of course, genetically superior to all other races, so I find it difficult to be less than modest. What to do?"

While I splutter into my tea, the astrologer rants about India's accomplishments.

"We invented the zero, the Taj Mahal is one of the Seven Wonders of the World and Varanasi is the oldest city in the world."

I'm brimming with all I can't say: I've heard that Damascus invented the zero and is also the oldest continuously occupied civilization on the planet, and that the Taj, while wonderful, is actually not an official World Wonder. I bite my tongue, until he continues.

"We are, of course, dear madam, also the land of peace and truth."

I crack and can't resist a snarl.

"Mr. Rakesh, if India is the land of truth, why have I been hassled and lied to and ripped off from the moment I got here?"

He nods sympathetically.

"Sister, I am sorry, there are some bad people everywhere, isn't it? Let me atone for my compatriots' crudity. You will do one thing. Tell me your details and I will tell you your future in our country for no charge."

Jonathan laughs and submits, giving his date and time of birth. Mr. Rakesh beams and somehow calculates his stars on the spot.

"Sir, you are loving India, you will work very hard here, next year you will face danger and have great success. This year you will finally learn to dance."

I beg to be excused, telling Mr. Rakesh that my mother has no idea of the exact time of my birth. The astrologer waves this aside.

"Madam, don't be worrying, I'll do it by numbers."

He allocates a number to each letter of my name, scribbles a long complicated equation involving dividing and subdividing and multiplication. Mr. Rakesh then leans back, scratches his head, rubs his butt and says, "Oh."

That can't be good.

He calculates again, sighs and leans forward with a stern expression and a tone that bids beware the Jabberwock.

"Well, madam, I will tell you one thing. You must listen. You are back in India for a good shaking. Here you will dance with death and be reborn. You will be a chameleon of karma and there are many guides to show you the way. You will search India's land of gods and find faith."

2 | Death, Rebirth and Sputum

We stagger back to our hut, Jonathan bent with laughter and me cursing India's futurists all the way home. But under my anger I'm freaked. If a beggar at an airport can correctly predict my future, why can't a jingoistic astrologer? I stand and watch the sunset over the Ganges, feeling superstitious and silly and sick of Indian soothsayers predicting futures I don't want. I wade into the waters, willing the river to cleanse my sin so I can avoid my fate. But the water doesn't feel holy—it feels freezing and silty and it smells like sewage. I dunk, scream with shock and look up to see a saffron-robed *sadhu* with long dreadlocks watching me from a cave. He waves his hand in half salute, half dismissal. I look back toward the room. Jonathan waves from the balcony with a Christmas drink. Much more attractive.

I have a beer and go to bed.

Just after midnight I'm thrown from my sleep—literally—and wake up on a floor that's trying to buck me off. Jonathan is white, wide-eyed and sitting bolt upright on the bed, which is lurching and banging against the wall like the bed in that scene from *The Exorcist*—he even slowly turns the possessed Linda Blair shade of green. I stand up punch-drunk and staggering and screaming with rage.

"That's it, I've had this country! This place is unfit for human habitation, it's mad! Why are we here? What the hell have I done? I've left my job, for this place! Why can't we be normal and live where we were born? Sydney is safe. What the hell do you wear for an earthquake anyway? Jeans?"

Jonathan suddenly de-stuns, jumps off the bed, grabs my hand and pulls me outside.

We sit on the lawn as the earth rocks. The Indian holiday hut and lodge guests sit in a circle, order tea and chat about the weather. It's as if they experience quakes daily and this is but a rumble. Jonathan drags me away from their party, for as I ride the aftershocks, I begin to regurgitate my repressed memories of why I never wanted to come here again. It's a vomit of hatred and a rambling rage against the bullshit, the pushing, the shoving, the rip-offs, the cruelty, the crowds, the pollution, the weather, the begging, the performance of pity, the pissing, the shitting, the snotting, the spitting and the farting.

As I hear myself rant I begin to hate myself for hating—for being so middle class and pampered and comfortable that I should now be so shell-shocked. I am shaken to my core; the ground, that stable and strong bed beneath me, has moved and it's stirred something once rock solid within. I put my head in my hands and cry. The astrologer is right; I need a new way of living in the world if I'm to stay in this country. Perhaps this is my dance with death that he predicted.

The quake does bring death to others. By Indian standards the damage is small—one hundred and ten people are killed and three hundred and eighty injured when an entire village slips down a Himalayan hill. It hardly even makes the news.

After the road rubble is cleared we return to Delhi, yet the city and our flat have yet to feel like a safe sanctuary. As I lie in bed at night, the traffic vibrations bring back memories of earthquake tremors and the cold, dark, empty flat feels like a tomb. The Australian Broadcasting Company office, directly above, soaks up all the available light and its rooftop washing area drips cold mold onto our ceilings.

Jonathan heads upstairs to get back to work. I set about getting to know the home staff, or the servants, a situation I've been dreading for its awkwardness and unfairness. I've worked as a cleaner, a waitress, a nanny and a cook, but I never, in my weirdest dreams, imagined I would one day have my own hired help.

Rachel, the cook, has a beautiful round face with deep dimples, dark skin and a huge white smile. Her first words to me (accompanied with a giggle) are: "Thank God you are here, sir has been sulky for a year."

This first sign of Indian cheek strengthens me with its familiarity, so I decide Rachel will be the first to stop calling me "madam," and I get working on it straightaway (I'm Sarah within a month).

Mary, our cleaner, never gives lip. She is rake-thin, sweet and shy with me. But she is great friends with Rachel and all morning I hear their rounded Tamil talk (they're both from Chennai in south India) and peals of laughter from the kitchen. I suspect they're comparing notes about their new madam, wondering why their spunky single sir has been missing such a weird-looking chick and probably concluding that it's because I put out before marriage. They must find this shocking. Rachel and Mary are devout Christians. As is Abe—his tiny flat above the garage is watched over by a portrait of a pale blond Jesus and a sari-clad Virgin Mary made of three-dimensional plastic molding. Abe's wife is also called Mary and he has three children—Angel, Assumpta and a son called Noah.

Our laundry man, or *dhobie* wallah, Moolchand, is a Hindu

who loves the mischievous cowherd god Krishna and makes sure our statue on the stairs is as shiny blue as possible in this pollution. Moolchand has a face like a comic actor—his round fat cheeks are cracked from ear to ear with a *paan*-stained grin. He has too much zest, too many teeth and too much happiness for one man.

Moolchand teaches me how to say a few words in Hindi: *namaste* and *kya hal he*—"hello" and "how are you." Every person I try it on says *teekay* (okay) in reply, but Moolchand is never okay. He's always "veeeeery happy, veeery happy" and he claps his hands and wiggles his head to demonstrate. He should be on television.

Our *chowkidor*s, or guards, are Lakan and Aamar. Lakan is tall and thin, Aamar is small and skinny. Neither speaks very much English but they're always smiley-faced, bored out of their brains and devotedly helpful. They run to open the car door (racing Abraham who often jumps to do it while the car is still moving), carry my parcels, open the house door and run up to the market for Rachel.

Downstairs is our landlord, retired General Kumar, who has an impeccable Delhi pedigree, and once owned a large slab of the West End. This suburb was originally built as a gated estate for high-ranking military personnel. Behind massive wrought iron gates grand homes rise reminiscent of *Dynasty* gone dilapidated; mock Tudor or Georgian facades are faded or filthy, and because Indians build onto their houses as their wealth and families grow there's quite a hodgepodge of styles within each house and each block. There are a number of small potholed parks complete with faded foliage clumsily cut into animal shapes. But these open spaces are difficult to access as they are surrounded by high fences and usually locked up to keep out the cows and commoners. The General has seen his suburb rapidly ringed by roads, suburbia and slums and watched former comrades die and move away to be replaced by foreigners and the new money set. But this doesn't seem to upset him. More British than the British, at eighty he has vim and vigor and still follows a jolly good army routine. He's up at oh-five hundred walking the neighborhood, upright but bandy-legged, swinging a small riding crop. At oh-six hundred he inspects his staff troops and then eats and reads papers until his afternoon bridge game.

One night over a pre-dinner whiskey the General entertains us with stories about being stationed in Delhi in the days of the Raj with his old friend David Niven.

"Of course that was before Niven took up with that frightful acting crowd. The old boy came to visit me here many years ago and telegrammed to remind me he would bring his wife. I wrote back to him saying, that's fine, old chap, but which wife?"

He gives his Nepalese houseboy a nudge with his evening cane so he laughs and we all join in. Indian humor appears to be an acquired taste.

The General tells me some of the history of my new hometown. Delhi is actually a series of eight cities ruled and ruined by sultans, slave dynasties, horse traders, Mogul kings and, of course, the British Raj. Each dynasty built their own city, and splendid buildings rot in ruins, except for the still vibrant Mogul center now known as Old Delhi, and the planned British parliamentary and diplomatic areas of New Delhi. The streets have run with blood several times, including when modern India was created in 1947. Yet the violent past is not as past as I would like. In 1984 two Sikh bodyguards shot Prime Minister Indira Gandhi, unleashing a wave of anti-Sikh violence; hundreds were bashed, shot and necklaced with burning tires. A mob armed with knives and guns even came to the gates of genteel West End and rattled for entry. The General huffed up to the gate and faced the madmen alone.

"I am General Kumar, there are no Sikhs here, go away."

The fifty madmen turned and tormented the next settlement down the road.

I should feel safer knowing the suburb's savior is so close but since the earthquake and the steady diet of sensory overload, I'm feeling increasingly vulnerable. New Delhi has a veneer of diplomatic nicety—but its mansions sit beside slums, and the traffic circles of rubbish and potholed paths lead to streets of poverty and despair. I feel as if I'm living on a thin crust atop molten madness and I can still sense the earthquake every time I sit or lie down. What's more, Delhi is supposedly cursed. It's said that whoever builds a city here is doomed to lose it. The General guffaws at my fears.

"Old codswaddle and superstition, my dear, but if you want to play it safe it's best to align yourself with the latest invaders."

"Who are they?"

"Those bothersome, tasteless, showy, nouveau riche, pushy people from the state of Punjab. They own the city now."

Luckily, just days before New Year's Eve, a Punjabi calls. And she *is* rather pushy. Jonathan looks confused as he tries to keep up with the frantic fast chatter she fires down the phone line.

"Hi, how are you? My name is Razoo Kapoor, I went to college in Australia and I loved it so, I rrrrrrrreeeealy miss it. I found your Australian Broadcasting Company number in the phone book, so why don't you come over for dinner? My mummy will be in so no alcohol please."

Jonathan says, "Sure." (He hasn't yet made many Indian friends and while this woman sounds very forward, we figure that just means she's a true-blue Punjabi and will definitely be worth knowing.)

Razoo stresses again no alcohol, gives her address, stresses no alcohol again, gives a time and stresses she really can't have alcohol in the house.

So, clutching limp roadside roses and no alcohol, we get Abraham to drive us for hours through the streets of Delhi at dusk. Smoke from cowpat fires clings to floating filth and smog, shrouding endless ruins of settlements and suburbs of decayed splendor. Abraham pulls up outside a nondescript apartment block and we climb steep dark stairs to a comforting port in the storm—a small flat that's lit up like a beacon. The door is opened by a bouncy beautiful babe with sparkling eyes, huge full lips and sleek jet-black thick hair.

"Welcome to India, I have a special surprise for you Ozzies, verrry special. Come come come in."

Razoo holds a bottle of nonalcoholic pink Spumante above her head, pops it ceremoniously and pours it into special crystal glasses. With a room full of strangers looking on, we are forced to drink and smile appreciatively. It tastes like warm, thick, sickly sweet bubble bath.

Razoo's mother (who insists I call her Auntie) pushes us down onto a couch of soft cushions and tells us about her visit to Australia. Razoo, she says, dragged her to a bar in Melbourne that was so smoky and smelly Auntie had to leave and then fainted on Chapel Street. As her daughter squatted down beside her, a crowd gathered to stare at her sari. One man inquired, "Is she drunk?"

This outrageous insult broke through Auntie's coma. She sat up and slapped him.

"I'm not drunk, I'm Indian."

Auntie is an international teacher of Gandhian philosophy and is adamant that good Hindus do not drink.

"Drinking rots the mind, the body and the soul and stops one from accessing inner truth. Hindus want that truth, we will not drink."

The young crowd listens intently. A circle of girls is sitting straight-backed, all with luxuriant long hair, wearing delicate earrings and *salwar kamiz* suits (long tunic tops over matching pants) teamed with pretty *dupatta* shawls. A row of boys is standing scrubbed clean, all wearing neat jeans and earnest auras. After the lecture, Razoo's three cousins turn to me, and the eldest announces proudly, "We are all studying to be dentists."

"Why?"

"It's a very honorable profession."

The room murmurs in agreement.

"But everyone is scared of dentists," I declare rather undiplomatically.

They all look at each other stunned.

"Why?"

"Because they hurt."

"Oh no, we won't hurt," the eldest smiles comfortingly.

"Doesn't your dentist hurt?"

Blank looks all around.

"We've never been."

"Never?"

"No, most definitely no. We eat food that's good for health and our teeth are perfect. Isn't it?"

It is. I've never met such good, dutiful and successful children with such good teeth in my life. The only sign of rebellion here comes from one guy who slouches in his chair, making a big show of his cowboy boots, and goes outside for a ciggy. Radical. The crowd appears not to have a cynical bone among them; our self-deprecating Australian sense of humor is mostly met with polite but stony stares.

All the same, I have a feeling Razoo will become an ally. She works in television, has a naughty look in her big beautiful brown eyes and a desire to go to New York. Her fiancé, Sunil, scowls when she mentions her plans, but she doesn't seem to care. Her best friend is nicknamed Billie (Hindi for cat) after her gorgeous green eyes. Billie has light skin, a shiny bob and beautiful teeth, and is quick to tell me she's not Punjabi. She is in fact a Delhi-bred Brahman of the highest class, with a family so strictly Hindu that even her dog is vegetarian. Razoo rolls her eyes.

"I am Billie's lower-class refugee friend from the Punjab who drinks street *chai* and ruins Billie's reputation. She shall never get a husband until I go to New York and stop making trouble."

I ask Billie what she'll be up to on New Year's Eve and she mentions television and her dogs. Thankfully Razoo overhears and swoops.

"You must come to a parrrrrrrrty with me, you will never see anything of Delhi if you ask Billie. I have five parties and will decide which will be the coolest and you will come."

I want to kiss her. But I dare not. Kisses are rather rare in India and Razoo has already mentioned how she found it difficult to walk in Melbourne's parks with "All those couples treating the parks like they were their bedroom—shocccckking!"

All the gang agree.

New Year's Eve gets off to a late start. In my new life, Jonathan's work comes before anything else and, as luck would have it, a big story breaks. An Indian plane, hijacked on Christmas Eve, has been stranded in Afghanistan in a seven-day standoff. India released three jailed Muslim militants who will soon be exchanged for the passengers at Kabul airport, and the plane is due to return to New Delhi two hours before 2000 begins.

Going to the airport could be a death wish. Computer companies are predicting chaos in the streets come midnight and the Australian High Commission is advising we stay inside with a flashlight and canned food. But Delhi already has power cuts, water shortages and hopeless communications, and I'm not sure I'd notice much more mayhem. Besides, Jonathan and I made a pact last year—we would see the new century in together, kissing or not. So I go with him to the airport.

After spending days on the tarmac, blindfolded, sick, and some pistol-whipped, the hostages emerge looking weak, traumatized and exhausted. But the crowd of about four hundred well-wishers couldn't care less. The hostages are gangplanked down the same ramp I fell down only weeks ago, and fed to the mob. The crowd surges and starts hugging them, touching their feet, shaking their hands, handing them flowers or looping leis of marigolds around their necks. The armed police, who are meant to be keeping control, are jumping up and down with excitement and giggling like goons. Some of the hostages collapse and faint, others cry and wail. Only the captain of the plane seems to be enjoying himself—he punches the air as he's carried on the shoulders of a mob of men cheering "Hip Hip Hooray" and "Indeeaaa, Indeeaa." A *sadhu* emerges wearing an orange robe, and I get close, hoping to hear a sensible comment. But he scolds the Indian government for saving his life.

"They should have let us die rather than give in to militants."

After interviewing a few passengers, Jonathan tries to film a piece with the only camera crew he could find to work tonight—five young blokes who don't speak English, don't own headphones and are far too excited to concentrate. When we turn the camera lights on we're mobbed. A man sticks his small smiling sons under each of Jonathan's armpits and a group stands directly behind him as starstruck and frozen as Marcia in the game show episode of *The*

Brady Bunch. The only one who is slightly animated slowly and carefully picks his nose. Just as Jonathan delivers a decent take, a tiny plump woman jumps into the shot, puts on her spectacles and begins to recite a poem she's written, called "Ode to a Hostage."

For a long cold week
Our Great Nation held its breath.
We prayed and wept
And held our faith
While you were at the mercy of Pakistani tyrants.
Welcome home, our heroes of Hindustan.

We film it, Jonathan claps and the crowd cheers. I dig my fingernails into my hands and try to look moved instead of hysterical.

By midnight we're back home so Jonathan can file the story. The brown, heavy, toxic smoke follows us up the stairs. The pollution is starting to get to me—it's slowly but surely leaching moisture from my face, blackening my skin, leaving an acidic taste in my mouth and starving my brain of oxygen. Tonight, I don't need a drink or drugs to feel out of it. We shiver on our roof as the new century begins. It's all bang and no beauty; not one firework makes it above the smog. Sydney's harbor extravaganza and happy face seem a million miles away.

We drive through an eerie silent streetscape to Razoo's preferred party. It's in full swing in a photographic studio in a village called Haus Kaus, and there's food, *chai* and even black-market alcohol. But the partygoers can't really handle their piss. It's a scene from my schooldays: girls are passed out with their heads in plates of food, guys are vomiting in corners and there's bourbon and Coke stickiness underfoot. Those sober are dancing up a storm on a dance floor straight from the set of *Saturday Night Fever* that lights up under their feet. We join in.

The DJ has an interesting style—mixing (or rather clunking) from the Beastie Boys, to *NSYNC, to a Hindi movie number where everyone sings along and perfectly performs the dance from the film. There are lots of hand signals, wrist flicks, head wobbles and pelvic thrusts. The boys dominate the disco. None are standing on the sidelines doing the Aussie drunk boy head thump; instead, they spin around, doing the Punjabi dance move (which involves a maneuver akin to changing a lightbulb).

A nice bloke introduces himself and shakes my hand, but a girl beside him slaps him across his face. We try to keep a low profile, but apart from a group of young blonde Russian prostitutes in taffeta dresses straight from *Pretty in Pink*, we are the only Westerners. The Russians seem to be gate-crashers cruising for business. While the Indian boys are standing staring at them with horrified horniness, the Indian women are throwing them daggers from big dark eyes.

We end up in the alleyway with Sunil showing Jonathan how to perfect his cartwheels while avoiding huge splatters of cow shit and green goobers of spit. The dancing and the ridiculous nature of this exchange with Sunil tickle me. I'm warming to the Indian exuberance and energy and for the first time I feel perhaps I'll learn to like this country after all.

At five we wake up our cab driver, jump in a taxi reeking of sleep and sweat and try to head home. But the smog is now so thick we can't see the road, or even the front of the car; we crawl along while the driver blasts the horn, coughs up his lungs and chants "*Bap re Bap*" (Oh my God). Jonathan dozes, I shiver. The warmth of the alcohol and the blood rush of the dance floor flow from me and the smog seeps in. I feel claustrophobic and a little crazed—as if suffocating from the cling of a desperate lover who now makes my skin crawl.

Suddenly the smog parts like a curtain. A being emerges. Naked, straight-backed, as gray as a ghost, his dreadlocks trail in the dirt. He carries a trident like the devil's rod. It's an *aghori*—a *sadhu* that lives in a cremation ground. A *sadhu* that smears himself with the ashes of the dead, drinks from human skulls and looks for salvation in stoned madness. His red eyes look straight at me and through me. It's a look from another world, a window to nothingness, and a black hole of emptiness. My bones snap dry, my blood freezes, my breath is suspended. I'm being shot by a supernatural shotgun. The *aghori* merges back into the mist. Jonathan wakes and I can't talk to tell him what happened.

• • •

In the morning I wake up feeling like a truck has run over me. It's my first ever full-scale flu. I blame the smog, or perhaps the Ganges Christmas dip for this bug. But after four days of huge headaches, body pains and coughing fits, I worsen. One night I find myself in a nightmare; I see dead bodies hanging from the ceiling, my lungs black and putrid on the outside of my body, my back impaled on a pitchfork, and there's a big beast sitting heavily on my chest. I'm gasping and retching and trying to push the thing off me but I'm blacking out and choking and gulping. The beast becomes the *aghori sadhu*, his trident has speared my lungs and back, his bloodshot eyes are gnawing into my pain. I know he has done this to me.

Jonathan wakes me up and calms me down. I breathe a rattled rasp and gasp like a goldfish in air while he makes a panicked call to the medical insurance company in Australia. Before I'd left home I'd joked with a doctor friend about getting sick so he could come and retrieve me. But of course I've got the one disease that means you can't fly.

Double pneumonia.

The overly respectful neighborhood medic somehow confirms the diagnosis while putting his stethoscope on top of my jumper and trying to listen to my lungs through thick wool and thermal underwear. He warns that pneumonia is dangerous in Delhi and can be deadly. It's hard enough to breathe here with healthy lungs, there's no such thing as an ambulance (some people buy a siren and stick it on their car in the vain hope that the traffic will part but it doesn't) and the only decent hospital is an hour away on the other side of the city. He warns me that if I stop breathing again I won't be able to get help. I've never been in a hospital in my life, I'm phobic of needles and all I can think about is staph infections, dirty injections, AIDS and a ward full of groaning people. Still, I'm too weak and terrified to argue. I get in the car. Abraham drives gingerly, grim-faced, and I pant in the back like a geriatric with emphysema.

Apollo is a private hospital that boasts first-world facilities. It looks like a wedding cake, has a Hindu temple on one side, a wasteland full of rubbish and cows on another and a train line across the way with a small slum stretched along it. At a small entrance FOR POOR PATIENTS families squat and cook. The large entrance is for the rich, and inside the place is dead posh, with clean(ish) floors and scrubbed nurses in starched white dresses and caps. I'm shoved into a wheelchair, pushed onto a bed, blood tested, X-rayed and delivered into a room of my own within an hour. An oxygen/steam mask is strapped to my face so I look and sound like Darth Vader, and a device like a plastic tap crossbred with a TV remote control is attached to my hand. On the end of it hangs a drip. Every three hours I'm injected with intravenous antibiotics, which feel like cold hard lard in my veins. The sweet nurse has a dreadful needle technique and only knows one word of English.

"Paining?"

She understands my answer.

"Bloody oath."

My hand swells, my rings are cut off and my arm flowers with green, purple and blue track-mark bruising.

Jonathan stays in the room on a couch bed (and not just because I'm deathly ill—apparently it's not uncommon for women in Indian hospitals to be raped). But even with him sleeping beside me, the first night is long and the fear is real.

At four in the morning I stop breathing again and press the buzzer. The nurse comes in and attaches the mask to my face, but I can't get the oxygen to flow and I panic. I can see the black tunnel of death. Of course, intellectually, I've always known I'm mortal, it's just that I've always pretended I'm not. I've gambled with my health, taking dangerous substances and pretending I'll be eternally young, strong and invulnerable. For the first time, my body has betrayed me. I now fully comprehend my vulnerability and my finite future and I'm entirely unprepared. I've been raised in a family of atheists. At school I'd chosen to attend nonreligion classes and developed a skepticism and disdain for faith that I expressed as open contempt. I don't believe in anything but never-ending blackness and aloneness and that scares me senseless. Yet in this hospital bed, with the nurse's tiny hand in mine, I glimpse the preciousness of existence. I realize that no matter how many spunky lovers you've had, how much you earn, what you do for a living and how groovy you look, all that really matters is how you live. I've always said such things, but now for the first time I truly believe them, deep in my bones and my diseased flesh.

Such blinding flashes of obviousness keep me awake all night and numb to the morning parade of care. Every fifteen minutes or so a nurse comes in to put the mask on me, take my blood pressure, stick a thermometer in my mouth or give me drugs. In between, people with clipboards come asking how I am and if everything is all right. There's an administrator, a trainee doctor, a big doctor, a dietitian obsessed with my feces, the head of maintenance, the tea deliverer, the soup deliverer, the main course deliverer, the mosquito eradicator, the men to make Jonathan's bed and the men to make my bed. I mumble absently to them all.

Then in march the "sputum brigade": a group of doctors and physiotherapists in white coats that make me feel like the world will end if they don't see green goo. The specialist tries to teach me the Indian morning croak and spit that I so detest.

"Madam, you must be getting all the sputum out, all must come, do it with me, come on. *Crrrrrrrrroooooooooooaaaaak.*" He runs to spit in my bathroom. "*Ppptttaaaaaaaaaaab*. Now you try."

I'm exhausted from my early morning existential crisis and can only manage a pitiful "croak, ppppppttt."

Another few medicos come in to help. Together they bend their legs and limber up.

"Let's all show her how to sputum. One, two, three, *cccccccrrrrrrrooaakkk*."

I just can't perform under this kind of pressure.

The senior doctor's patience snaps. He huffs, "Madam, you are not leaving this hospital until you fill this."

He slams a specimen jar on the bed and marches out.

For the next week I'm forced to frequently suck on a huge china bong full of steaming water, wear the fighter pilot mask, blow into a machine and suffer ten-minute sessions of being whacked on the back. It's all to little effect. I'm just not a snotty person. Eventually I hack up a blood clot and they seem slightly impressed.

"It's a start," the specialist says gravely.

Today, exhausted by all the effort, I sink back in my bed to watch the afternoon cleaning team—three guys with a talent for slapstick. Their supervisor is Jim Carrey trapped in an Indian body. Tall, lanky and elastic, this Indian Jim has a rubber face and impossibly white teeth. While the others clean around him, he stands at the foot of my bed and performs a bizarre routine where he impersonates both Shane Warne and Sachin Tendulkar, famous cricket players, using my drip as the umpire, his broom as the bat and the head of his second-in-charge as the ball. I laugh, which starts off a wretched round of coughing. Indian Jim stops the performance and gets serious.

"Are you going to die today?"

"No."

"Why not?"

"I'm not that sick."

"Ah, madam, but you could and you must be ready."

I close my eyes. He's immune to the hint.

"We Hindus accept death is there, death is our fate. You Western people, you pretend death is not there, you plan and plan as if life is chess game, is game but you not playing. Isn't it? Your karma and kismet is playing, God is playing, and only thing for sure is you will die one day, isn't it?"

"So what to do?" I borrow the Indian phrase and head wobble. Indian Jim grins and wobbles back.

"You must die while doing your duty."

"But I don't have a duty."

He steps back from the foot of my bed, disbelieving.

"No job? No husband? No children? No being good daughter?"

I shake my head at each. He sighs sadly.

"It will come, madam. Get your health good and be rich, be good, be enjoying, it will come."

Reducing my ambition and simplifying my life; that's a prediction I should heed.

A week later I'm sent home in a different body. Thanks to a lovely little hospital souvenir, a stomach bug, I'm gray and scrawny and sickly. Puffing and panting, I slowly climb the stairs. Rachel, Mary and Moolchand stand at the door with flowers, openmouthed at my transformation.

Rachel gasps, "Oh no, you look terrible."

Mary raises a hand to her heart and Moolchand begins to cry.

In India, skinny is not sexy. Fat is beautiful and bountiful and befitting a good woman of pedigree, and I am causing shame to the compound.

Rachel pulls me inside and quickly shuts the door. "You are not going out until you look better."

Jonathan leaves to cover some stories in southern India and Rachel and Mary become my loving jailers. Our water purifier wakes me at nine by singing a dinky digital version of "Jingle Bells" to alert us to the fact that it's working. I eat fruit and vitamins while Mary makes my bed and I'm ordered back to it at ten. Three times a day I lean over a bowl of boiling water and eucalyptus—Rachel demands more sputum and less sick and I dare not disobey. Mary worships symmetry—she organizes my medication in order of bottle size, with a second classification of color, and aligns all the cushions diagonally to the couch. I give up control of my personal belongings and sacrifice privacy and spontaneity for Indian-style slobbery.

My Australian friends ring and tease me about having a cook and a cleaner but my days of feeling like a dickhead are fading fast. I'm already so desperately dependent that when I'm alone on weekends I feel quite helpless. The sickness is slowing me down but so are India's idiosyncrasies. It takes hours to put the tap water through the jingling purifier, boil it to kill the remaining bugs, strain it to remove the white flecks of pipe and pour it into the storage urn. All the tiny, tired-looking vegetables have to be washed with purified water and purple iodine, and even then I'm not sure what to do with them; I can't buy pasta and I don't know any Indian recipes. I have to watch the washing machine because it clicks off every time the power cuts and it takes four hours to clean one load. It takes all day to do a few household chores and by nightfall every surface is covered in a thin layer of black dust. A part of me thinks I should be working—perhaps writing some freelance articles for newspapers and magazines—but most of me is aware that I'm too worn out to even make a phone call. The ambitious career girl has gone, replaced by a spoiled skeleton in need of some rest and recuperation. I've worked my butt off for ten years. Perhaps it's high time to take off a year or two.

But without a job or a focus I feel vulnerable and useless. In New Delhi even simple acts like shopping are highly specialized skills that require a great deal of training. There's no such thing as a supermarket, and I have no idea where to go for safe fish and decent veggies.

One day, when the weather is warm, Rachel takes me to the market. Head high, red *dupatta* shawl rippling in the wind, she breezes through the masses of stalls like a queen, ignoring the stinking open drains, the grazing goats, cud-chewing cows, the hawkers, beggars and pushy Punjabis. I trot behind her like a pesky child, spellbound by the way she swoops on certain foods, demands a discount and flicks a wrist to signal a coolie to collect her purchase in an enormous basket on his head. The coolie—a little boy perched on skinny stork legs and dressed in rags—joins me in her train. The stalls display their products in wonderful artistic designs; gorgeous splashes of color and beauty flash among the filth, the flies and the forlorn.

The narrow shops and stalls are crammed with so many staff that we customers can't get too close. There is no self-serve in India; jobs are strictly demarcated and structured for organized chaos. One worker gets the fruit, another cuts it, another weighs it, another wraps it, another takes the money and another will give the change. Most workers are obviously underemployed and very bored. They sweep dirt from one place to another, dust, rearrange things and sit on their haunches watching the world go by with infinite patience and passivity. When a customer comes close they leap up from stupor to frenzy in seconds.

India's frantic lethargy is catching. Within half an hour I am walking in slow motion like a zombie with a blank-eyed stare.

The doctor's latest tests have shown I'm anemic, so Rachel now grabs my shawl and leads me like a lamb to the slaughterhouse. Down a dark alley we lift a grimy curtain and enter a dark round room. Dead sheep and goats hang from hooks and a row of Muslim men wearing white square caps squat with huge knives sitting between their black toes. (Many Hindus do not eat meat and most won't kill animals, so India's Muslims have cornered the butcher market.) Rachel selects a chicken to die and waits while its neck is wrung. As a Christian, she doesn't mind the carnage, but I consider Hindu vegetarianism for the first time as I head back to the car gagging.

We drive home in the opposite direction from which we came. New Delhi is Canberra behind the looking glass—endless traffic circles ensure that when you head off in the opposite direction to where you want to go, you always get there.

I begin to live out an Asian Jane Austen existence and in my weakened state submit willingly to the protocols of the new Raj. The neighbors begin to call, have tea, inquire about my family, chat about arranged marriages, passionately debate whether milk is good for health, hand me their calling cards and slightly bow as they leave. It's a truth universally acknowledged that one must be polite and charming on the surface but bitchy beyond belief just below the veneer, especially when one is talking about ones lower than oneself.

Mrs. Dutt, who lives in a pink mansion at the end of the street, is my most frequent guest. Enormously fat and caked with white powder, she huffs and puffs into my room, tells me how terrible I look, runs a finger along the mantelpiece, pulls a face at the black diesel dust (which resettles ten seconds after Mary wipes it clean) and complains.

"One just cannot get good help these days. My dear, Rachel is on the phone again, don't let her be so idle, you are paying her good money, get her to do something."

"Mrs. Dutt, if she's made the food, she can do what she wants," I bleat naively.

"No, impossible, don't be stupid, yaar, get her to make jam or rearrange the shelves and, by the way, I must tell you that that Mary is selling your garbage."

"People buy garbage here?"

"Yes, of course, she will be getting a couple of rupees a week, you know."

"Well, she cleans it up, she can sell it."

Mrs. Dutt splutters and turns pink under the white over the brown.

"You are spoiling them, they will turn on you and cheat you. They all steal, and cheat and lie and connive. By being soft you are ruining them for us."

If she only knew the worst of it. My staff are not only being corrupted by my Western slackness, but also by my Western morals. I hear a huge debate raging from the kitchen one day and go to investigate. Rachel has been reading Mary an article from my *Vanity Fair* magazine; they are discussing "fluffies"—fetish folk who dress up as fluffy toys and fuck each other.

I have only one gripe with the workers of India. They just won't say the word "no." Taxi drivers tell me they know where something is and get hopelessly lost, waiters insist something is "most definitely" available and then don't deliver it, Abraham drives me to a market that he knows is closed, shopkeepers say they have something, then hide because they don't. It's bizarre. Perhaps it's an honor thing, perhaps it's a hangover from the Raj, or perhaps "yes" can mean "no," like the head nod can mean "no way" and a side-to-side shake can mean "of course." The puppet-like wobble mixture of a shake and a nod can mean anything or nothing.

Razoo comes over, takes one look at my new scarecrow look and summons a beautician to make me presentable.

Indian women are incredibly obsessive about their looks, and whether they wear *salwar* suits, saris or shawls they're always tastefully dressed with coordinated accessories and makeup. Razoo always looks divine. An only child and a self confessed "brat," she is woken up every morning by a woman massaging her with almond oil. Every third day she's given a scrub, and once a month she has a facial, an arm and leg wax, eyebrow shape and manicure and pedicure. This is all before breakfast and without leaving her bed.

I have never been a girlie girl but I submit to a pedicure, manicure and facial, which altogether costs about twenty dollars. It's wonderful and well needed. Thanks to the Delhi pollution my skin is leathery, as dry as a stringy bark and clogged with black dust and brown dirt. But the beautician, Rupa, touches me like I'm a rare doll.

"Madam, my first white skin, so nice, pale is good, very good, so lucky."

With Rachel translating, I tell Rupa that in my country we put on fake tan and lie in the sun. She's horrified—she's been using skin-whitening cream every day of her life.

"No, pale is best, pale is most beauteous. Stay inside, madam, bestest for staying pale."

I decide to submit to paling into Indian significance and sensuous spoiling. If I can't have convenience I may as well have luxury.

And power. India's boundaries of behavior are still dictated by caste, upbringing and wealth. I may not have good breeding, be a Brahman or be related to the Minister for Railways, but I'm considered filthy rich and that means I can treat people dreadfully and get away with it. In fact, it's expected. Mrs. Dutt tells me to stop being so sucky crawly all the time.

"Why are you saying please and thank you all the time to your servants? It's not necessary, you sound too desperate to be nice. Have some backbone, you're very annoying."

We all hear Mrs. Dutt screaming at her cook every night and it's rumored she belts her cleaner, but mostly she shows her power by pretending people don't exist and complaining about how stupid they are when they're standing right behind her. It's appalling, but it rubs off. I'm beginning to get a little impatient and short sometimes when people are slow or stare too much. But Rachel pulls me up by saying "yes, madam" when she hears snobbery in my voice.

Other "servants" fight back with the weapon of knowledge. Dolly, the General's cook, is the compound gossip. She's a round and happy woman who feeds me apple pies and badly kept secrets. This genteel suburb is hiding a lot. The Christians around the corner are divorced but both names stay on the gate to save face. The girl across the road had a husband who beat her and has been on a "quick visit" to her parents for four years. Her neighbor married an Indian man from Seattle but when she traveled to the United States she found out he already had an American wife and family—she stayed to save face and is now the nanny. And Mrs. Dutt, the suburb's moral guardian, actually lives with a man she's not married to, because her husband left her for a white woman. Even Dolly has a secret. The General's cleaner says Dolly had a daughter who was either kidnapped and forced to marry a brute or went off with him (no one is quite sure). Saving face is so important that living a lie is accepted practice.

I should have been prepared for this. I have an Australian-Indian friend Padma who grew up in Sydney but has been increasingly forced to live under the yoke of Indian face-saving deception. Strikingly handsome, tall and sporty, Padma has only returned to India once. She came to New Delhi with her mother after high school but found it difficult to make friends and maintain her active lifestyle, so she returned to Sydney to go to college and have a career. Her mum stayed in Delhi and remarried. I always thought Padma rather conservative—she works in banking, doesn't drink much, never does drugs and doesn't believe in sex without love. She never mentioned a dad and I just assumed her parents were divorced. Of course I didn't find it shocking that she had been brought up by a single mother and didn't blink when she moved in with her Aussie boyfriend. Then one night last year Padma's boyfriend rang me from a hotel.

"She chucked me out."

"Have you broken up?"

"Worse, her mother's in town and she can't know I exist."

For the next month Jason had a better time than his girlfriend did. Padma's mother spent her entire visit displaying emeralds, topaz, gold and diamond solitaire rings and slyly teasing her daughter.

"Look, but don't touch, not until you are married."

Padma laughed. Her mother began to pray aloud to her Shiva statue.

"Oh god of marriage, please let my daughter be married. Don't let me be a failure as a mother."

The pressure was on. After a campaign of blackmail, tears, threats and angry fights, Padma promised to come to Delhi to meet marriageable men. Jason moved back in and she delayed the trip time and time again with work excuses. Then a friend of a relative of a friend saw Padma kissing Jason on the Bondi beachfront and wasted no time in calling Delhi. Padma's mother wrote a one-line letter.

Beti (child), it's me or it's him, if it's him you won't exist anymore, to me you will be dead.

Love, Mummy

At the time I thought this disgusting, but one night, while tipsy, Padma told me why her educated, intelligent mother was so strict. India didn't have a swinging sixties, so when her mum committed the ultimate crazy trip of marrying a man for love, her family handed over her inheritance (which she handed on to her husband) and disowned her. They never talked to her again. Seven months later, while heavily pregnant with Padma, she met a woman on a bus who told her that her husband already had a wife and child in Poona. The shock triggered an early labor and Padma was born by the side of the road two months premature. When her mother confronted her husband, he beat her. With no family and no social services to help, she suffered his violence for four years while she secretly went to college and stole enough housekeeping money and jewelry to escape. She went to Australia to get a job and to get as far away from him as possible. She's never got over the shame and she's never seen her family again.

Padma doesn't even know her father's full name, where he is, or whether her grandparents are still alive. She has grown up being told that only she can pay for her mother's sins. Finding a girl a suitable man, filling a huge glory box with jewelry, clothes and sheets, and throwing a massive elaborate week of wedding festivities for the couple can absolve past bad acts and help earn better future lives. But I only half believed Padma. It all sounded too clichéd, too melodramatic, too movie. Until she announced she would obey her mother.

"I can't let Mummy be all alone in the world and I can't make her relive the shame and the isolation of rejection," she flatly explained after she dumped Jason a few months ago.

"But she's married again, she's not alone," I tried to argue.

Padma just shook her head sadly and promised to see me in Delhi. At the time, I couldn't understand and didn't know how to comfort her. Of course my mum hasn't loved all my boyfriends and I get the impression she wants me to marry someone with prospects, but I know she would always support my choices and never reject me. Now I'm in India, Padma's life makes a little more sense. Here, life is lived so publicly and saving face is all-important.

One night Padma calls, her voice low and soft.

"I'm here."

"You're in Delhi?"

"Yes."

"Great. Come over!"

"I can't, I'm here to meet men, wish me luck."

Every night for a week we whisper on the phone while her mother sleeps. At first we laugh about the dorky boy who went to Oxford and wears a cravat, about the guy with dreadful acne and a lisp, about the military officer who demanded her measurements, about the bloke from Calcutta who's obviously gay.

"He's ahead so far," Padma says. "At least I could have my own life and he'd probably love to move to Sydney."

But as the days go on she sounds more and more depressed. Despite being slim, spunky and super-smart, Padma is not considered a great catch. She is old (twenty-eight) and she hasn't got a father or a star chart (her mum is not sure where the bus was when she gave birth). What's worse, she grew up in Australia, where everyone drinks and most girls are considered "damaged goods." Her mother must scrape the bottom of the barrel of her caste, and Padma is forced to sit and smile and be interviewed as if she's applying for a job as a lifelong slave. They fire questions like "You will quit work after your marriage, won't you? Career girls are so crude and masculine, don't you think?"

"Do you know how to cook proper Indian food?"

"Do you know the rituals of fasting for your husband?"

The interviewers are also savage in giving her performance feedback.

"You're very dark, too tall and your nose is funny," states a short, fat, ugly guy with a monobrow.

As the rejections pile in, Padma's mother gets increasingly desperate, setting her up with a guy crippled by polio, an albino and a forty-five-year-old divorcé with a harelip.

Padma sneaks out to meet us for dinner one night. She sighs with hopelessness but can still crack a joke.

"Imagine if I told them I ate meat and wasn't a virgin."

There's a spluttering and coughing as the eavesdropping woman at the next table chokes on her food.

"What are you going to do?" I whisper.

"Fuck them all." She slams her fist on the table, loudly defiant. "We're giving up on the Delhi boys and going to London, where they're taller and maybe equally damaged. Mum's going first to set up meetings, and I'm leaving for Thailand tomorrow to go to an international banking conference for a tax dodge and a final fling."

The woman at the next table chokes again and almost has to be resuscitated.

As Padma flies to Bangkok, I stop judging her for living a lie. In India, it's easy and expected. I, too, have succumbed. This country does not recognize de facto relationships, socially or bureaucratically. Sick of the disapproving looks and murmurs, I've started telling people I'm engaged or married.

When my visa nears expiration, I apply for a new one, dressing demurely in a *salwar kamiz* and carrying a letter from Jonathan saying we are engaged and I need to stay in India until our marriage. After lining up and filling in four forms, I sit in a dark room until my number is called. A huge hairy man in a safari suit comes out with my application and the letter, looks me up and down like he's buying a leg of lamb (or a tub of *dahl*—a spicy souplike lentil dish, the staple meal of North India—if he's vegetarian) and yells, "You are not married?"

"No, sir, I am engaged. We are organizing the wedding. That's why I need to be here."

"No. Get out, you can't stay until you're married."

"Just two months, sir."

"No. You're no good to India if you are not married."

He stamps REJECTED on my form and strides off. I leave hyper-ventilating with anger.

A week later, Jonathan puts on a suit and sneaks in with me. The same man comes out with his hands on his hips and a growl in his voice.

"Look, madam, I told you, get out until you are married. Go away."

Jonathan jumps up, gives the man his card and shakes his hand.

"G'day. I'm from Australian Broadcasting. I'd like to see the manager."

The bureaucrat bends and smiles.

"Of course, sir, come this way."

I sit in the back of the room while Jonathan, the manager and the middle manager have *chai* and discuss cricket. I'm given another visa. We walk out smiling a snarl—this country would be easier with a strap-on penis.

Saving that, I now decide to arm myself with language. India has hundreds of languages, but Hindi is the common tongue in Delhi. The Australian Broadcasting Company office finds me a teacher and he arrives bowing low.

Hari Lal (whose name means "green red") is tiny, balding and has shiny skin the color of warm walnut. Softly, sweetly and firmly, he tells me that he's one of the few people in Delhi who speaks proper Hindi and he's glad to be of assistance. His first insistence is that I attach a *ji* to everybody's name, as this is a term of high respect and means "soul one." Hari Lal tells me the Hindi hello, *namaste-ji*, means "I recognize the divine in you." It's a lovely sentiment I'm happy to adopt. But Hari's Hindi is more practical than spiritual. It's memsahib Hindi; the language of the lady of the manor. I repeat after him:

"Clean the table."

"Make Indian dinner tonight as we are holding a reception."

"Please send this telegraph to London."

"Go call sahib."

And my favorite phrase: *Agar magar mudt kidjeaye*—"No ifs and buts please."

Jonathan and I lay a bet on who will use it first.

But as I haltingly begin to use the phrases, Rachel laughs, Abraham startles, taxi drivers stare at me and the local beggars retreat in shock. I ask the Australian Broadcasting Company office researcher—a young funky woman called Simi—what I'm doing wrong and try out a few sentences on her. She tries to stop herself from laughing but her eyes twinkle and her shoulders shake.

"Sarah, the thing is this. Hari Lal is teaching you formal Hindi and Urdu. No one speaks it here. You should speak Hindustani. You are being too polite."

I feel like an idiot. I've been talking a language that died out with the British Raj. When I thought I was asking a taxi driver to take me somewhere I was really saying, "Kind sir, would thou mind perhaps taking me on a journey to this shop and I'd be offering you recompense of this many rupees to do so, thank you frightfully humbly." And I've been greeting filthy naked street urchins with "Excuse me, oh soul one, but I'm dreadfully sorry, I don't appear to have any change, my most humble of apologies."

I carefully and respectfully suggest to Hari Lal-*ji* that perhaps I could learn the informal way of talking and perhaps some street Hindi.

His cup of *chai* clatters into the saucer, he pulls himself up to his full height of four feet ten and sharply and sternly states, "Madam, please, these people of Delhi are uneducated and rude. We will not speak like filth. We shall speak properly, as befitting your station. I will not talk like that. I absolutely refuse."

There begins a battle of wills that keeps me from communicating with the locals for months to come.

When I ask him how to tell a taxi driver he's ripping me off, he suggests a phrase that translates as: "Is your taxi made of gold, dear man?"

When I want to tell a man to stop staring at me, he suggests: "Haven't you a mother or sister at home?"

And when I ask what I should have said to the man in the visa office, he suggests: "You are making my mustache droop."

"But, Hari-*ji*," I protest, "I don't have a mustache."

"No, madam, but it means 'you are threatening my honor.' Mustaches must always twirl upwards."

As Hari sticks to his principles, fewer and fewer students stick with him. He's a relic of a forgotten India, a gentle, congenial land of courtly poets, and he's slightly lost in the increasingly crude and brutal present. I keep having lessons to protect him from the world and because I like his company. He even encourages me to get fit and get out.

"Sarah-*ji*, life for an Indian woman is like a frog in a well. You should jump out before you forget how."

But getting out is not easy.

It's almost spring and a weak sun is striving to lift the winter smog. After taking three sets of anti-amoeba antibiotics, I've gained some weight and strength and I want to walk. Rachel tries to talk me out of it, Abraham wants to drive me, and Lakan doesn't want to open the gate. When I finally get outside, I'm only halfway down the street when the General's driver pulls up beside me in his car, beseeching me to get in.

"The General doesn't like madam walking. Please get in, please, madam, it's not looking good for the house."

"No, I'm walking. Don't worry, it's okay."

"No, please, madam, please, pleeeeeeeazzze."

I've learned to ignore. But the driver won't give up. He cruises behind me for three blocks, waiting for me to change my mind.

A rickshaw rattles up.

"Yes?" smiles the driver as he sticks his head around the windshield.

"No," I snap.

He drives ahead one meter and maintains speed in front of me.

A taxi pulls up.

"Yes?" the driver grins.

"No!"

His face falls and he drives beside me. I now have an escort convoy and am exercising in a pall of black smoke. I give up and get in the backseat of the General's car. The driver smiles proudly, chauffeurs me around for twenty minutes and takes me home.

A compound conference is held and a yoga teacher is hired to help me work off some steam.

Yogesh is not what I'd expect from someone whose name translates as "King of Yoga." He's less a stretchy *sadhu* and more a King of Camp—a pouting, flamboyant, slim hunk in a polyester body shirt and tight pants that show off a great little behind. Yogesh's voice is exactly the same as the gay salesman's in *Are You Being Served*? but with an Indian accent. I loved yoga in Australia and had a great teacher who taught gentle moves and deep breathing, but Yogesh's style is less slow stretches and more Jane Fonda aerobics combined with British Army calisthenics and a high-octane bitch and gossip session. In Yogorobics we do leg squats, leg circles, push-ups, sit-ups, back bends, toe points, tummy tucks and repeat each ten times. When I try to make it a bit Indian and spiritual by putting on a mantra CD, Yogesh flips and flusters.

"Saaaaarrrrrrah, I hate this stuff. It's too religious. Have you got anything funky?"

Yogesh's favorite soundtracks are Café del Mar, the Cream Nightclub collection and his own voice. Jonathan is his favorite subject.

"Jonaaaathhhhhhaaaaaaaaan (giggle giggle), lift your buttocks up. Loverly, Jonaaaaathhhhhhhaan (giggle giggle). Oh you are stretchy for a boy, Jonaaaaaatttthhhhhannn. Don't push it too hard, you don't want to strain yourself. Ooh loverly."

If Jonathan's away or busy, Yogesh goes into girlie gossip mode, giving me a running commentary about all his other expat "ladies."

"The Bhutanese ladies are sooo skinny, Sarah, the Singapore ladies are toooo fat, the French girls are too thin, and they always talk about this and that, and as for those Punjabis, I won't teach them, they are so crude and flabby, and they have no style, no style at all."

I stretch, pant and puff out "really?" a lot.

Yogesh is Bengali. Born in Calcutta, his parents died when he was young and he was sent to a private Christian boarding school near Delhi.

"I was so lucky to keep my name. The non-fee-paying orphans were converted and rechristened Matthew, Mark, Luke and John. It was drrreeadful and, you know, really, on weekends they would take us to the village and tell us to bribe the people to turn to Christ by giving them chocolate milk. I don't even like chocolate, you know."

Hence Yogesh is anti organized religion. But while he may not go to temple, he is a good Hindu; he exercises the body, doesn't eat meat or dairy or any foods that make the genitals hot, like onion and garlic. And he knows the philosophy of yoga and follows it.

The poses we do in the West are only one minuscule part of yoga. Yoga is a Hindu philosophy of attaining superconsciousness that can involve work, breath control, meditation and asceticism. The stretches are *asana*s or poses that were copied from animals and compiled in the Veda scriptures written hundreds of years before the time of Christ. But Yogesh says it's best to start slowly on the path to enlightenment.

"Make the body healthy and the soul will follow," he chants.

"What soul?" I tease. Yogesh giggles.

"Oh, Sarrrrrrah, everyone has a soul. Just let it breathe and relax before the next crrrash of karma."

"Karma crashes?"

"No, *you'll* crash into karma. One minute tra la la la tra la la la, and the next minute crrrassh bang smash, so you need to be fit. Now pant with me: OohhAhhOohhAhhOohhAhh."

"I've had my crash, Yogesh, my brush with death."

"Ah yes, but your bang and smash are still to come." Yogesh smiles and his eyes sparkle. This yogi is not bringing me inner peace.

4 | Three Weddings and a Funeral

New Delhi's winters are short. By February the smog has gone, the shadows shorten and shawls are abandoned as spring springs. This is the season for love to bloom, but preferably after the wedding.

Sunday mornings we sit sipping *chai* and laugh at the newspaper's marriage classifieds. Razoo drops in to teach me how to interpret the spouse ads.

"*Tall*" means above five feet five.

"*Handsome groom with green card*" means butt-ugly brute with an American work visa.

"*Homely girl with wheatish complexion*" is an ugly girl with fair skin.

"*Broad-minded match wanted*" means the person on offer is divorced.

"*Extremely beautiful girl wanted*" means

a vain but probably funny-looking bloke wants a babe better than Miss Universe.

"*Caste no bar*" means we are lying.

"*Wanting a homely wife*" means a mama's boy and his family want a slave who'll cook, clean and massage their feet every night.

Razoo reads, wobbling her head like a multijointed puppet, throwing her arms around like a mime artist and twisting and turning her fingers like a Balinese dancer. She is furious grace.

"Sarrrrrrrrrrah, these drrrreadful boys get beautiful girls and it drrrrives me mad." (When Razoo's upset she rolls her "Rs" much more.) She summarizes her thoughts on marriage with the Punjabi adage "Look at God's carelessness, that donkeys always get the cream." Razoo knows many women like Padma and she's frustrated that brides should be fair-skinned and gorgeous with a couple of degrees, a high-paying job and a big fat dowry, while most grooms should just be ready, willing and, hopefully, able. I try to calm her down.

"Razoo, don't be upset, you have a fiancé."

She grimaces.

"I've got to get out for a while, I'm going to New York to work. They love the ethnic thing. I'll get a great job and trade on being a poor and put-down Indian woman. I'll get married later, maybe next year."

She leaves for the Big Apple and I lose my only girlie mate.

But luckily it's the wedding season and Delhi is becoming a party town with plenty of opportunities to meet and greet. White horses with gold saddles canter through the traffic, baggy gray elephants with pink-painted trunks lumber along major roads and houses are lit up like fairy kingdoms. Restaurants are full of awkward first dates chaperoned by older sisters and toothless grannies, and the shops are crowded with women buying saris and gold jewelry and silver toe rings.

Jonathan and I explore Wedding Street in Old Delhi. It's a winding narrow alleyway smelling of sweet onion, rotting garbage, boiling milk and acrid urine, and crammed with cycle-rickshaws tangled up in pedestrians. Tiny alcoves are stacked to the ceiling with crowns, handmade invitations, Indian sweets, gaudy red and gold silk saris and *lengas* (skirts), silk suits and turbans, tiny lights, plastic and wooden bangles, necklaces made of money, miles of fabric and mountains of gold jewelry. A man squats to feed old wedding saris into a fire while an old lady watches her past burn; she will collect the heat-resistant gold to decorate her grandchild's dowry box. Gold is a girl's best friend—an Indian woman's social security, insurance and alimony if abandoned or divorced. The street's finery and the frantic fuss are overwhelming and I understand why Razoo wants to escape all the work involved in getting married.

Moolchand dances on our doorstep giggling and jiggling as he hands us a card emblazoned with the Hindu swastika. It's our first wedding invitation.

"Madam, I'm veery haaaappy, soooo happy."

He claps his hands and wiggles some more; his grin beaming so wide his face must hurt.

"My daurrrrrrtttttter marriage is coming, I have found good boy who has a house, a good government job, he doesn't dreenk or smoke and is verrrrry young and sooo handsome, you should see, sooo handsome."

Moolchand is now jumping, dancing, clapping his hands and head-wobbling so much that I'm getting dizzy just watching.

"Is your daughter happy?"

He stops his jig, stands still, cocks his head to the side and looks confused.

"Of course." He shrugs his shoulders and gestures at Rachel as if to ask "is this a trick question?"

Rachel shuts the door and tells me it's possible that Moolchand's daughter wasn't asked if she was happy, but she most likely would be. She'd have met the man and trusted her father's choice.

The day before the big night, though, we see Moolchand's grin is gone. His face is shut, his eyes are red and he hangs his head with grief. The father and the bride have been up all night weeping, for tomorrow she will leave her home and live with her husband's family.

"They will be her family now, my daughter will liiiive with them, coooook for them, love fooor them, not my daughter anymore." He sniffs as he melodramatically collapses onto the office couch and pounds the pillow.

The following evening, the Australian Broadcasting Company family leaves together for the wedding in a jolly mood. Abraham is driving, and Rachel and Mary sit primly, dressed in their gold jewelry and best silk saris. Jonathan is in a suit and I wear a shawl over a Western evening dress that's a bit too sexy for an Indian party. We travel for two hours alongside rickshaws heading for weddings all over the city and bulging with entire orchestras—bottoms, arms, legs and trumpets stick out and bass drums balance on top.

The wedding we're going to is to be relatively small; only five hundred of Moolchand's closest friends, relatives and neighbors are attending and they are all there buzzing with excitement as we get out of the car. The entire street is blocked off with a long white tent erected along its length. At the entrance a massive mechanical peacock welcomes us by opening and closing its fan-like tail in a shuddering motion; powered by a huge noisy generator belching at its rear, the auspicious bird looks like it's farting black smoke. Glittering plastic chandeliers hang from the roof, garlands of bright orange flowers are twisted around every pole and two long blocks of row upon row of red velvet chairs face a stage where two gold thrones await the couple. Moolchand must have spent a fortune on showing off for the neighbors.

For an hour Jonathan and I sip warm Coke, surrounded and stared at by a huge circle of guests that jabber and comment on our each and every movement. Rachel listens in and translates: apparently they like my shawl but think my hair is far too short and I'm too skinny; Jonathan is very tall but far too young to be a bureau chief. We're saved from inquiries about our marriage and childless condition by a great commotion at the tent entrance.

The groom is approaching.

Uncomfortably lopsided upon his white horse, he's dressed in white silk, topped with a gold tinsel crown, and his neck is garlanded with a necklace of money. The horse stops at the tent entrance and ten men stand below it struggling to hold up massive neon strobe lights that bathe the groom in glare. His baby face sweats with the heat but is frozen in terror. The wedding band—twelve men in white starched uniforms with red and gold epaulets, cummerbunds, pith helmets and grand mustaches—tumble out of a rickshaw and start blowing and banging on their instruments.

It's the worst music I've ever heard; a discordant, anti-rhythmic blast of twelve different tunes in the key of off. Somehow the groom's family finds a beat to dance to, and swirl their saris and suits in a circle around the boy, gesturing and yelling to him in Hindi, "Stay with us, don't go in."

Moolchand's family comes to the front of the tent and starts screaming back, "Come on, time to get married."

The bride's family tries to pull the groom's family toward the tent while the band blasts faster and faster and at a higher and higher pitch. It looks like there's going to be a fight. But Rachel tells me not to worry; it's a ritualized performance and all in good humor. Indians are great actors (if a little melodramatic).

Of course the dutiful boy, his family and his friends finally enter the tent and the horse bolts off to the next event. The boy, who's aged about twenty, is repeatedly blessed in a huge huddle at the door of Moolchand's house; the women anoint his forehead with sandalwood, throw rice into his hair and chant up a storm. Moolchand pushes me to the front.

"See how verrrry handsome he is, madam?"

"Yes, Moolchand, very good-looking and he has very pale skin."

I've said the right thing; the father of the bride cheers and claps with glee.

The guy *is* cute but he's freaked, caked in sandalwood, green with fright and reeling from the clouds of incense, as his drunk friends hysterically jostle him while somehow managing to balance sacks of presents for Moolchand's family on their heads.

The bride emerges into the melee. Her baby face is heavily made up, her body weighed down by tradition, expectation, a red and gold sari and tons of bracelets, nose rings, earrings, necklaces, headpieces and rings on her fingers and toes. She keeps her head bowed but tries to take a covert peek at her husband before they're jostled and pushed onto the stage above a mosh pit of blessings.

We royal white employers are crowd-surfed toward the front and pulled onto the platform by Moolchand's bouncers. The punters roar as we stand behind the thrones and make the V sign above the couple's heads for photos. When we get down, everyone follows us to the wedding buffet to watch us eat; the bride and groom are left forlorn and forgotten. Worried we are stealing the newlyweds' thunder, we give them an envelope of cash, wave to our fans and leave. Most of the guests are also heading home—the actual wedding ceremony won't take place until five in the morning, the auspicious but antisocial time selected by the *pundit* (priest).

In the morning, still sleepy from the night before, we are handed another invite. This is for a love match wedding. Simi from the Australian Broadcasting Company office is marrying Vivek, a freelance filmmaker with a goatee who often comes to pick her up from work on his motorbike. Simi is always giggly, fun-loving and friendly and I begin to drop by her office daily to hear her tales of wedding organization delivered with a dimpled grin, a tinkle of her earrings and a banging of bangles on her desk.

So far things have been going well—the venue is booked, the invites are printed, her mother has bought the jewelry and hundreds of forms have been filled out for the bureaucrats. But a week before the ceremony Simi comes into work less and less, then not at all. She's been missing for two days when Jonathan expresses concern, but no one in the office seems to find this unusual or unprofessional; it's assumed she's too busy with preparations.

But there has been a disaster. When Simi returns to the office her eyes are downcast and her laughter gone. Vivek's parents have suddenly decided they're against the match and are refusing to talk to Simi, her mother or even their son. Simi says she's been too upset to work or eat. The worst thing for her is that no one knows why her future in-laws have gone so cold.

"It's so strange, you know, his parents are quite liberal, his dad is a journalist, they let Vivek have an earring and long hair, they know we have been dating for years. Maybe it's because my dad is expired or because of my age. I'm twenty-eight, a year older than Vivek."

"Why would it matter if your dad is dead?"

"Well, you know, Sarah, in India a woman is not much without a husband. Once, a neighbor told my mother that my dad mustn't have cared for her much because he left her."

"But he didn't leave her, he died."

"I know, but widows are considered worthless and bad luck to know. My poor mum has been having a tricky time of it."

I'm getting good at hiding my shock at India's social cruelties and instead of screaming I shake my head and tell Simi I'm sad for her. But she doesn't want any pity. Simi picks herself up and pushes ahead with the plans, and Vivek decides to disobey his parents—a radical act in India. I admire them both.

Simi and Vivek may be unconventional but Simi wants a traditional wedding with all the warm-up gigs. Jonathan's mother Meg is here for a holiday and is quickly invited to the first pre-wedding party. Abe drives us across the slimy oozing black mud of the empty Yamuna River to Simi's family flat in north Delhi. The tiny living room is packed with gorgeous girls in silk saris and matriarchs with barrel bellies wrapped in delicate, delicious chiffon topped with cardigans. A few blokes roam the room wearing white *kurta* suits (long shirts and baggy trousers) and children run underfoot in stiff little nylon dresses looking like Kewpie dolls.

Simi's voluptuous and beautiful mum (another Auntie-*ji*) welcomes us with a formal *namaste* (placing her hands in prayer and bowing her head a little), a guffaw, a hug and a gift of toe rings that she insists I wear to the wedding party. I love her immediately. She speaks little English but drags me into her bedroom for a lecture endlessly repeated by Indian middle-aged women: I should be getting married soon. To encourage me she displays the wedding jewelry piece by piece. Gold chains, an emerald necklace, a garnet bracelet and topaz earrings, delicate anklets, cute toe rings, a heavenly headpiece and a diamond stud for Vivek.

I'm not a jewelry girl but I make appreciative noises and Jonathan's mum promises she'll hassle her son on my behalf. Thankfully Meg then winks at me; she can sense my discomfort and is merely amused rather than affected by the Indian marriage obsession. Deep inside I hope and suspect marriage is where Jonathan and I are heading, but I want to be sure that we can be together forever. My parents and Meg allow us to make such huge life decisions privately; I'd be furious if they didn't. But I forgive Auntie for her lecturing; she is Indian and I'd hate to take away one of her great pleasures in life. Besides, I'm touched by feeling so included in the festivities and so welcomed within the family. Indian hospitality is warm, welcoming and loving, and I lap it up to counteract my frustrations with the country.

We eventually squeeze into the main room for a ceremony called *naani mukh* that involves asking the ancestors to bless the match. Simi's gentle, sweet and quiet brother sits on the floor with the *pundit* surrounded by trays of orange flowers and offerings of bananas, apples, *dahl*, rice, curd and pineapples. Sanskrit prayers fill the room and sandalwood and rice are applied to a huge garlanded photo of Simi's "expired" dad. Simi is Bengali, so the women occasionally blow plastic conch shells and make a high-pitched ululation. Apparently all the married women are supposed to make the sound at certain moments but the younger ones are a bit too inhibited and don't know quite when they're meant to let rip. Simi's mum and the grannies are in their element; screaming, berating and bossing everyone around one minute, and then collapsing into tearful laughter over *chai* the next.

But while the ceremony looks very serious and intense, Jonathan's mum and I are the only ones being respectfully quiet and attentive. There's food bubbling on the stove, a tiny puppy is barking and running around, the kids are screaming and Simi's uncle is stretched out behind the priest, snoring louder than the chanting and the ululating put together. The doorbell rings every few minutes and more relatives cram into the two-room flat.

Simi emerges from a milk bath looking stunning in an orange sari; her feet are painted with a little red Hindu swastika. Meg and

I admire the work and a girl giggles and squats to paint ours with the same pattern. It feels weird wearing an emblem I associate with hatred but Simi's friend and foot-painter Sonali assures me that Hitler perverted the swastika's intent. It means luck or well-being. Soon all the women in the room have little swastika feet.

We sit on the common roof for the *aaye buro bhat*, the daughter's last meal in the maternal house (Simi will be fasting from now until the ceremony). Sonali serves us banana-leaf bowls full of Bengali fish stew and fish heads. She is not married and is kind of like the bridesmaid/slave who has to do all the work while looking cute, demure and available in a pretty pink suit. I tell her I've been three times the bridesmaid and never the bride. She looks upset.

"Did you fast properly?"

"Fast? I don't fast."

"Well, there you have it, your first mistake. You must. I'm fasting and luckily today is Tuesday, so if I do this right, my future husband will be like Tuesday's god—Hanuman the monkey god."

"Is that good?"

"Oh yes, I quite like him, he's mischievous and strong and loyal and steadfast. If Simi was getting married a day earlier I'd have to fast for a husband like Vishnu."

"But isn't he really powerful?"

"Sure, but personally I think he's a bit of a control freak." She winks a long-lashed eye. When Sonali is not starving herself, serving food and painting feet she's writing her doctoral thesis about businesswomen in Orissa.

Simi is now dripping with gold and swathed in silk, and her dainty toes are being touched up with red polish. But she has one more grooming activity to endure. A tiny young beautician with a thick plait that stretches to her knees squats and painstakingly applies *mehindi* (a red mud-like henna) in intricate swirls and pictures on Simi's hands; she paints peacocks, flowers and tendrils of ivy. I just can't resist asking for a swirling pattern of circles and twirls. As I wave my new hennaed hands in the air to dry, the entire brigade of Aunties wake from their afternoon snores to check the work.

"The warmer the heart the darker the henna," they chant. The largest of all the Aunties nods appreciatively as she pats my wrist. "Ah, you have the hottest heart of all. Look, girls, be like this one." No one seems to notice the advantage of white skin in the staining competition. I'm surrounded and rewarded with more *chai.*

Vivek arrives. We sit in a circle and bless him with sandalwood, and he in turn has to touch our feet in a gesture of respect. Technically this means that now and until the day I die I can demand that Vivek bow before me, but as I'm leaving he pulls me aside and whispers in my ear, "Sarah, don't even try the feet thing with me. The boundary for traditional behavior is set by the range of my mother-in-law's eyes. By the way, can I borrow some Massive Attack CDs?"

We head home for a costume change (I'm ordered to wear a silk *salwar kamiz*) and, while Meg rests up from an exhausting day, Jonathan and I return to Simi's flat for *sangeet*: the music night.

A crowd squeezes onto cushions around the room and a group of girls form a rainbow of silk surrounding Simi's mum. Massive Attack is not on the agenda; Auntie plays an ancient piano accordion-type thing and sings in screeching Hindi. The ancient wedding songs start off like soft laments, then pick up speed and energy and get quite raunchy. The girls clap in time and sing the chorus but Simi's mum steals the show. The act culminates in a sexy song to Vivek where she beckons him to come hither with fabulous eyelash fluttering, shoulder shimmying, pelvic wriggling and a flapping of her floppy arms. The girls squeal, the men kill themselves laughing and Vivek blushes all the way to his bare feet. Women should only flirt with husbands or sons-in-law and this is a rare show of sexuality. I must say I'm shocked—it's been two months since I saw a woman and man hold hands, hug or even touch.

The unmarried dutiful Sonali is pushed to dance for us. She performs a Bollywood hit beautifully, twisting and turning and lip-synching like a professional; her head wobbles and pelvic thrusts seem coy and sexy all at once. Jonathan and I are ordered up to join a circle around the nearly weds; we imitate the others, clapping and clicking our fingers and flicking our hips. Simi's mum even tries to teach Jonathan to do the Indian shoulder shimmy, which causes everyone to fall over in hysterics. The matriarchs then decide Simi's friends must perform. A guitar appears and a very serious boy picks it up and begins to strum and sing.

"It is a noyne aclock on a Saturdey, and the regulars of crowding shuttle in."

"Piano Man" is a bizarre contrast to the other songs, but the oldies clap along anyway and at least we know the words.

The next morning Vivek sends Simi saris and some turmeric to apply to her body and luckily some falls on Sonali, which means she will be married next.

Rachel takes me shopping and I buy a gorgeous deep pink and gold silk sari for the same price as a pair of jeans. At dusk Rachel stands me in the center of the room and wraps me up in the six and a half meters of silk. I feel fabulous but too scared to walk, terrified I'm going to step on the hem and unwrap myself in front of the guests. Rachel's final orders are: "Do not take drink so you don't need to pee, do not eat much and have fun."

The wedding is at the National Press Club. Simi arrives stunning in red and gold, laden with jewels and covered in makeup; the gaggle of grannies order her into the corner and demand she look coy and meek.

Vivek's family has left town in protest; there's no one to pay for a horse, so he arrives in the Australian Broadcasting Company car which is covered in red roses and driven by a hysterically careful, nervous and proud Abraham. Vivek is dressed in cream silk baggy pants and a cream shirt and wears a white pointy cone hat that looks like a tampon on his head; it's meant to make him look silly and humble for one last time before he's honored for the rest of his life. It works. Vivek looks very embarrassed and worried he will never regain his cool image.

His friend Ravat throws his head back and laughs. "Vivek will go from being a sheep to a tiger, loved, adored and respected for the rest of his life. From now on he can be a proper little shit if he wants to be. It's the Indian man's birthright."

Simi, surrounded by a wall of saris and seated on a wooden platform, now has to suffer the part of the wedding I know she's been dreading. She's of good Indian roly-poly frame and has to be carried to Vivek and circled around him seven times. Her face is hidden behind two big banana leaves but I can tell she's shitting herself as her brother and his friends groan and threaten to drop her. Finally, after lots of laughs, ululating and conch blowing, Vivek is lifted up too, the leaves are dropped and they grin at each other. Simi's brother and his mates practically throw her down and run off to steal a shot of whiskey in the parking lot, as the matriarchs in saris march up to the couple to bless them one by one, hand-feeding them sweets. After fasting all day they both nearly throw up.

Simi and Vivek enter a little pavilion and sit with the *pundit*. Everyone ignores the actual ceremony, except we foreigners. After a lot more chanting, ululating, conch-blowing and feet-touching, Simi and Vivek are tied together to circle a sacred fire seven times. Each circle is accompanied by its own mantra—mostly all to protect the husband. Vivek places red powder on Simi's central hair parting to mark her as a married woman, and we surround them and throw red rose petals.

There's no kissing of the bride, but this is a groovy crowd, so we line up and get a hug.

After all the buildup and exhausting observance of tradition, and perhaps too much Pepsi, everyone is tired and emotional. Suddenly the entire wedding party bursts into tears; the grannies mop their eyes with their cardigans, Simi and Vivek rock with sobs, and the sweet sari-clad girls whimper. When everyone calms down, the newlyweds sit on the thrones and we all eat.

But as we're happily stuffing our faces, Jonathan, Meg and I are grabbed and practically pushed under a table. The eunuchs are here. Eunuchs are men who were kidnapped in childhood and castrated to give them this career, or sometimes transvestites who've chosen the operation. None do drag well. Skinny and small-hipped in tacky saris, their eyes are ringed with blue shadow and their lips slashed with pink. They seem sad and crude. Eunuchs are considered bad luck, and they trade on this to extort newlyweds. If they don't get big bucks, they'll create a scene and they don't mean a Kylie Minogue dance act; vulgar ditties, crude dances and even a display of their mangled sex organs will bring the family into terrible disrepute. If they see us white guests they'll demand an exorbitant amount. After a long and labored negotiation someone pays them off and we're allowed to show our faces again.

The guests leave soon after dinner, but, despite all the buildup to the event and the days of intense, emotional and draining rituals, the newlyweds are not even allowed to go home and pass out—let alone have sex. This is because of an ancient Bengali legend. A holy man once told a bride that it would be dreadfully bad luck to have relations with her husband on their wedding night but she lustfully ignored the advice. A poisonous snake bit her new husband and he died. The holy man revived him only after she vowed all future women would abstain on wedding nights to pay for her error. So, even in present-day India, Bengalis guard the groom against his wanton wife. Simi's mum and friends will sleep between the newlyweds tonight, and this is one tradition I think Vivek would like to do without; he doesn't look happy as he's led away in a fist of family.

A week later, weary from the wedding madness, I'm slobbing about when there's a knock on the door. I scream as it opens. It's Padma—and a tall, cute Indian guy with a thick long rope of a ponytail sticking out of his New York Yankees baseball cap. She introduces him as "Surinder, my husband."

We scream again.

Rachel and Mary linger after delivering *chai*, widemouthed and open-eared for the story.

"Well, so I'm at the Thai conference and on the last day I look up and see Surinder, and I do a double take. My heart starts going into arrest, I can't breathe, I feel dizzy, the whole bit. He walks over and we just know, it's karma, baby, we just know. We talked, we walked out of the seminar, got on a boat, went to an island, got off and got married in the local church."

They hold hands and look lovingly into each other's eyes. I

nearly fall off my chair, Rachel drops the teapot and Mary freezes, too freaked to move.

India is in love with the idea of romance. On the television, men woo women with soppy songs, flowers, teddy bears and heart-shaped balloons, or shed teeming tears of unrequited love. And then there's reality. Dutiful sons and daughters do not fall in love and marry without their parents' blessing.

I shriek, "Shit, Padma, what did your mum say?"

Padma looks down.

"You haven't told her?"

"No, I just said I couldn't get to London to meet men and she's flying back to Delhi today. Sarah, I can't pay for the sins of my mother all my life and, besides, Surinder is perfect. She'll be happy. He's Indian, he's a doctor, he must be the most suitable boy in the country. He studied in the States and he has a green card. Sure, he's Sikh, but that's a part of Hinduism. He's perfect, we're perfect, love and Indian, who'd have thought?"

Surinder smiles sweetly and adoringly. He also hasn't told his parents, who live in the Punjab, and he sets off to do so. A gossip honor guard sees him through our gate; the compound is buzzing with scandal.

I can't sleep with worry, but Surinder rings in the morning. His parents are cool—upset, hurt, but accepting. Padma and I celebrate the relief with a cup of *chai*, and I apologize to her for my worry—perhaps I've misjudged Indian conservatism. Padma sets off happy-hearted to break the news to her mother.

But when she gets there it turns out her mother already knew. It says so on the note that was found below her hanging body this morning.

Beti, you have ruined my life, I can't live with the shame,
Mother

Her mother's second husband blocks Padma's way into the house. He hands her the note and speaks to her feet.

"You have destroyed this family. Your mother has restored her honor but yours is gone for good. You are dead to us now. I own this house and the one in Australia, she signed them over to me. You get nothing, now get out."

Padma stumbles to our house, retching and wretched. Surinder rushes back to Delhi to hold her. She cannot speak with grief and no one except Surinder, Jonathan and I will talk to her. None of her mother's friends visit, call or seem to care. Suicide seems common here. I have given up reading Indian newspapers because of stories about women hanging themselves with their *dupatta* scarves. Girls who are shameful spinsters or forced into bad marriages seem most at risk, but I've read much about women who are widowed or abandoned also resorting to suicide. It seems in a land where death is ever present, the cultural taboo of self-killing is slightly reduced. For women with few choices, death can deliver status and honor. The pull for respect and the shame of living in disapproval are stronger than the lust for life.

Padma is not invited to the cremation but we watch from afar. At a funeral ground beside the scum-filled Yamuna River her mother's shrunken body is wrapped in white cotton, carried aloft, dunked three times in a pool and placed on a pile of wood. She burns blue flames, black cinders, singed hair and popping bones. Her husband stands straight with righteousness until he does the son's job: smashing the skull to let the soul out. As it cracks, Padma stumbles and falls. She stands slowly with her fists clenched into her stomach. An orphan of Mother India, she is drained but determined.

"My mother didn't have the strength to turn her back on her family and her country. I do."

"What will you do?"

"Surinder and I are going to the States. This country is too small and nasty for me."

She turns from the smoke and the smothered love and walks toward the car.

We drive from the loneliness of the funeral pyre to the crowds of the back streets of bedlam that constantly assault with sounds, smells and sights. Padma sits numb while I'm high on sensory overload and sick from Wonderland's roller coaster of extreme emotions.

Amid the manicured lawns of the embassy district cars slow down to avoid what appears to be a branch on the road. But it's not a branch. It's the twisted limbs of a beggar who's been hit by a car; he is lying in the middle of the road crying and reaching out his hands for help. We pull over and Jonathan jumps out. But as he approaches the stricken man, a bus lurches to a halt; its driver gets out, grabs the beggar by his arm, drags him to the gutter and dumps him, his face and abdomen bleeding from the bitumen. He's dragged in anger, not in sympathy; human debris removed. The driver, his route now clear, jumps back on his bus and drives away.

India is the worst of humanity.

At the traffic light, Pooja runs up to our car; she is a local beggar who knows we are the softest touch around. We've given her clothes, food and pay good money for the paper she sells. She has rat-tail Rastafarian hair, dimples and dirty teeth but still manages to be the most beautiful child I've ever seen, with a smile that would melt stone. She moves to tap on the window but sees we're upset and hesitates. She gives me a newspaper and pats my hand.

"Poor memsahibs. *Ap teekay hoga*" (You will be okay).

The pity in her liquid brown eyes is an extraordinary communication of kindness from a child who has nothing to a woman who has everything.

India is the best of humanity.

Padma and Surinder travel to New York and Jonathan sets off for Pakistan. Left alone again, I feel the germ of a desire to cope with such shifts of extremes. Living a dutiful life as an Indian memsahib is not the way to do it. Padma's sorrow has made me sick of the nasty gossip delivered in rapid, loud, high-pitched singsong voices; such secrets and judgments are soiling my soul. I have almost died physically and now I feel I'm dying spiritually. I've crashed into another wall of bad karma and in the process lost my lightness of being. I miss silence, space and solitude, the luxuries of my country with its empty lands and calm cities. I realize Indian Jim's suggestion of "doing my duty" is not enough to sustain me anymore. Being healthy and wealthy won't get me peace of mind, body and soul.

I must find peace in the only place possible in India. Within.

5 | Insane in the Membrane

I decide to start my quest for inner peace with a brain enema.

A couple of my friends have undergone this treatment with the extreme meditation called Vipassana at a camp in the Blue Mountains, west of Sydney. I'd always thought Vipassana was a Western practice but it's actually a Buddhist technique that began in India.

Buddhism was born in India but its teachings were lost to the country after Islamic invasions. The Vipassana meditation teachings were preserved as a trained technique within Burmese monasteries and only recently reemerged via an unlikely guru. S. N. Goenka is a small pudgy man with a tendency to snort like a bull and squint like a squatting bullfrog. Born into a strict Hindu Indian family, he grew up to become a rich industrialist with stress migraines so bad he required morphine fortnightly. He found Vipassana meditation was the only thing that could eradicate what he called the "snakes, scorpions and centipedes" within. On a trip to India some years later he taught his parents and twelve of their friends; they then wanted courses for their friends, and the method mushroomed in India (and beyond) after twenty-five centuries of absence.

Goenka's courses are based on the original teachings of the Buddha, but without the robes, head shaving, chanting, bell ringing or begging—which is a good thing because I'm hardly ready to be a monk and my impressions of Buddhism are that it's a rather extreme religion that requires followers to spend too much time inside their own skull. I would never have considered a ten-day date with my mind in Australia, but here, I have the time, the need and the desire to remove the blockages of the past and find a new way of living.

Vipassana centers are all over India but I choose one that I hope will be the quietest in this chaotic country. An overnight train trip across the green Punjab, a five-hour taxi ride below snow-covered peaks and a long walk up a steep Himalayan hill beyond the meditating monks of Dharamsala is the small town of Dharamkot.

I approach the green metal gates of the meditation center with caution, for from tomorrow talk is forbidden. On the train I had nightmares of the horrors of being alone inside my own head. I saw my mouth bursting with forbidden words and my body gripped in a straitjacket surrounded by white coats. My friends' laughs and warnings echoed in my head—few think I'll make it and one even offered me a case of beer for every day I survive. The general impression is that I can't shut up for ten minutes let alone ten days and nights. I kind of agree with them. I am slightly scared of going psycho.

The center doesn't look like a loony bin, it actually seems peaceful; surrounded by pine trees are numerous small cottages, a large meditation hall and bathroom blocks with showers and pit toilets. A small fence strictly divides it into male and female sections. After handing in my passport, my book, my diary and my pens, I'm given the only thing I can read for ten days: the rule book and schedule.

Over the next week I'll study that pamphlet to such a degree that I'll know the composition of every dot and mark on the page. Yet it won't speak to me in the same way—I won't see alien life forms, or secret messages, just a way of life I never thought I'd embrace. The rule book contains my vows as a temporary monk. For ten days I'm not to kill, not to lie (easy when you can't talk), not to steal, not to speak and not to have sex. I find a pen at the bottom of my backpack and decide to write a few words every day on the back of the rule book. I feel sinful already but I'm keen to remember the experience.

I'm given the number of my "cell." The word is apt. It has a damp concrete floor, a tin roof and plastic walls, and is just big enough to allow me to stretch my arms out. Inside are a hard bed, a shelf and a hook. I've stayed in some pretty depressing rooms in India but this feels like a self-imposed prison.

I put my backpack down, hang up my jacket, put my mineral water up on the shelf and sit on the bed. I open the door and watch the mangy monkeys swing through the mossy pine trees. I explore the boundaries of the center like a caged animal, return to my cell and sit on the bed. I'm bored already and day one hasn't even started. We are still allowed to talk and to leave, and I hear people planning to go out for coffee. So I go back, get my money and have my last caffeine and cake.

This late snack makes me not really notice that dinner is only stale *numkeen* (salty spicy Indian chip things) and a banana (which I don't like). I love a big dinner but for the rest of the course this is it—a great breakfast and lunch but a tiny dinner. Soon my stomach is rumbling louder than the first Goenka video in the meditation hall. My last words are to complain about a bad back and plead for a position by the wall. Mouths rammed shut in case they leak, we troop off to bed like prisoners to the gallows.

DAY ONE

A gong breaks the silent, dark, dead hour of four. I ignore it. At four-twenty it rings again and a little bell is jangled outside my room. It's dark and cold. As I stumble to the hall I notice the fat white moon bulge with luminosity. I'm not a morning girl but I instantly feel excited by this new adventure of dawn. The thrill doesn't last long, as dawn is spent with eyes shut, focusing on my breath; this is most uninteresting and I fall asleep a lot. I frequently jerk myself awake and take a peek to see if anyone has noticed; my classmates (mostly foreigners) all look very focused, except for the Indian woman in front of me who is snoring.

Two and a half hours later we're gonged for breakfast. The routine then involves a one-hour meditation at eight and a two-hour sit from nine until lunch. Then there are three more long meditation sessions before the pathetic excuse they call dinner, another meditation, a video from Goenka and another little meditation before bed.

It's a boring technique. There's no mantra to focus on, white light to receive or god to picture; we're just told to observe our breath. All damn day. Apparently we need to learn to concentrate and to focus the mind so we can realize subtle truths. But my realizations for the first day are hardly subtle. They are:

1. My nostrils breath differently. Most of the time my right nostril takes in air on a sideways angle, while the left sucks in air directly below it.
2. I always need to have a song in my head and they are rarely good ones. Today's major tune is "Breathe" by Kylie Minogue. It's very boring when you only know the chorus and can't do any Kylie dance moves.
3. I'm impatient. By the second meditation session, one part of my mind has already dictated the unread chapters of the novel I had to hand in for locking up yesterday. Another part has finished the novel and determined it's not a bad book. A third section is worrying that when I do pick up the novel again it's likely the wrong things will happen.
4. Wonderland is within. I'm hyperactive and insane: one thought leads to something ridiculously unrelated and never comes back to the first. My thoughts don't make sense, or come to any conclusions or insights. And there's

rarely one thought at once; there are layers of boring, repetitive, crazed snippets. I'm regurgitating memories, plans, information, music, movies, *Friends* episodes, *Dr. Who* highlights and daydreams. It's mayhem in here.

5. My body is weak. It's aching already.

I'm kind of disturbed by the fact that there are thirty girls around me I don't talk to, or touch, or acknowledge in any way. No body language is allowed—no smiles of reassurance or grimaces at recognized or shared experience. A few girls are already crying and it feels selfish not to comfort them. I crack after lunch and squeeze one girl's elbow and smile in sympathy. Obviously, for some, meditation brings up less rubbish and more pain.

I feel like I'm trapped in a TV episode of *Survivor Spiritualists.* The last one left gets enlightenment.

DAY TWO

Song for the Day—"I Was Made for Loving You Baby" by KISS

Today I realize that my brain is beyond mad. It's now sprouting huge paragraphs from novels I've never read, using language I don't even understand. Unfortunately, it doesn't last and I come out of the meditations as moronic as I go in. I feel like I'm on drugs but there's no one to bring me back to earth or share the experience with. My brain is so desperate for friends it's started talking to itself, taking on male and female characters with strong accents and weird attitudes. I've heard the Dalai Lama warn that too many Westerners come out of meditation retreats thinking they are Buddha. My self-image is not that good: I think I'm Sally Field in *Sybil* with a major multiple personality disorder. Conducting my own psychotherapy, I half hope for repressed childhood memories; all I come up with are ABBA and KISS songs.

After five more hours of pussycat T-shirt dresses, glittery high heels, bad makeup, silly tunes and long tongues, Goenka reveals I'm not the only one doubting my sanity. But the teacher is not here. Vipassana is too popular for Goenka to teach courses now and he appears via a scratchy videotape, starting every little lecture with a heavy sigh and an ominous drawl.

"The secccoooooond daaaaaaaay is over. You have eieeeeeeght days to gooooo."

Tonight he drones that we have wild "monkey" minds, and while reining them in takes time, it will be worth it because controlling the mind is the only way to truly realize the expression of goodness and decency. My mind is most definitely wild ape territory. So, rubbing my painful joints as I fall into bed, I decide I'm willing to give Goenka's way to peace a chance.

DAY THREE

Song for the Day—"Raindrops Keep Falling on My Head"

Today I realize I've spent more than thirty-six hours concentrating on my nose and lips. It's only slightly less boring than focusing on breathing. I don't even like these areas of my body and damned if they feel any different for all the attention. I'm starting to get cranky. Why am I wasting ten days of my life learning to sleep sitting up? At one stage I begin to doze and jerk awake so suddenly that I bang my head against the wall. I crack up as quietly as I can. I'm actually dying for a good laugh; this meditation stuff is intensely serious and most of us look very depressed.

Yet, through the crankiness, cold, back pain and exhaustion, I feel a slight tinkling of emerging exhilaration. Unfortunately it's not yet coming from within. Spending twelve hours a day shut up inside makes me feel the outside world more keenly. At times the silence is deafening. Over the last five years I've slowly been losing my hearing from too many loud concerts, dance parties and radio headphones. I now realize what it will be like if I go deaf. Silence is strange, isolating and scary. But silence is sensual, for my other senses are becoming heightened. I nearly explode with joy at the feeling of sun on my face and tree moss under my fingers. Sitting having lunch, I notice a raindrop clinging to a railing. It's shining like a perfect diamond. I move my head down and the light hits the raindrop through another band in the spectrum—it glows red like a garnet. I dip my head again, it becomes sapphire; again, and it's topaz; and then I lift my sights to transform it back to a diamond. I spend forty-five minutes moving my head up and down making rare jewels out of a drip. Have I discovered the true wealth of nature, a natural drug of the brain, or am I just missing TV a little too much?

The two Indian women in the group have left—they kept talking and couldn't hack it. There's only us foreigners now.

Goenka tells us that soon the mental defilements will pass away and we will have healthy thoughts. I'm not sure if the raindrop love affair counts as healthy. He insists wisdom is within us all. I find this hard to believe; I seem to be regurgitating anything but wisdom. Tomorrow we will learn a new technique to find this inner truth. I'm just thrilled I will be able to take a break from focusing on my nose.

DAY FOUR

Song for the Day—"Hush Little Baby, Don't You Cry, Daddy's Going to Buy You a . . ."

Today I'm feeling very dizzy and faint and I have a horrific headache from coffee withdrawal. My bowels are also missing caffeine and it seems I'm not the only one; everyone is scoffing tablespoons of laxatives. How are we meant to cleanse our brains when our bodies are as clogged as India's toilets? I'm also suffering sensory deprivation and feeling exhausted beyond all tiredness. And I realize now why there's a vow not to kill. There's a mad Indian down the hill who's been yelling some political slogan through a distorted loudspeaker for four hours; I'm meant to be cultivating tolerance and infinite compassion, and all I can think about is how I'd like to murder him.

Our new meditation technique involves observing sensations on the body. We are told to focus on its parts bit by bit and feel heat, cold, tingles, tickles, air, etc. I feel nothing except huge blocks of pain in my back and legs. We're told to be aware, but not to react; then we'll break down the barrier between the conscious and unconscious mind and be able to live in a state of equanimity. It's mission impossible. Goenka has started to chant a Sanskrit tune at the end of each meditation that sounds just like the lullaby about Daddy offering to buy a child a rocking horse and a diamond ring. Inside I sing along. I have no self-restraint at all.

DAY FIVE

Song for the Day—"It's All Over Now, Baby Blue"

I'm beginning to think there are some people not suited to Vipassana and that I'm one of them. I have a mind that has prospered on an ability to do more than one thing at once. I can interview someone, put on a CD, read a screen, calculate the number of minutes to a newsbreak and think about what I'm going to have for lunch, all at once. So now, while I'm focusing on my body parts, my brain just can't cope with something so one-dimensional. To amuse itself my mind has decided to dump its mental inhabitants and take up with floozies residing in each body part. All my limbs and organs have names and personalities. My ankle is Christine (I think that's because "ankle" sounds like "uncle" and I had an Aunt Christine). Christine is very obstinate. My elbow is a cranky old Doris, my back a stubborn trucker called Stan, my thighs are two lesbians wanting to get it on and my neck is a hysterical old Indian woman. This is not normal. Physically, I'm faring no better. A new rule requires us to sit still for one hour—it's agony; my legs have such bad pins and needles I fear I will never walk again.

I can't do this.

By training our mind not to react to body sensations such as pain or pleasure we'll supposedly learn to reduce aversion and craving, thereby leading us to liberation and true happiness. I'm flunking Freedom 101. It's halfway through the course and if I could walk I'd run. Extracting deep cravings and conditioning by meditation is like psychological dental surgery.

DAY SIX

Song for the Day—"I Could Be Happy"

It's starting to happen. I'm feeling happy. I have self-control. I've sat still for one whole hour! It's exciting to know I can take charge of my mind and body and focus away from pain and discomfort and unhappiness.

Of course I'm not there yet. After six days of close proximity to thirty other women, I'm feeling a desire to categorize them all. This is kind of like a silent boarding school—factions are forming and I'm feeling annoyed by some women who have never even looked at me and who, of course, I've never spoken with. One I've christened "Old Mad Bag" always pushes for one of the few seats in the dining hall and today she moved my raincoat which clearly marked my spot. Another I've named "Piggie" because she refuses to wash her greasy curly ponytail and slurps her tea like a sow. I've decided "Miss New York" is a designer, "Hippie Trippie" is an E-loving raver, "Monkey Rapper" adores Puff Daddy and "Rattie" should stop twitching her nose. They probably call me "The Freak" because of the way I've started giggling at myself. Perhaps I'm going mad, or perhaps the realization of my craving and negativity is making me happy. Goenka is right: accepting suffering doesn't have to be pessimistic. A new mantra forms in my mind.

"The only way is up . . . for me and you now."

Shit! Another song.

The others don't look happy yet. Several are still crying and most are acting strangely. One girl is creating bizarre artworks from seedpods, another one is wearing a Jesus-like crown of twigs and hugging trees. I find myself watching another girl imitating a ladybird. Unfortunately this leads to the "Ladybird Ladybird" song about the house being on fire and all the children gone. Music lodges in my brain like chewing gum in hair; it's the hardest thing to dislodge and while I can't imagine living a life without it, I just wish the songs would get better.

DAY SEVEN

Song for the Day—"Feelin' Groovy" by Simon and Garfunkel

Today we've been told to really observe ourselves, and the course has morphed into the part of the movie *Fame* where the students do drama class. Everyone is very slowly putting food to their mouths, placing one foot in front of the other as if they were under water, and sitting down deliberately and demurely. My observations so far today are that I've kicked coffee cravings and my sexual visions are minimal. Before I'd got here a couple of friends had e-mailed me with warnings of sexual fantasies such as "mountains of vulvas" and "piles of penises." They sounded like nightmares to me. Luckily, the closest I've come to titillating thoughts are a few images of Jonathan smeared in chocolate handing me an ice-cold vodka.

Lying in bed I see my brain in visual form as it was and is now. At the beginning of the course it was like that first scene in the movie *Contact*, looking and sounding like all the radios and televisions of the world were switched on and set at different stations playing a mad symphony of senseless sound and images. I've now got to the stage where my brain is like a television left on at night after the station has gone off the air—all static snow and white noise.

We are told we should now be observing a flow of energy throughout the body. I hear girls whispering to the teacher about waves of tingling from head to foot, but I'm still feeling pain and occasional tickles. What's wrong with me? The Vipassana theory states that unconscious thoughts create physical sensations, so letting sensations arise and pass without reacting gets rid of unconscious pollutants within our mind. Obviously I have a lot more pollutants than I realized. Yet I can feel a tingle of something. It's as if my cells are realizing that suffering is temporary and my mind has moments where it can move above the pain and feel in the groove with another level of being.

DAY EIGHT

Song for the Day—"King of the Road"

It's the eighth day and I've almost stopped craving for the end of the course. There are times when I'm actually enjoying the process. I'm in love with the peace, the self-control, the self-discipline and the calm. The world outside seems daunting, brutal, loud and ugly; can I ever maintain this state out there in the madness?

Tonight I realize where a lot of my hate comes from. It's anger at my own faults or a manifestation of my inability to counteract the actions of another. This comes to me while watching the Goenka video. I feel a wave of boredom and can't concentrate, I feel hate toward Goenka; in my mind he becomes a fat toad who's imprisoned me. Then I realize I put myself here and I'm actually angry with my own bad body and mad mind. He begins to make me laugh instead. Every day there is more and more chanting on tape and there is one new section in which I swear Goenka is singing about "gay protection." Probably not what the Buddha had in mind, but it could be a cool new anthem for a meditation float at a Gay Pride parade.

According to Goenka, we are carrying tanks full of gasoline in our minds, so one spark from past action ignites other sparks and explosions. Vipassana is emptying the tank and eventually the petrol will be replaced by the cool water of love and compassion. At one stage today we all showed we have a lot of petrol left. The audiotape went on double speed and our large-girthed guru sounded like a chipmunk. Hardly hilarious stuff, but all of us exploded like a refinery bombed from above. After eight days of taking ourselves seriously, none of us could stop giggling for about ten minutes, while the assistant teachers and helpers remained absolutely impassive, as if laughter was a defilement they had kicked long ago. I keep giggling in my room for hours. I miss the emotion of joy and I can't see why mastery of the moment doesn't allow for its expression. If nonattachment and equanimity don't allow for hilarity, I'm not sure I want them.

DAY NINE

Song for the Day—"Oh What a Beautiful Morning"

Someone's cracked and is starting to hum. I must be progressing, for the tuneless fool hardly annoys me.

It's been ten days without a mirror and not seeing the thing that most people recognize as me makes me less aware of the boundary of self. My concerns about losing my identity while unemployed in India begin to fade into irrelevance. And for just a few seconds today I did lose myself altogether. While observing my sensations, I felt sick when I could feel the blood pumping through my veins, but I kept calm, and slowly the vibrations within and on the surface of my body melded together with those in the air around me. I couldn't sense where I ended and nothingness began. For one brief moment I realized I am just vibrating matter—arising and falling away like all the other particles in the universe. I lost it soon enough but I've caught a glimpse of the Buddhist and Vipassana notion that there is no "I," no "permanent self" to cling to. I lost my ego, my core. This, apparently, is the "ultimate truth" and the way out of self-obsession and self-importance. I do feel some bliss, some generosity and kindheartedness growing within me.

Then I freak myself right out. I go to ask for some advice (quiet talks with the course assistants are allowed). After nine days of silence and supposed getting of wisdom, this should be the first uttering of a new conscious being. Unfortunately the old me blurts out: "I'm a bit confused."

The new me freezes in shock as the words boom from my mouth, hit the concrete walls, bounce back and whack me around the head. It takes me a while to work out what I'm hearing. I sound so intrusive and so loud that for the first time I feel infinite compassion—for the assistant and for all the people who've ever had to listen to me.

Goenka's video chat congratulates us for starting to dissolve our egos. By renouncing our creature comforts, observing moral precepts and trying to gain wisdom through self-observation, I should have also developed tolerance (which I've failed to do), truthfulness (which is easy when you can't talk), strong determination (which I've needed) and pure selfless love (which I've begun to desire). Last but not least are equanimity, or detachment, and charity, qualities I've shown I do have beneath my mad monkey mind.

This course is free (Goenka refuses to receive payment for teaching people to observe reality) but donations are encouraged and I pay enough for at least two more people to attend. I try to show tolerance to the Israeli in front of me who pays five American dollars as a contribution and others who are noticeably absent for this part of the course.

DAY TEN

No Song!

The final speaking is sort of an anticlimax. After a morning meditation, we walk out of the hall and for the first time in my life, I find I have absolutely nothing to say. The young Israelis are whooping, laughing, screaming and chatting away in Hebrew. I walk away from them a bit shell-shocked at the exuberance. An Australian girl bursts into tears, shattered by sounds. A Canadian girl and I start up a gentle conversation, but within half an hour I feel the strain of social interaction, that growth of something dividing us, the boundary of awkwardness between beings. We're back in the real world and while I've gained great skills I feel I've lost some as well.

At dinner the hall is raucous. Smiling, open, happy faces grin at each other and whoop in delight. There's a vibrating bond between us—we're survivors reveling in each other's success. I realize the mad one and the piggy are sweet, the designer is a designer and the hippies, hippies. But I feel I've weeded out some past conditioning that dictates my preferences and prejudices; right now these people are as beautiful as I make them, things are as scary as I allow them to be, and as ugly and nasty as I create them. The world's a beautiful place.

We're told that to maintain this new state we'll need to meditate an hour each morning and night, and come back to the center in a year. This sobers me up. Vipassana has been the hardest thing I've ever done and I'm not sure I could do it again. Brain enemas are not pretty. I also don't see how I will be able to find two hours a day to climb back into my head. In India, if I'm not working, then maybe, but back in my hectic Australian life? Doubtful.

FREEDOM DAY

We're given a sugar hit for breakfast; after ten days of no sugar or coffee this hits like double-strength Ecstasy. But there's no teeth grinding or wanting to be sleazy, instead we clean up like a pack of happy Brownies. For the first time in my life I feel a level of mental and physical control I've never experienced before. We take some group photos and I hug my fellow survivors good-bye.

I skip out the gates, down the hill and back into India on air. My mind is clear, my heart is open, everyone is beautiful, everyone is worth loving, the world is wonderful and I feel universal love and compassion for all. For the first time in my life I'm living in the moment and I no longer miss my job, perhaps because my need for outward success to feed the ego has diminished. I go to an Internet café to read e-mails, ring friends and leave hysterical rants on their answering machines.

But within an hour my peace of mind is challenged. At the bus stop in the town of Dharamsala a beggar boy begins to hassle me. I stop, look into his eyes and then give him the dinner I've bought for the train trip. An old Tibetan monk watching starts clapping and laughing; the boy and I join in. An ordinary Indian begging transaction that normally makes me feel depressed and guilty has become a human and humane exchange of laughter and true compassion. Sure, I haven't saved his life, but it feels like a greater gift than money handed over out of guilt, anger and resignation. I definitely feel I've purged something and I'm ready to be reborn.

Unfortunately, I have more dead parts of myself to shed.

6 | Sikhing the Holy Hair

India has a hair fetish.

In terms of faith, the Sikhs are not meant to cut it, the Muslims wear it like Mohammed, the Buddhists are bald and the Hindu *sadhus* refuse to groom or remove their dreadlocks. In terms of facial fashion, '70s mustaches like Mr. Kotter had are common, the handlebar is still cool and the Willy Wonka twirl waxed and twisted upward is much admired. In the main, the more head hair the better—men still adore the Travolta *Saturday Night Fever* mullet and the Liberace wig look. Beside the roads several sit in the dentist chairs of the roadside barbers, peer into cracked mirrors and preen, lovingly fondling their facial hair, patting down their bouffants and combing their curls.

"A hair is a woman's glory," Rachel recites as she washes her hair every week at our house (her place is low on water). She and most Indian women have thick, long, shiny, bouncy and beautiful locks. Every Sunday the parks are full of girls sitting in a circle massaging oil into each other's scalps, and the salons buzz to the sound of hair dryers. But Indian girls are paranoid about body hair. They shave their arms and legs and pluck their faces free of dark down.

Babies' scalps are shaved on their first birthday so that their first hair can be given as a gift to God, and their little heads are massaged with sandalwood to encourage thick regrowth.

Hair is just another reason I don't fit in here. I've never had good hair. It's thin, curly, ratty and neither brown nor blonde. And now India is killing it.

Every morning since Vipassana I've been waking up to notice strands on my pillow. When I shampoo, my hair comes out in my hands and the drain clogs with knots and nests. If I brush my hair it fills the bristles within three strokes. By April I'm leaving strands and knots wherever I go.

Rachel says it's just the onset of summer shedding and she oils it for me; greasy and smelling like fries it just falls out faster. Rupa the beautician applies mashed frangipani leaves and flowers, mayonnaise, eggs, henna, coconut, curd and eventually even bootleg beer—it grows thinner. Hari Lal suggests a purifying bottle of water before breakfast, Yogesh makes me stay in headstands for ten minutes and Simi prescribes vitamins, but still it falls. It's now so thin I start getting sunburned through my part. The girls at the local beauty salon hold a crisis conference and decide on a weekly head massage with a giant throbbing vibrator hand mitt. It's wonderfully relaxing until the hairdresser yelps—a huge chunk of hair is wrapped around his mitt. Within weeks I have so little hair I can pin it up in one bobby pin. Mrs. Dutt books me in to see a nearby legendary Ayurvedic miracle healer, P. K. Jain.

It's standing room only in the packed waiting room and everyone is scrunched close and staring. I smile weakly, until a man wearing a tight white T-shirt tucked into ball-crunching black jeans walks straight up to me, stops inches from my face and with a completely serious expression on his, whips a comb from his back pocket and does a slow-motion Fonzie-like flick through his well-oiled mullet. I'm rigid in shock. Is this a come-on or a pose-off? I'll never know, because at that moment my name is called.

"Missss Seeeeraaaaaaaah, please be coming."

In a tin-walled cubicle I tell Mr. P. K. Jain my hair woes. He shrinks back from me, nervously runs a hand through his thick locks and then yells, "Eureka! I see what is happening. You are shedding your Western identity and becoming Indian. Take this, it will help you become one of us."

He hands over a huge envelope of cocaine-like powder and ushers me out the door.

I snort every morning but my hair falls faster.

At the Apollo Hospital a skin specialist gingerly and disdainfully picks with his pen at the remaining strands and says it is situation hopeless. According to him, when my body needed energy to recover from pneumonia it shut down the growing phase of the hair cycle. Now, three months down the track, all that hair is in shedding phase. He gives me an injection and some medication for my scalp. I read out the contents of this medication to a Sydney doctor who says it's illegal at home and demands I throw it out.

It's too late anyway as I'm now almost bald.

I've never been good-looking or very vain but this is devastating. Obviously some of my resident ego has survived Vipassana, because I feel ugly, freaky and depressed. Meditating doesn't help, the neighbors begin avoiding me and Jonathan isn't around for sympathy. Telling me he'd still love me bald as a billiard ball, he flew to Sri Lanka to do some cricket stories.

After a lonely week of tears and moaning "why me" I decide to accept the inevitable and shave my head. But the hairdresser refuses, horrified I could suggest such a thing. Instead she offers a short haircut. I agree. She lifts what's left of my ponytail up between two fingers and snips it off.

"Finished."

She walks off.

My ears stick out and my scalp is ugly. I walk out weeping, straight into the arms of a gang of Sikh teenagers.

"Hey, baby, what's up," one drawls in what he thinks is an American accent.

I look up to tell him to shove it, but instead struggle not to laugh. The lads are swaggering around in tight blue jeans kept high under their armpits by belts tied twice around their tiny waists. Their heads are covered in white cotton twisted into a bump. The material is so tight it stretches their eyes into slits and pushes their ears out. It's hard to look tough in a topknot; their vulnerability makes me trust them.

"I've had a bad haircut," I blubber.

They all look at each other and nod in agreement.

"Mmm, not so cool. What's wrong with your hair?" (The bravest and the smallest of the gang seems to be asking out of concern but sometimes I hate Indian directness.)

"It's falling out."

Dropping all pretense at tough, they stare at each other and back at me openmouthed and upset.

"Oh man, that sucks big time, baby," squawks their spokesman, forgetting to keep his voice low and Yankee style. The others chorus "yeah" as they step back, wary of my misfortune. Only the littlest stays close.

"You should go to Amritsar, the best town, the best people, the Sikhs, man. We fight misfortune and weakness. Maybe at the Golden Temple God will help you get your hair back."

Amritsar is in the Punjab near the border of Pakistan; a half-day train trip from Delhi. Padma's husband, Surinder, always raved about it and I decide to go and check it out. Of course I don't really think a town will make me hirsute but I don't have much hair left to lose. While I don't believe P. K. Jain's explanation that my hair loss means I'm becoming Indian, I do believe that trying to understand more about this country will make my life easier. Besides, Jonathan will be away for another week and I've nothing better to do.

From the Amritsar train station I catch a cycle-rickshaw through flat dusty streets bustling with business. And bristles. This must be the hairiest holy town on earth. The men wear their long head hair wrapped up in bulging blue or orange turbans. Beards hang loose and long in ZZ Top style, or are groomed with neat central parts. There are beards in buns and beards in pigtails, there are beards separated into two braids each tucked behind an ear. There are beards tied down with a cord so tight it puffs out cheeks and thrusts fat lips forward. Some men even wear a facial hair net. But my favorite look would have to be the big bandage wrapped over the beard and tied at the top of the head—these guys look like they're the victims of a permanent toothache. With my balding scalp I feel more naked and vulnerable than ever and put my *dupatta* shawl over my head as I travel along the facial hair parade. At a delightful guest house that smells of mothballs and faded glories, I sleep to dream of hair.

Sikhs are urged to worship early in the morning and I'm up before the sweat, filth, exasperation and exhaustion of a typical Indian day can build up. A cool wind blows through almost empty streets lined with the humps of beggars under blankets. En route to the Golden Temple my rickshaw cyclist sings softly under his breath and a light mist swirls around his skinny ankles as the bitumen starts to warm with the early summer sun. We pass squat square shops paying tribute to the ten Sikh gurus who founded the faith. There's a Nanak Tailor, a Har Krishnan Secondary School, a Hargobind Car Parts and a Tegh Bahadur Guest House. Nanak is the most popular name; he was the first Sikh guru. Born in 1469, when there was much violence between Hindus and Muslims, he urged Indians to worship one God whose name was truth.

At the end of a warren of dark narrow alleys we come to the bright white walls of the Golden Temple. This is the Vatican of Sikhism, the most important *gurdwara* in the world. After removing my shoes, washing my feet and covering my head, I walk through one of the gates just as the fat fireball sun plops over the horizon. It kisses the faces of Sikhs washing the marble walkways with milk, and ignites the Golden Temple Sanctum which sits in the center of the sacred pool. The rippling tank waters turn orange, shimmering like the sacred nectar (or *amrit*) that gives the town its name. A knot of nervous men gather on the stairs, all dressed in bright white turbans, their deep blue tunics teamed with gleaming silver swords.

I ask an official-looking man with a name tag what's going on. Temple officer Subedar Dalbir Singh is only too happy to help me; a jolly, rotund man in a safari suit, he proudly congratulates me for arriving on a special occasion. His Punjabi-accented English is a punchy bombardment delivered at breakneck speed with strong nods of his hair-heavy head. I think he explains that Sikhism doesn't really have a ministry as such, but at the Golden Temple four men, or *granthi*s, are paid to recite the entire Sikh bible by heart in the sanctum, and today two new *granthi*s will be ordained. These guys are starting an important job. Before he died, the tenth guru, Guru Gobind Singh, told his people there would be no more living gurus and they must follow the Guru Granth Sahib, which consists of more than one thousand pages of poetic meditations on God, guidance to good living and hymns. This book is not just a bible, it's more a living saint—every morning it's carried in a procession to the sanctum and put to bed at night with just as much reverence.

I follow the new *granthi*s and their pushy families across the narrow bridge to the Golden Sanctum for a rare glimpse of the book in daylight. The silent crowd of Sikhs gasp as we watch the unwrapping of a birthday present from God. Two men fold back beautiful orange felt that's intricately embroidered with gold flowers. They carefully peel away five more layers of felt, followed by layers of white cotton. Finally, the Guru Granth Sahib is revealed. Beautifully handwritten curved script travels over thick massive sheets. The new *granthi*s nervously begin their recitation. I can't understand it, but the communal singing, or *kirtan*, they lead is divine. I have to stop myself from crying out "Alleluia!," for these Sikhs seem to be the only Indians who understand that music sounds better if it's not making ears bleed. In shops, movies, restaurants, festivals, weddings, temples, train stations and parties music is always distorted beyond all comprehension, but here the harmonium and tabla are soft and clear, and the human voices rise unadulterated by sound systems. Influenced by the Sufi hymns, the music is designed to prompt a particular devotional mood or emotion. I feel sweet joy, a sense of a shared serenity within the human spirit.

The sound of huge kettledrums signals the end of the ceremony and reminds Sikhs of their most fundamental religious practice—*sewa* or service. Subedar shuffles along beside me muttering, "Doing duty serves God and rids us Sikhs of selfishness, ego and misery."

We head toward the *gurdwara*'s communal kitchen, where aluminum dinner trays tower high and massive cooking pots bubble on fires large enough to bake an elephant. Topknotted boys peel piles of potatoes and carrots, and about fifty women squat rolling dough.

A beautiful young girl with a plait down to her bottom stands up, grabs my hand and pulls me down into the *chapatti* circle. The *chapatti* is the basic foodstuff of north India—round hot bread that starts as a blob of dough and is then pinched and rolled into a perfect circle with a series of deft wrist actions. Through sign language and giggles, the girl shows me, her mother shows me and *her* mother shows me; but the three generations fail. My *chapatti*s look like the playdough failures of my childhood—lumpy, wrinkled and torn. Grandma snatches my rolling pin and pushes me away. Sacked, I walk out amid gales of high-pitched hysteria.

The communal kitchen is the Sikh faith's "up yours" to the Hindu notion of caste. Hindu Brahmans will not eat with lower castes or let them touch their food, but in the Sikh dining room all eaters are equal—beggars, Western tourists, Hindu *sadhu*s, pilgrims and school kids eat spicy chickpeas, vegetables and perfectly round *chapatti*s with their hands.

But while the Sikhs can dish out food, they usually won't accept it or anything else. Subedar shows me the Akal Takhat Sahib, the

Sikh parliament that was destroyed in a 1984 shoot-out between the government and separatists wanting a Sikh state. He gruffly growls, "The government rebuilt the building and we knocked it right down and built it again ourselves."

"Why on earth did you do that?"

Subedar puffs out his chest.

"We are not beggars. Dependence leads to guilt and shame. You will never see a Sikh beggar ever."

He's right, I never have.

Subedar pushes me toward the museum, looks at his fob watch and bustles off.

The Sikhs are the Irish of India, portrayed as the fools, the losers and the clowns. The latest gag I've heard involves a game show host asking a Sikh contestant, "Sadarji, what is your name?" The Sikh stumbles, ponders and then responds, "What are the options?"

But Indians also have a deep respect for the Sikhs, believing them to be honest, tall, tough and not to be trifled with. Perhaps that's because the Sikh faith has been hard won with bravery and blood. The community calls itself the Sikh Khalsa—the Army of the Pure—the long hair, knives, bracelet, boxer shorts and comb are its uniform. Hair is never cut so the God-given form remains intact, and the comb keeps it tidy. The knife symbolizes a willingness to fight in self-defense or to protect the weak. The bracelet handcuffs a Sikh to God, and the boxer shorts, which are long and baggy, show modesty and restraint.

The first Sikh gurus were allowed to propagate their new faith during the rule of the most tolerant of all Mogul leaders, Akbar the Great; but when Akbar died in 1605, the fifth guru, Arjan, backed the wrong son in the war of succession and Sikhism was punished. In the temple's museum a huge painting celebrates the first Sikh martyr by showing him calmly sitting on a red-hot pan while burning hot sand is poured over his lap. Another large work shows the ninth guru's comrades being boiled alive and sawed in half; the oil painting beside it shows their master beheaded. Other gorgeous exhibits show Sikhs hanging, dragged behind horses, rammed on the head, shot from cannons, knifed in the mouth, scalped alive, turned on spiked wheels and run over by trains. Special reverence is given to Baba Deep Singh, a warrior who was almost decapitated but somehow held his head on and kept fighting to get to the Golden Temple. Children's comic books of gore are on sale. The captions are curt: "*There is hardly a mode of torture which the Sikhs have not suffered, and not one has cried in pain or relented.*"

I'm not the only one gasping in horror. Beside me an extraordinary creature stands still, a hand to her mouth. She's a fragile, delicately boned girl with ivory skin, wearing a white turban, a white flowing head scarf, a white *salwar kamiz* and a huge knife in a black holster. I ask her if she's all right and she whispers, "Yes."

We leave the museum to sit and watch the calming waters of the pool together. Her name is Keval and she is a Western Sikh. In a Texan drawl she tells me that a couple of years ago she was a normal nineteen-year-old all-American girl who drank too much and partied every night. But one day she took a Kundalini yoga class. The teacher was an Indian Sikh called Yogi Bhajan. Her face flushes a light pink with the memory.

"As I was walking up to him I was the happiest I've ever been. It was total relief, comfort and peace. It was like we had known each other forever and I'd been missing him for so long."

Soon after, Keval dropped out of college, started a yoga ashram and was given her new name according to her numerology. She says she's one of ten thousand Western Sikhs and Yogi Bhajan has converted them all. I know that Indian Sikhs don't really get into yoga and the only thing I've heard about Kundalini yoga is that it's great for sex. Keval is anything but sexy, yet I am fascinated by her. She is intriguingly self-contained, so pale she's almost translucent, and despite the strange outfit and her bright beaming face, she's somehow bland and vacant. I find it amusing that ten thousand Americans are dressing themselves up in a religion that has such an Indian look and character, and I can't help but further question her about her life. When Keval invites me to a nearby school for Western Sikhs, I quickly accept; I'm keen to see if her kin are as strange as she is.

• • •

The Miri Piri Academy squats low in the green flat fields where the sixth guru, Hargobind, was born. A pale, skinny and acne-scarred American with a stringy ginger beard comes to meet me at the office. He's the school's academic director, his name's Kirpal and he's happy to show me around. In the late sixties Kirpal was one of America's long-haired army of the impure—the baby boomer hippies who were dodging military service, rejecting discipline, authority and weaponry to worship drugs.

"I was doing every drug under the sun as an avenue of opening up my consciousness, but I was just creating knots in my psyche. In the first yoga class I experienced uplifting inspiration that was clean, there was a sense of transcendence."

He stares into the distance with watery blue eyes and sighs. I guess what's coming—Kirpal met Yogi Bhajan and found a guru who got him high on Kundalini yoga and addicted to love.

This is obviously not your average American school. The bell rings for assembly and the kids come out of class in a calm and orderly manner. The boys are wearing blue tunics and the girls are wearing pants, all of them wear turbans and huge side knives. This must be the only American school in the world where the children are ordered to carry a piece and punished when they don't. They form a lineup and stand at stiff attention, except a tiny little girl who makes soft groans as she does push-ups for punishment. Just when I'm thinking it strange that former peace activists are running a military academy with strict discipline, the children break assembly for cuddles and a game of soccer.

As I watch them kick the ball around lazily in the heat, the few hairs left on my head stand up on end. The children all seem to have blue eyes, lily-white skin and are strangely self-possessed and reserved. They remind me of the telepathic alien children in the movie *Village of the Damned*. One little girl with her turban slightly askew approaches to hand me a tube of thirty-plus sunscreen.

"Here, you must have sunscreen, you have to wear it every day to keep your skin pale and unwrinkled."

These white Sikhs are more obsessed with pale skin than most Indians! I feel calmer when a woman with freckles and sun damage joins us. She is Kripal (Kirpal's wife).

"These children are very different, aren't they?" I understate the obvious. She stares at me unblinking.

"Yes, they are very special. They're on a mission, you could say."

"A mission?"

"Yes. In the seventies, Yogi Bhajan started working with us women. We went to power-raising camps where he told us we had to give birth to the new generation. We worked toward raising our consciousness to attract souls that will transform the planet. It was very lofty, we were idealistic hippies. We got married, had babies and these are the children we wanted to do all the work."

I'm not sure this is going to get my hair back. Yet it's an entertaining diversion and I marvel anew at the different kinds of people that India attracts.

I attend a class of final year students who will soon be sent out on their divine mission. Their guest teacher is Guru Singh and he is obviously a hero; the kids sit around him and practically pant with happiness. I whisper to a girl next to me, "Why is he so famous?"

"He's the first white Sikh," she whispers back.

Guru Singh is so pale his edges blur in a ghostly hue. His sharp, emaciated face falls into a snowy-gray beard that straggles thinly into his lap. His delicate pink fingers softly pluck his guitar as he tells us about these "dark times on earth, the Kali Yurga." From what I've heard, most Hindus and Buddhists believe we have centuries left of these dark ages, but Guru Singh predicts it'll all end in 2012.

"This will be the Age of Aquarius, a golden age of truth, but the transition period will not be easy. All the conditions that rule this age will lose their dominance and they'll lead to mind distortions and freak-outs. There'll be insanity on the streets and we will be like the Red Cross."

The kids sit rapt, straight-backed and cross-legged, almost holding their breath in excitement. Guru Singh lifts his voice louder.

"That's why you're going to school. Your generation is at its most creative point right when the age is shifting."

He strums stronger and rocks, raising his voice again.

"The frequencies of the universe are rising. You are the arrowhead. We are here to help you, but you have to burrow through time and space. It's going to be fun."

He rocks faster and points wildly up in the air.

"It's going to be in your face, Mr. White Man, Mr. Politician and Mr. Organized Religion."

The students breathe out, lean back and grin. I almost choke. I know teenagers need their egos pumped up, but isn't this going too far? They'll be thirty in 2012 and very pissed off if no one calls their emergency number.

After the class I ask some if they feel special. They all quietly say "yes," but can't explain why, except for pointing vaguely at their turbans. Many seem just ordinary kids wearing a strange costume; they come late to class and giggle in the corridors. But there are too few signs of rebellion for me. Kripal says more than forty have even volunteered to get up at two-thirty in the morning for forty days to wash the Golden Temple floors. I wore red stockings and Doc Martens to school for a year in a futile attempt to stand out and be different; these kids are Western students who embrace strict rules, a uniform and a path in life as saviors. But perhaps my reaction only shows my own prejudice. India's young don't rebel much—Razoo is the most radical under-thirty I've met so far and she believes that because Indians are raised with a strong identity they don't need to experiment much or reject what their parents believe. Perhaps the identity these children get from being Sikh might be giving them a strength and self-confidence they wouldn't get in the West, where children are overloaded with options. But then again, maybe they are brainwashed. I'm not really sure.

The new white Sikhs train for their divine mission in life with intense three-day meditations and Kundalini yoga, both of which are intended to open up their *chakras*, or energy points, in the body. I'm invited to join a Kundalini class and curiosity wins out over cringe. We start sitting cross-legged and circling and grinding our pelvises while sighing. I feel pathetic, if not a little perverse, with pubescent children pelvic-thrusting and moaning and groaning all around me. Guru Singh drawls directions.

"You're barely getting into it, be creative, you are unique, FUUUUUULFIIIIILL yourselves."

I try to let go, but I'm not the only one feeling silly; some kids are chewing gum and looking down. This seems a cruel command for adolescents.

Finally we are fulfilled enough to sit with our arms up in the air for ten minutes and pant. After a few minutes of hyperventilating, I begin to feel happy, dizzy and light-headed, but I'm not sure it's God, I think it's oxygen saturation. Guru Singh starts strumming his guitar, and with our hands on our heart *chakras* we chant:

I am what I am that is me,
I am what I am that is me,
I am what I am that is me,
Thank God I am.

A student joins in with a tabla and Guru Singh strums louder and louder, yelling at us to "Siiiiiiiiiiiiiiiiiiiiing it out."

It's "Young Talent Time" meets Christian holiday camp. We send out all our loving by lifting our hands over our heads and shaking them down chanting:

May the longtime Sun shine upon you (arms up),
All love surround you (arms up),
And the pure light within you
Guide your way on.

And we finish with a long-drawn-out "*Sat nam*"—which means "truth is the name."

For a time my cynicism is suspended and I'm in on the group

high. The singalong of self-love has created a New Age ring of confidence in the room. Guru Singh oozes happiness in himself, his faith and his music. He gives me a CD of songs he's made with Seal, called *Game of Chants*, and shows me references by Jane Fonda and Pierce Brosnan. I tell him Courtney Love said *sat nam* at the MTV awards and showed me some Kundalini yoga moves when I interviewed her at Triple J, but I can't resist adding that she then put her cigarette out in my coffee. (Obviously the oxygen-induced high is fading and I can't help challenging his confidence—smoking, drinking and other drugs are not welcomed among New Age Sikhs.) The song and panting stuff may be kind of fun but I'm skeptical of this form of yoga; mainly because the first Sikh guru was critical of the practice and believed service to others was a better way to God. This new version of Sikhism seems to be a synthesis of age-old knowledge and modern self-loving Americanism—its saccharine self-absorbed smugness is a bit much for me.

The Indian Sikhs seem even more confused by the turbaned white people. The next day I run into Keval again at the Golden Temple, and as we sit down for a final chat, a small crowd gathers around us to watch. For once I'm not the center of attention—they are all staring at Keval. Indian Sikh women don't wear turbans or carry a knife, so her outfit confuses them. And the fact that Keval is white and wearing such a getup obviously amazes them. A man is pushed forward to speak to her but he's too intimidated; instead he asks me, "What she is?" I explain in Hindi that she is a Sikh. They pass this around the circle in Punjabi, shocked and murmuring. I ask them what they think. Some say "very good," a few are amused that rich spoiled Americans come to them for help, but a few shake their heads angrily.

"She can't be a Sikh, she's not Indian," an elderly man spits as he wags his finger at me sternly. "Sikh is not just religion, it's our birthright of blood, it's not for foreigners."

I see his point. I'm kind of uncomfortable about people adopting a cultural identity because they perceive their society lacks its own. I vow that if I further explore India's smorgasbord of spirituality I won't end up in a costume or in cheesecloth.

Although I'm enjoying not working, the journalist in me wants to collect more information and perhaps court some controversy about the white Sikhs, so I wander around to the nearby headquarters of the faith—the Shiromani Gurdwara Parbandhak. Here, Sikhism is protected with machine guns as well as swords, and the Committee Secretary, Gurbachan Singh Bachan, plans propagation of the faith while sitting behind a desk as large as a small boat that's surrounded by weapons and *chai* wallahs. Gurbachan is a fierce-looking, hairy version of Rumpole of the Bailey and his thick-lipped permanent scowl sends the message that meeting me is a waste of time. His face lifts when I mention Yogi Bhajan.

"He is my friend."

"What do you think of his focus on using Kundalini yoga in his teachings?" I ask.

Gurbachan Singh laughs long and loud and his office assistants join in.

"Yes, Sikhs don't do yoga, but Yogi Bhajan is just attracting those Westerners by yoga to get them to be Sikhs. It's a tool for accelerating Sikhism."

"So that's all right, is it?"

"Yes, madam, isn't it? Look, Sikhism will solve the world's three main problems. Firstly, mental depression will go, as Sikhs remain in an ascending mood. Secondly, AIDS will be wiped out, as Sikhism makes mankind free of HIV because we be faithful to a single partner. And thirdly, cancer won't happen, as Sikhs don't smoke and they don't get skin cancer. The hair of the Sikh will absorb the sun's rays."

He leans back and frowns at my pathetic scalp.

"You need it most, madam. Your hair is not much and in Aus-[illegible] you haven't got the ozone layer, you need hair to protect you even more. Join us, sister, become a Sikh missionary and stop cancer."

How do I tell this man that if I went down to my local Sydney beach looking like Celine Dion in her turban phase and told the gay boys in G-strings that they must give up waxing, they'd banish me? If I then proposed they grow their facial and head hair, I may need the Sikh sword for protection. I respect the Sikh focus on living a moral life, doing good deeds for others and speaking the truth (a relative concept in India), and for being spiritually strong to fight weakness and fear. But I hate a uniform and I'm not ready to leap to a faith in God yet, let alone a religion. As for the white Sikhs, while the old me would have rejected them as sick freaks, the Indian-based Sarah seems reluctant to judge them too harshly. It's as if their tragic guitar playing has awakened heartwarming images of kids singing Kumbaya around the campfire as well as my Kundalini, for on the train home I sing their chants about being what I am. Their friendliness and gooey openness have disarmed me, and while what they teach might be a bit over the top, I think they're harmless. What they have shown me is that India has many lessons to teach and many paths to travel to peace; I'm encouraged to find my own.

Back in New Delhi I realize that something transforming did indeed happen in Amritsar. As I shampoo my few hairs clean of the filth from the trip, I feel little stalks. Regrowth. It's as if I've now shed the old body, mind and hair. I joke with Jonathan that I am a newborn babe budding in India's spiritual supermarket.

7 | Indian Summer in Suburbia

A week after I leave the Army of the Pure, a civil war erupts at the Australian Broadcasting Company compound.

Moolchand fires the first shot. One morning he runs down from his laundry room on the roof and barrels straight into our flat crying fat tears, shaking with sobs and wringing his hands.

"Irrrreeen is gone, sir, help, irreeen is gone."

Jonathan and I look at each other. We beg Moolchand to slow down and to calm down, but he sobs louder and louder. "Irren, irren, priess, priess, gone, gone."

We shake our heads, failing to understand the tragedy at hand. He yelps in real pain and Rachel comes running.

"The irren, my good, number-one, excellent preisser irren, totally, one hundred percent gone."

Moolchand's mustache quivers and droops, he sinks to the floor like a runner shot in a trench. Rachel translates as she revives him with *chai*.

The iron has been stolen from the laundry.

The news spreads around the compound in fearful whispers. Gossip, conspiracy theories and finger-pointing follow. Angry shouts come from the rooftop; the Australian Broadcasting Company office manager Peter tells Jonathan he must act decisively and defensively to keep control of the staff. Jonathan is a most unwilling commander but we trudge upstairs to the office for a council of war. Mary, Rachel, Abraham, Moolchand, Lakan, Aamar and "Mr. Peter" sit in a semicircle, eyes downcast, feet shuffling; Abraham is shaking, Moolchand sniffling and Lakan emits a nervous cough. The new Australian Broadcasting Company staff reporter, Neeraj, stands at stiff attention beside Jonathan. Neeraj should really be in the army rather than journalism; General Kumar loves him as he always wears camouflage fatigues, sports a number-one haircut, keeps a well-preened sergeant major mustache and insists on calling Jonathan "skipper." Today he offers to translate for clarity.

Jonathan sighs deeply and in his most solemn reporter's voice begins.

"As everybody knows, the iron is missing."

Neeraj jumps his legs apart, clasps his hands behind his back and clears his throat.

"*Hum-ko maloom yeh press missing he.*"

Everybody nods. Jonathan continues.

"This is a most serious crime and I am most upset."

Translation and tears, shakes and sniffles. I stifle a giggle.

"There will be an investigation. But I don't want to hear rumors, innuendo or suspicions, just facts."

They nod sternly as one. I dig my fingernails into my hands.

"This brings shame on me, shame on the Australian Broadcasting Company, shame on Sarah and shame on your good selves."

I bow my head and shake with laughter. There's a ripple of eyes and a Mexican wave of gasps. The staff think I'm crying. They shuffle out stooped, supposedly sad and shamed, but, like me, they are faking it. Moolchand beams as he sets off to buy a new iron, and tells me he likes the new Jonathan.

"Mr. Jonathan is real boss now. We love having tough guy, you and sahib-sir are too nice really. Too softy."

Whoever says India is spiritual has no idea what it's really like to live here.

All the same I'm feeling energized by my brush with Sikhism. It's as if the buds of my new hair contain the seeds of a new strength. A desire to take action grips and propels me to move the Australian Broadcasting Company away from this dreadful dark, diesel-stained dungeon of a flat on the highway. I'm warned it's mission impossible. Many correspondents and their partners have failed—even our predecessor, the debonair Edmond Roy, who speaks four local languages. I ignore all the doomsayers and begin juggling real estate agents, landlords and staff requests for suburbs with the best shops, churches and temples. Jonathan seems amused, touched and cheered by my stories of Vipassana and Amritsar and my subsequent transformation. While he's made me promise I won't become a white Sikh or a Hare Krishna, he's encouraging me to make the most of India and to travel as much as I want, starting with a tour of Delhi's rental properties. He, too, would love to move from the West End—he's sick of the pollution, and the traffic is coming through as background sound in his reports home.

This year, anyone who is anyone is moving into farmhouses south of the city. We bump and bash down brown potholed tracks to view mansions with colonial columns, sweeping staircases, dust bowl courtyards, dried-up fountains and high mud walls topped with ugly shards of broken bottles. I cruise sedate bungalows within Delhi's diplomatic suburbs; all full of faded glory, with elephant foot umbrella stands, grand gray chandeliers, stained conservatories and moldy drawing rooms. I view ex-embassies filled with tiny dark windowless rooms that possibly served as torture chambers. All are too expensive for the Australian Broadcasting Company budget. Delhi rents are almost as high as New York's.

We rein in our search to one affordable village (Delhi is more a collection of villages than suburbs) called Vasant Vihar in south Delhi. It's not near anything much, bar the homes of our staff and the airport, but it does have a shopping center with a classy movie theater and an ice-cream shop. I fall instantly in love with a house modeled on the starship *Enterprise*—the huge living room is dominated by a wooden bar, three revolving chairs and a set of huge curved windows displaying a Milky Way of splattered bird shit. In warp speed we tell the agent we'll take it, but he rings the next day saying the owner will not let non-Indians pollute his property. This is an unusual triumph of bigotry over big bucks, as most landlords jump to fleece foreign tenants.

Then we find an apartment shaped like a ship, with porthole windows and a staircase built in the shape of an anchor—we adore it. But the owner sees that we're white and triples the rent before we've even made it to the front door. We get lost in houses with labyrinths of crescent moon-shaped rooms added on as families expanded. We see marble mausoleums and subterranean dungeons that are worn down, half torn down, dirty and degraded. We inspect new properties all kitsch and crass with green marble floors, brass fittings and copper art that have been modeled on the Alexis pad in *Dynasty*.

Then, just as I'm about to admit defeat, we tour a gorgeous, light, private house with a huge terrace of trees. The price doubles but is still right. I ask the real estate agent (all slick hair, big blazer and huge belly) if I can see the staff quarters. He looks at me as if I've farted.

"The what?"

"The staff quarters."

"What?"

I give in. "The servants' quarters."

"You want to see the servants' quarters?"

"Yes."

"Why, madam?"

"To see how our driver and family will live."

Abraham (listening in from the car) begins to sweat, shake and swallow rapidly. The real estate agent and elderly owner glare at him suspiciously, stare at me contemptuously, wobble their heads and scratch their balls. I climb alone up a spiral staircase to a tiny windowless room and a filthy toilet. I yell down, "That is it?"

The owner shakes his stick at me.

"What more do they need?"

"Our driver has a wife and three grown children."

"So?"

We reject the house despite the owner's attempts to bribe us with moonshine poured into a Johnnie Walker Black Label bottle. Some of the staff may think we've gone all soft again but Abraham and his family are grateful.

Finally we find a red brick house with round windows, a seventies sunken den, light shades shaped like fig leaves and an inner garden open to the elements (this is good *vastu*—the Hindu equivalent of *feng shui*). The building is self-contained, with no interfering landlords on site, and has enough room for an upstairs office and a downstairs home, plus it has a roof terrace and a tiny patch of scorched earth for a garden. The owner is a colonel who doesn't rip us off too badly. We're thrilled, but our old landlord, General Kumar, is distraught; we are deserters, abandoning him for a lower-ranking officer's home.

On the morning of the move a small army of skinny men swarm into the flat on the highway and wrap every single CD, bowl, toiletry product and safety pin in separate huge balls of newspaper. They work rapidly and diligently, until one finds our only bottle of Stoli vodka. The day ends with the truck half full, three boxes stolen, four of the mover-wallahs vomiting in the stairwell and a group of them asleep in the driveway.

It's worth it.

In our new home our sleep no longer vibrates with car horns, truck rumbles and screeching brakes. We wake up to the rumble of wooden wheels of vegetable carts, the clip-clop of cows, the ping of bicycle bells and the cry of "*aiiiiiiyeeeeeee, aiiiiiiiiiiiiyeeeeeee*" (please come) from the garbage collector. We have breakfast to the sweet songs of the broom man and are further serenaded by the plant seller, the rug cleaner, the curtain maker and sometimes by the flutes of the snake charmers. Occasionally an elephant will clang its bell, or trumpet as it trundles past on its way to perform at a birthday party. By lunchtime the air is filled with the soft thud of ball on bat and cries of "howzat!" As summer builds, the afternoons grow so still that only the crackle of badly tuned transistor radios and the whisper of suburban snores carry through the thick air.

Our home is also a hotel—troops of Australian friends begin to stagger in from their travels, limp, filthy, skinny and exhausted. They collapse onto the couch and into the loving embrace of Rachel's cooking, Mary's coffee, Jonathan's bootleg beer and Moolchand's laundry. Many of them refuse to leave until their plane's due date. One good mate from Sydney, Pete, lifts his head from slumber one afternoon to christen our new home the "Biosphere" and threatens to put us in the *Lonely Planet* under the recommendation: "A hotel that seals out the heat, the dust, the dirt and the exasperation to create a pod that reenergizes the traveler for reentry to the infuriating furnace that is the Indian outdoors."

We buy some small sculptures, recover the couches, get curtains made and place big cushions on rugs. At last a home! I'm comfortable in my sanctuary of sanity, my safe house on the other side of the looking glass, where things are in their place.

By May, however, I'm less comfortable. Pete and all our friends have left; only the most foolhardy or ill-informed tourist would dare venture to India from April to September. The staff is slowing down for summer, too. Only Rachel has vim and vigor. She also has a glow and sings as she works. Rachel is in love. Akash, a friend of her brother's, has asked for her hand in marriage. She shows me the photos of his conversion from Hinduism to Catholicism that won her heart. He stands small, slight, serious and confused as the priest wets his head and renames him Ronald. They travel to Madras for the wedding and Rachel returns from the honeymoon vomiting—pregnant from the wedding night.

As summer builds in intensity we begin hibernating from the heat of the day. Jonathan and I wake floppy and dehydrated before dawn and drag ourselves out for a brief break with home. We walk wet with sweat to our local park, a square of brown, dotted with dirty, raggedy gum trees. A couple of ancient Muslim tombs add ambience but their rotting walls are scratched with graffiti like "Sita loves Ramesh" and "Hai Hindustan!" Mangy dogs lie deep in mounds of sand, black-bristled pigs and local slum boys compete for scraps, and tiny girls collect and carry huge piles of rubbish and firewood on their heads. It's hardly Hyde Park. Under a sky that's a white-hot sweltering soup of pollution we join middle-aged men in shorts pulled high over round paunches as they stride and clap their hands to applaud their own efforts. Young men play cricket to an audience of cows, and old men leg-squat, star-jump and gather to comment on the weather or to congratulate each other on being Indian. There are big beaming smiles the day India reaches the one billion population mark and handshakes and pats on the back when Delhi overtakes Mexico City as the most polluted city on earth.

"Good to be number one at something, hey, boys," shouts an old codger to his friends.

At seven the local laugh club meets.

I haven't seen many people really laugh a lot in India. Perhaps it's the bad jokes but perhaps it's also the fact that the country lacks the lightness of being that a belly laugh requires. Instead, laughter is a serious form of exercise best practiced in a circle of about forty men and boys and best sounding like a pack of hyenas in pain.

One morning the chief laugher calls a sweaty Jonathan and me over. Fat and happy, he stands with his legs wide apart and stomach out.

"Come, laughing is good for health. We will exercise the lungs and fill the heart and body with joyful energy."

So we stand like him, with our hands on our hips, chins to our chests and pelvises forward. We take a deep breath.

"Now laugh," yells the leader. He bends his head back, expands his girth and waves a hand like a baton.

We exhale, yelling: "Hhhahhhhhahahahahahahahahaaaaaaaah-hhhhhhaaaaaaaaaaaahhhhhhha!"

I'm feeling a bit dizzy.

"Put all your body into it now, come on. Breeeathing in and exxxpiring with laughter."

"HAHAAAAHHHHHHAAAAAAAAAAHHHHHHHHHHAAHHHHAAA!"

I think I've popped a blood vessel in my head.

"Are you getting it, madam? Don't be shy, laugh your cares away and wake the gods with your noise."

I take a deep breath and mime like a Bollywood movie star. Jonathan lets rip a huge laugh that collapses into a fit of giggles. The group looks at him oddly—as if by showing true mirth he's breaking the rules of forced laughter.

We head home light-headed and loving our new suburb.

By June it's getting too hot to laugh, in fact it's getting too hot to do anything. Temperatures are over one hundred °F and I can't even leave the house. Jonathan travels to Afghanistan, where he will require a cool head to secretly film in a land where cameras are illegal. While he's out of touch for two weeks, I shut myself inside. But there is no escape. The power cuts increase and the air-conditioning breaks down. My head feels like it's full of cotton wool soaked in oil, and I am as weak as Superman struggling with a necklace of Kryptonite. I drag myself around the house and flop onto the couch in a semicoma. Thoughts drift like light cloud—the moment I try to catch one it dissipates. I adopt the Indian blank-faced straight-ahead stare, as I can't be bothered to shut my eyes or to focus them. At times it feels like my pupils have been sucked dry and collapsed into withered raisins. Arms too heavy to move, head too heavy to lift, I lie and watch the fan like a placid infant transfixed by a mobile. At times I'm so hot I cry, but the tears evaporate before they reach the corners of my eyes. My Sikh-inspired spiritual strength is melting away and my brain is too fried to meditate. I begin to worship the air-conditioner and pray for fewer power cuts. Outside the Biosphere, those not wealthy enough for coolers, fans or air-conditioning are asleep in hot heaps under snatches of shade. The city cooks us slowly.

At the end of June the rains don't come. Delhi and Rajasthan are drying up under a crippling drought; the trees are drooping, leaves are shriveling, and the grass is dying. Everything is coated with a thick layer of desert dust. Tables and chairs, bookcases and floors, carpets and doors, beds and lamps, fridges and stoves, paintings and lamps are all brown. And so am I. At night I wash a putrid paste out of my ears, nose, hair and mouth; it's a cocktail of dust and chemical residue mixed with a dash of Indian sweat. I now smell like a local as the spices from Rachel's cooking seep from my skin. Indian sweat has an aroma like nothing else in the world—it's a sickly sweet mix of onions, turmeric, chili and chutney. A cloud of thick, tangy perspiration hangs over Delhi, pulled down by the stench of boiling diesel fuel, rotting garbage and fetid drains.

Then we run out of water. Moolchand may now be able to iron but he cannot wash my cruddy clothes. The water pump screeches in rage as the supply dries up, and a tanker comes to dribble a brown murky stream of groundwater into the tank. The shortages are already bringing disease; the papers are reporting more than seventy percent of children have chronic diarrhea, and there's a new health hazard on the roads—streams of vomit cascade from bus windows as commuters overheat in their honking saunas.

At night I turn my face to the east, waiting for that Sydney southerly that smells of salt and freedom; I'm blasted with desert dust and flies. Sometimes after 10 p.m., Abe drives me around traffic circles splattered with spread-eagled sleepers and floppy children to take in the Delhi summer show. On a stadium of car roofs, families stand and watch planes land, while small, sweaty, skinny men push carts of melting ice cream along the strand of spectators.

The only people immune to the power cuts are the diplomats. I attend some dinner parties in High Commission homes of Igloo-cooler opulence to chug beer and pig out on seafood bought from a special commissary shop. It's a bizarre scene—full of foreigners attempting to figure out India. I'm beginning to think it's pointless to try. India is beyond statement, for anything you say, the opposite is also true. It's rich and poor, spiritual and material, cruel and kind, angry but peaceful, ugly and beautiful, and smart but stupid. It's all the extremes. India defies understanding, and for once, for me, that's okay. In Australia, in my small pocket of my own isolated country, I felt like I understood my world and myself, but now, I'm actually embracing not knowing and I'm questioning much of what I thought I did know. I kind of like being confused, wrestling with contradictions, and not having to wrap up issues in a minute before a commercial break. While the journalist in me is still curious about the world, I'm still not really missing the way my old job confined my perceptions of life. My confinement here is different—I'm trapped by heat and by a never-ending series of juxtapositions. India is in some ways like a fun house hall of mirrors where I can see both sides of each contradiction sharply and there's no easy escape to understanding.

What's more, India's extremes are endlessly confronting.

Jonathan returns from Afghanistan and we've missed each other madly. While we may be living together he's proving to be gone a lot more than I expected. He suggests a weekend in Kesroli in the countryside away from the constantly ringing phone, fax and telex machine. Driving in a heat haze through fields as dry as a cracked heel, we pant and bake, too listless to scream at the near-miss head-on collisions with huge trucks, buses and farting Jeeps bursting with a cargo of cooked country folk. The roadside is littered with plastic, dead dogs, stiff cows and the twisted corpses of smashed-up metal. The relics of dead trees stand mutilated by villagers' long blades. Their branches have been hacked for firewood and their knobbly limbs look like the truncated stumps of lepers. At the construction site for a giant concrete Krishna, sweating swamis jump in front of our car, forcing us to stop and take offerings of sugar. Highwaymen who call themselves "officials" hold a rope across the road and demand a "safety tax" or "land tax" or "road tax." We give enough to buy us a blessing and permission to close the window. Our tempers are frayed and our faces bloated and blotched.

Heat shimmers off a town whose major industry is as a waste dump for shattered enamel basins and toilets. We stay at Kesroli's four-star hotel set above fields of limp yellow mustard, where women move slowly collecting cow dung and patting it into round, flat cakes they'll dry in the scorching sun. On the edge of each field are stacks of cowpats modeled into little storehouses for hay. The dried chalets of shit are beautifully carved with patterns of swirling loops and flowers.

From a turret of the small hotel, which was once a fort palace, we watch the town prepare for dark. In courtyards below, men lie on charpoys chatting and playing cards. The women are herding goats, feeding cows, brushing buffalo, stacking cow patties, bringing in washing, sweeping, cleaning, lighting fires and cooking meals. The acidic, slightly sweet aroma of a hundred cowpat fires wafts up, intertwined with snatches of sound. Religious music, the laughter of children, the pings of bike bells, the braying of buffalo, the snarls of mad dogs and some soft singing rise to our ears.

In the early morning I awake to the throb of a smoking generator. Below our hotel a black pump spurts two jets of water into a square concrete public well with three levels. The men make the top their open-air locker room; they strip down to their undies and disappear behind a frothy lather, then reemerge bared brown again by the strong jet of cold on their backs. Below them, small nude boys do cannonballs; hugging their knees to their chests, they leap into the deepest pool, scoring splashes and screaming with joy. They then hop out and run up shivering to jump again.

They soak a young girl on the lowest level; she ignores them as she concentrates on washing her baby brother. She soaps him up, pulls his hands above his head and dunks him; he comes up spluttering but never screaming. Around her, women lather, pummel and slap saris, shirts and suits against the concrete. They carry sodden heavy loads on their heads, hang the clothes on the nearest tree and return to fill the buckets with water. They'll wash at home, hidden. In many parts of rural India women are forbidden to even defecate in daylight, let alone wash in public.

A small boy calls me down from my turret. I'm hardly Rapunzel and he's no prince but I succumb to his performance. Indians are incredibly friendly to strangers, and it seems it starts young. Down at the well the boy and his friends surround me chatting like chicks—confident and spirited and charmingly candid. The lead ruffian struts like a rooster and brags in Rajasthani Hindi that I find hard to understand, but I think he's telling me about his family, his farm and his friends. As a school bell jingles, he stops suddenly, cocks his head, pulls his uniform over his glistening body and announces boastfully that he and his boys must go now.

"We are going to school. It's only for boys, no girls like you can come."

"Why?"

"School costs money. Girls can't be costing for study, they must work."

I bury a snarl, shrug and stay with the women.

A girl aged about ten laughs as I try to help her lift her huge bucket of water onto her head. She then saunters off unbowed with a baby on her hip. She turns, sinewy, strong and divinely gorgeous, and motions me home to meet her mum. I follow.

It's only seven o'clock and I'm sweating and slick, panting and putrid. My hostess looks like she should be in a *Vogue* model shoot, as long-limbed, dark and beautiful as her daughter. In a concrete bunker of a home decorated with tin cigarette posters we sit on the baked courtyard floor and compare my tiny rings to her huge silver anklets and the bone bracelets that adorn her arms up to her shoulders. She giggles and offers me *chai*. Her name is Suntre and she's in constant motion, swinging a tiny baby as she chats, makes tea and rolls *roti* bread. The courtyard fills with neighbors who pinch my skin, laugh at my Hindi and look sadly at my spiky hair. We compare our days. I'm planning on breakfast and being driven back to Delhi. They will clean their huts, sweep the yards, tend the fields, make lunch, wash down the buffalo, go back to the fields and then return to cook dinner for their husbands.

"Every day is the same. I make *chai*, I make *roti*, I work. Our lives are not easy like yours."

I nod. "What's your favorite time of the day?"

Her mother-in-law answers for her: "In bed when we're asleep."

"Ha," the women chorus. "Yes."

The crowd in the courtyard builds, the heat is stifling, but the conversation becomes more intimate. Suntre tells me she came to Kesroli to be married when she was nine, and now, at the age of twenty-three, she's the proud mother of four children and two buffalo.

"And two girls," she adds as an aside.

"In Australia, girls are counted as children, too," I stammer.

The women laugh. Then the crowd parts as a neighbor rushes up and thrusts a tiny package into my hands. I'm sweating so much it slips and I nearly drop it. It squeaks. A tiny baby screws its face to mine; it's an eight-week-old girl, and I'm asked to name her. I choose Priya, after the current pinup woman of the Indian modeling scene, and because it's a name I can pronounce. The mother pulls a face, shrugs and Priya is christened. Born in the shadow of a motel that charges one hundred dollars a night, Priya won't be able to go to a school that costs eight cents a day. I consider taking her home. But she will be happy here. Suntre insists I don't worry: "We are all very happy, we have no other choice."

A man appears and breaks up the fun. He speaks in English.

"Of course she is happy."

The women scatter.

"And I'll be telling you why you white people are not happy."

He adjusts his penis.

"We Indian people, we look at the people more poor, more low, more hard than us and we be thanking God we are not them. So we are happy. But you white peoples, you are looking at the peoples above you all of the times and you are thinking, why aren't I be them? Why am I not having that moneys and things? And so you are unhappy all of the time."

I think of the times I've walked around my Sydney suburb wishing I could buy a house or a flat near the beach; I think of the magazines of envy I've drooled and dreamed over and I nod my head.

He spits and walks off.

The women go back to work.

How I miss Australia, where destitution comes via television images, and I can press the off button. India makes me feel anything but lucky and happy. As the Vipassana high wears even thinner and my Sikh strength further fades, I feel increasingly dismayed and guilty. I feel guilty for not giving these women money and guilty for knowing it wouldn't be enough. I feel guilty for being in a position where I'm privileged enough to be a giver rather than a taker and I feel guilty for wanting more than I have and taking what I do have for granted. At times I feel angry at the injustice. But most of all I feel confused and confronted. Why was I born in my safe, secure, sunny Sydney sanctuary and not in Kesroli? India accepts that I deserved it, but I can't.

I wait for understanding and for the monsoon.

By July the rain still hasn't come. Hot winds make us paper-skinned and full of red rage. The city's sanity snaps and Delhi descends into mass madness. A beast is on the loose, leaping from roof to roof, attacking people sleeping above their hot homes. The stories begin with a small monkey and, as the heat and humidity build, he transforms from monkey to ape-man to monster, from one foot to ten, from having brown eyes to boiling red, and from having hairy hands to wielding clubs with long sharp spikes. A pregnant woman trying to escape his clutches falls down the stairs to her death. Two others die of fright while jumping from a roof. The authorities investigate and put it down to the "usual summer-induced mass hysteria." But the beast within continues to grow and the bile rises in the most mannered of throats. A model is shot in an illegal bar, a movie star gets drunk and violent with his girlfriend, and there's a coup for the leadership of the Australian High Commission Women's Committee. I don't understand the politics but the women now in charge have heard I know how to use a microphone. They give me my first Indian gig, as the host of a women's fashion show.

Looking ridiculous in a designer Indian *salwar* set, I use a lot of words like "elegant, stunning, gorgeous, delicious and exquisite," while commenting on clothes I know nothing about. Pink flesh is on display—shoulders, knees and calves and in the finale out pops a Western nipple. It's all too much for my Indian assistants—the cameraman trips over the catwalk and the man meant to be fading the music is too transfixed to do his job on cue. My new career is a failure and I decide it's really time I did some freelance writing—if I could only make my brain think of a story . . .

The only time I feel human is when Jonathan and I leave our still house to climb the ancient tombs of Muslim Delhi. In this ugly city the past provides rare grandeur and beauty. Our favorite spot becomes the shady crumbling Madrassa of Haus Kaus village, a long high-domed hall with numerous small round balconies that project out over a dried-up lake. In the fourteenth century, medical students would sit here on lush carpets to discuss the philosophy of medicine. Patients would be prescribed good food and music, poetry and dance; their medics viewed them as complete physical, mental and spiritual beings that could heal themselves by diet and lifestyle. Somehow the place still soothes despite the fact the tombs smell of urine and are full of men holding hands and grunting in shadows. It's said the descendants of the *fakir* healers still see patients in some Muslim-dominated areas of Old Delhi, but it would be hard for them to prescribe the tender treatments of old in the dried dust bowl of modern-day Delhi.

Yet it's a member of the Islamic community who offers me a

respite from the heat and insanity. Javed is a tailor recommended by a friend at the Australian High Commission. At twelve percent of the population, there are more Muslims in India than there are in Pakistan. While relations between them and the majority Hindus are presently peaceful, Javed is from a state racked by violence. Large, strong and with a slow-forming sweet smile, he fits Jonathan for a denim safari suit with red buttons, and strokes his wispy hennaed beard as he weaves a passionate tale of his home and India's most dangerous state.

"My beloved Kashmir, you must go, it's the most beautiful place on earth and we have twenty-one types of mutton. It's as cool as dew on the grass and we have twenty-one types of mutton. The snowcapped mountains kiss the indigo sky and we have twenty-one types of mutton. Kashmir people are the best people in the world . . ."

"And you have twenty-one types of mutton," Jonathan and I chorus.

Javed stares unsmiling as he checks the flare of the suit pants. Then, with his hand on his heart and his eyes elsewhere, he promises us heaven.

"It is paradise. It will touch your soul and bring you to God."

We look sheepish. He smiles sweetly and adds a rare joke.

"Providing you eat the mutton."

8 | Heaven in Hell

My first glimpse of paradise is five coffins.

At the airport at Srinagar, the summer capital of Indian Kashmir, heat shimmers off badly camouflaged hangars and the tarmac is white hot. The only shadows creep from the five oblong boxes of death. Inside are the bloodied corpses of Hindus gunned down while on pilgrimage to Amarnath, a cave containing an ice *lingam* (a penis-shaped stalactite) worshiped as the all-important Hindu god Shiva. More coffins wait in the terminal, which is a low room ringed with soldiers standing at stiff attention. They carry massive machine guns and sport major mustaches and bizarrely big smiles. They salute and shout out to us, the only foreigners.

"Welcome to Kashmir!"

Military formation and formality break as the men surround us, jostling to shake Jonathan's hand. We escape to the parking lot; there's a yelp of joy as a man jumps, punches the air, runs toward Jonathan and struggles to pick him up in a bear hug. It's Mukhtar, the Australian Broadcasting Company "fixer" who organizes interviews, translates and helps Jonathan film his stories in this region. Mukhtar has a handsome, full face with liquid brown eyes, sparkling teeth and dimpled cheeks. He wells up with tears as he shakes my hand and flings his arms out wide.

"My brother Jonathan, my sister Sarah, welcome to Kashmir, welcome to heaven on earth."

It's only a week since Javed planted the seed of desire in me to see Kashmir and Jonathan has been called here to do a story on the latest cease-fire and peace initiative in the state. I've tagged along because I'm sick of being left alone to fry in Delhi and I sense an opportunity to do some freelance stories on Kashmir. It's now been more than eight months since I've worked; my leave pay has run dry, my paranoia about losing my career has raised its ugly head and once again I feel I'm losing my sense of identity. For ten years my work has largely defined who I am, and while I'm keen to be more than my job, old habits die hard.

Jonathan is glad to have my company but Mukhtar is a bit jealous that I'm here. Again and again in the car he asks Jonathan, "You still need me, don't you, brother?"

"Yes, Mookie, I need you and so does Sarah."

Mukhtar beams. He loves Jonathan dearly, especially since the day they were caught in the cross fire of a Pakistan-Indian conflict at Kargil last year and Jonathan gave him his flak jacket. When Mukhtar tells me this, I'm not impressed. In fact I'm growing more somber by the minute. Kashmir looks closed and fearful.

We drive along roads lined with cute chalet homes that all seem dourly shut up behind barricaded doors and boarded-up windows. At crossroad checkpoints the fat barrels of machine guns peek over sandbags. On the outskirts of the city a sign boasts WELCOME TO PARADISE. And another underneath pleads PLEASE DO NOT BE URINATING HERE.

Indeed the people of Kashmir have been pissed on from a great height for many years—by the British who sold their state to a Hindu king for a paltry sum, by India's army and by Pakistan's militants. These nuclear neighbors have fought two wars over this Muslim-dominated territory that is split between them. The disputed Himalayan border here is the highest battlefield on earth. The toll has been devastating. More than thirty-five thousand people have died here over the last ten years; that's nine a day. Yet for some reason, no one wants to abandon the fantasy bequeathed by the poet Fir Daus: "*If there is paradise on earth, then this is it, this is it, this is it.*"

As I nervously take in the submachine guns, shuttered shops, abandoned homes and barricaded buildings, my heart begins to pound with "*This is shit, this is shit, this is shit.*"

But Mukhtar is enraptured; his eyes devotionally caress his town and the distant mountains and he sings sonnets of praise.

"Jonathan, my brother, have you ever seen such green fields, such a majestic mountain, such sky of blue?"

"Yeah. It's kind of like Switzerland," Jonathan teases. Mukhtar nods.

"Ah yes, but brother, these mountains are real."

Jonathan laughs, while I try to look astounded instead of scared. We cross a canal clogged with weeds, foamy with pollution and black with grime to stop at a modern military checkpoint. Waved on by soldiers, we halt at an ancient wall, a gate opens and our car is surrounded. We are pulled out, sprinkled with red flowers and garlanded with orange leis. Mr. Bhat's houseboat workers are welcoming their first guests in months. The boss stands tall and pale, bar a large mole on his face. He claps his hands and hugs us both as long-lost friends. The staff constantly fall over each other in competition to take our bags and show us around.

Tiny, worn and worried, gentle Lassa, the boatman, has worked here since he was seven. As Jonathan and Mukhtar discuss their schedule, Lassa takes me on a tour of the photos of the people he has served. He remembers George Harrison playing sitar on the lawn, Nelson Rockefeller calling for more pancakes, Ravi Shankar drumming and the "beautiful songs of John Fountain."

"John Fountain?"

"Yes, John Fountain, very nice."

Lassa nods energetically. I must look confused.

"John Fountain was great singer, don't you know her?"

He points to a photo of Joan Fontaine.

The most famous recent visitor is Peter Jennings from ABC in America; journalists are practically the only people who visit Kashmir now. George Harrison's boat is sinking low in the muck, Rockefeller's is partially submerged, the photos are faded and the articles that rave about this place are yellowed and curled.

Our houseboat is floating faded glory, featuring a carved wooden deck, a den with paisley cushions, an enormous dining table, a huge chandelier, a king-sized bed and a tiny pink bathroom. It smells strongly of sandalwood, mothballs and dust. And it creaks and rocks on a breathtakingly beautiful field of lotuses. Towering green stems stretch to flowers as large as a giant's outstretched hand with petals the color of pearl kissed by pink; giant leaves shaped like elephant ears sit flat and green on the dark waters and, below the surface, pods bulge with peanut-shaped seeds. Bouncy frogs, bright blue kingfishers and tiny terns dance from leaf to leaf. Stilt-legged, knobbly-kneed herons place their feet as gingerly as ladies trying to step across a puddle.

I eat the lotus landscape as dusk drips down. Beyond the lake, the jagged line of the snowcapped mountains softens and merges into a mauve sky; the water darkens to purple and then black. The lotuses bend and bow to the setting sun, neatly folding their huge petals and giant leaves inward as if to hug themselves warm. Lights twinkle from across the lake and I feel the unfamiliar rise of a goose bump on my skin. The first touch of cool is as delicious as the moist misty clean air that fills my scarred lungs. The Muslim call to prayer wafts down from the nearby mosque, swifts swoop for mosquitoes and a dark canoe floats past; a small girl squatting on the bow plops a paddle and nets into the water.

Kashmir begins to cast its spell on me.

• • •

We are jolted out of bed before the sun; the call to prayer harsher, more insistent and less romantic at four-thirty than at dusk. But it's perfect timing for a boat ride, and Lassa is superkeen to earn his first cash in six months. He knocks on the door and waits, silent and small in the dark of his boat, as we emerge into a cool new day.

As Jonathan films a sequence for his story, I lie down on the big red cushions of a beautiful blue gondola with a canopy of flowered cotton. Lassa hacks the thick tangle of lotus roots with his oar and the leathery leaves groan as they set us free; drops of dew move like mercury on those we don't disturb. As we glide across the glassy silver waters, the sky grows purple, orange and pink. I wake with the warmth and stretch with the lotuses; together we grow tall and wide to greet the light. Egrets walk from leaf to leaf, dogs bark from the bank and the ghats start echoing with the sounds of material being slapped clean.

Lassa brews green Kashmir tea with cinnamon, cardamom and crushed almonds, and breaks warm, fresh flat bread. We munch as we pass canoes of giggling girls and cheeky boys in bright white school uniforms and old men on their way to market. Gardens bob on the surface of the water—plants grow in big bowls of matted bulrushes that float gently above their long roots. Strong-faced women squat on flat wooden canoes cutting red tomatoes, orange pumpkins and giant zucchinis for harvest. We disturb a family of ducks and then there's silence, bar the plop of the paddle, the buzz of dragonflies and Lassa's soft singing. I doze in languid bliss, as if we are in a heavenly realm.

We come back to earth on the other side of an ancient rotting wooden bridge. The weeping willows part to reveal a floating market of boats so close that we could walk from one to the other without getting wet. There's a noisy jumble of wood on wood and shout on yell and a strong smell of river reed, mint and the other wares for sale: lotus roots, cucumbers, beans, flowers, saffron, woolen shawls and timber. Men squat on the tips of the overloaded low boats arguing ferociously about price and weighing produce with ancient measuring scales. Occasionally there's a yell and a laugh and a thrown potato whizzes past our heads to plonk into the dark waters. Leathery old faces with no teeth split open as we give the Muslim greeting, "*Assalam alaikum*"—may peace be with you.

"*Alaikum assalam*," they wish back.

But peace is anything but with these people.

I spend the day helping Jonathan film a story of a valley shattered. In a lunatic asylum four lank bodies and dead faces share one bed and Prozac is handed out like candy. In shuttered streets Hindu temples are boarded up and homes have been abandoned. The Hazratbal mosque, which holds a hair of Mohammed, is sandbagged; the ancient Mogul fort is occupied by the military; the gardens are closed and the marketplace is somber, shut by dusk for an unofficial curfew. Srinagar is jumpy, and now so am I. Standing on a bridge filming Jonathan's piece I turn to see a glint of light—a soldier in a sandbagged bunker is pointing his gun at us. I freeze and, for a moment, forget to breathe. I feel fear in waves and see scared people in small pieces. Furrowed foreheads flash above sandbags, eyes peek through veils, cheeks clench behind beards and fingers loop tight to triggers.

Life here is also in pieces. We interview politicians and bureaucrats, police and journalists, militants and soldiers, and all talk of life before and after militancy. Before 1989 there were tourists, film crews, famous musicians, trekkers, cherries, jobs and complete families. Now rows of houseboats called *Noah's Ark*, *Heavenly Tiger*, *New Australia* and *Sydney* slide low into the waters, rotting and empty. Shawl shops are dusty and deserted. Young men are sent south to make money or sent skyward by death. In 1989 the peaceful push for an independent state ended and militancy began. Most people we meet want Kashmir to be an Asian Switzerland; an independent peaceful state. But few seem to blame the separatist militants for the violence. They talk of terrible atrocities by the Indian army—prison deaths, shooting of suspects, torture, bribery, thieving, corruption and prostitution. Terrorist bombings are dismissed as "Indian setups," and shootings as political conspiracies.

I spend a day in Srinagar listening to rumor, suspicion, conspiracy theories and gossip, and only once do I find anyone who wants to verify a rumor they've heard. It's a weaver I'm interviewing for a story on *shahtoosh* (beautiful fine shawls worth around ten thousand dollars each but now illegal because of the risk of extinction to the chiru—a kind of antelope—which provides the fiber). He leans close and whispers, "Is it true you Western women live with a man, really live with a man, before marriage?"

I shift my biggest ring to my left ring finger and say a slow, hesitant "Yeeees, sometimes."

All the weavers in the shop then clap and smile happily, excited that sinful women will wear their weaving work. But when I try to scotch rumors that Hindus eat steak, or that the government is banning *shahtoosh* to punish the Kashmiri weavers, they refuse to respond.

We think differently, these Muslims and I. I have been raised in a culture of skepticism, but they see my requirement for proof as a burden on my back. The eldest weaver shakes his finger at my constant questions.

"You Western people are all science, all fact, all show me. You don't even believe in God anymore because you think we came from a monkey."

The weavers chorus a cackle, as if evolution is one of the funniest things they've ever heard. Business banter is dismissed and our talk turns to higher truths.

"You are Christian woman?" a young lime-eyed weaver across the room asks me, head cocked.

"Yeeeeeees," I reply hesitantly again. (I've given up explaining atheism in India. It's rarely understood or respected.)

The man and his friends murmur.

"You are like us, you are of the book," one states while his father claps. "Your Jesus is good man, he came to Kashmir here, he is buried here, so we respect you, and Jesus and you are our honored guests."

"He came here? He's buried here?"

"Yes, yes, of course, all great saints come here, this is Kashmir, holy place. But Jesus is not the best. Mohammed, peace be upon Him, is the greatest and latest prophet."

Back at the houseboat I find a Koran in the drawer of the nightstand and start reading in the soft light of dusk. Raised in an Australian society that, in the main, seems to believe Islam is a barbaric religion that treats women dreadfully, I'm actually amazed at how familiar the holy book seems. Mohammed's teachings are revealed to him by the archangel Gabriel and contain references to the stories of Adam, Noah, Moses, Abraham, Sarah, Jacob, Isaac, Ishmael, Mary and Jesus; stories that I have read in some form or just absorbed over my Australian childhood. Like the Old Testament, the Koran is repetitive, at times contradictory and frequently scary. The all-powerful Allah seems at times loving, sometimes severe, and there's much mention of Satan and Judgment Day. Yet I'm comforted by the familiarity of its teachings, its code for truthful living, and the mercy and goodness of a prophet who shows the way to the divine. Islam is not so alien as I'd believed, and after eight months of living in a country where life and religion are so intertwined I'm less harsh in judging the faith of others. I now feel being an extreme atheist is as arrogant as being an extreme fundamentalist.

The prophet of Islam—Mohammed—was born in C.E. 570 and in his twenties he began to be visited by the archangel Gabriel. The divine messages Mohammed received are contained in the Koran; they advocate Muslims surrender to the will of the one true God and strictly adhere to Allah's laws, which cover all aspects of daily living from marriage to banking to conduct.

I hunt for the passages on women and dress codes, but I find only that Mohammed urges women to guard their modesty. I also read that the Koran advises men they shouldn't wear tight clothes across their genitals. I can't help but note there's still a lot of stretch denim in town.

I am choosing to cover up more and more in India—it's now been seven months since my legs have seen the light of day and I always wear a *dupatta* shawl across my breasts. But to me, the *sal-*

war kamiz is not a religious duty or even a free choice; it's a resentful surrender. The north Indian men on the streets stare so hard and are so sleazy that I often feel like I've somehow starred in a porn film without knowing it. In Muslim Kashmir they seem to look a lot less, but they still stare. Why should I have to cover up because men are weak and cannot control their eyes? I try to discuss this with some of the women I meet in Kashmir; most women don't wear the veil here, preferring the head scarf, but nonetheless the bounds of female modesty are strict and clear. All agree with me to some degree that the dress code and male attitudes are unfair, but they are pragmatists not idealists and they accept responsibility for male desire. The most common refrain is "Men should change, sister, but we all know they never will, so we protect our modesty for them, for us and for Allah."

As with Christianity, Islam is interpreted differently across the world and varies to some degree from culture to culture. With the exception of Kashmir's mostly imported Islamic extremists, Indian Islam has a unique style that shows the faith can be adaptable and accepting of differences. It has to be, for India's one hundred and fifty million Muslims are living in a land of idols, the likes of which were smashed in Mecca. There are idols beside the road, on street corners, at the roots of trees, in homes, in offices and in paddocks and some are even washed, dressed, fed and paraded before being put to bed at night. This must be confronting for people who don't believe God should be depicted in any form, but by and large Muslims seem to get on well with their Hindu brethren.

However, horrific exceptions loom large. When the British pulled out of India in 1947 they divided the country into Hindu India and Muslim Pakistan. As people moved sides en masse, the new nations were stained with the blood of a million. In Kashmir, the Partition was complicated: the Hindu ruler dithered and decided to go to India, Pakistan invaded the state and the border between the two has been in dispute ever since. Indians and Pakistanis—neighbors who were once compatriots—now dislike and distrust each other. Of course the dispute over Kashmir is about land as much as religion, but straight-out religious Hindu-Muslim violence occasionally flares in other parts of India as well. In 1992 a Hindu fundamentalist mob destroyed the sixteenth-century Babri mosque at Ayodhya, triggering religious riots in which more than two thousand Indians were killed, most of them Muslim. And there's always a level of political tension caused by the fact that the current Indian government is dominated by a hard-line Hindu party, the BJP—the Bharatiya Janata Party—or Indian Peoples' Party, which has been linked to groups involved with the mosque's destruction. But violent flare-ups are not as common as peaceful lives lived side by side. Hindus are supposed to accept all paths to God and Muslims are aware of their minority status.

But a friend of Vivek's, Asaf, once told me it isn't just fear of the majority and the government that keeps India's Muslims tolerant, it's a unique Islamic attitude. One day his two little girls were bowing deep in prayer to his Hindu wife's statue of the elephant god Ganesh. His Muslim mother screamed at them to stop. They turned to her saying, "It's all right, Noni, we are reciting the Koran to him."

"Such good girls," said Grandma as she walked off happily.

Asaf believes such tolerance and togetherness stem from Indian Muslims' strong tradition of Sufism. Sufis are Muslims who rely less on the strict rules of the Koran and instead try to conduct a more personal ecstatic relationship with God through music, song and poetry.

Here in Kashmir, though, Sufism is struggling.

Shopping for shawls, I have the required tea and the required chat about cricket with a handsome, tall, young shopkeeper with dull green eyes. He quietly tells me he's a Sufi and that he wishes he could organize a singing night for me.

"You have never heard such rapture, such ecstasy. When I sing and hear that music, I am with God."

"I'd like to hear it."

He shakes his head sadly. "So would I."

Sufi gigs are too dangerous at the moment. As is being a Sufi. The shopkeeper hangs his head as he softly says he was once bashed by extremists for not being at the afternoon prayers in the mosque. He adds that two women wearing jeans were shot in the legs last year and that two without head scarves had acid thrown on them. The young Sufi says Kashmir's Muslims aren't extremists but they're making use of imported fundamentalists from Pakistan to help them get rid of the "Indian occupation."

"How do you know you'll be able to get rid of the extremists even if you do get independence?"

He stares at me and gulps.

"Do you want a discount on that shawl?"

I get one. Business here is bad.

Death seems to be the only growth industry in town. In the blazing heat of the afternoon we visit a graveyard which has overtaken a sports arena and stand above men buried in the dry dirt of the playgrounds of their youth. The graves are decorated with tinsel and plastic flowers. Headstones are carved with the gentle curves of Urdu and the straight strokes of English:

"*When slaves are martyred they are relieved of all their pain.*"

"*Don't weep on my grave because thanks to Allah I am a martyr.*"

"*Do not shun the gun, my dear younger ones, the wait for freedom is yet to be won.*"

The sound of soft weeping wafts from one grave. A woman is sobbing over the hump of dust that entombs her son. Mukhtar stoops toward her and asks permission to intrude on her grief with a camera and questions. She sits up and pulls aside her veil to talk to the camera like it's a confessional and a comrade. Her name is Mehmooda and her son Mohammed was a twenty-two-year-old militant who died in a gun battle with the security forces last year. Mukhtar translates.

"I handed him over to Allah, he would take care of him. He used to pray five times a day that he would be a martyr fighting security forces. Allah heard his prayers. He wanted to belong to Allah. On the day of judgment he will speak for me in front of Allah. His blood should not go to waste. *Inshallah*, his death will help Kashmir."

Inshallah is a common word in Kashmir. In this state nothing is taken for granted. Everything is "if God is willing." The word "Islam" actually comes from a root of a word that means "complete surrender," but Mehmooda's fatalism astounds me. In India I've slowly been learning that I'm not in complete control of my life. I got sick, Jonathan is constantly called away and India's general disorganization means things never really turn out as I expect, but Mehmooda's faith and fatalism make me realize how much I still cling to the belief that I have power over my destiny. Perhaps it's time to let that go. Back at the boat on the lake of lotuses I shiver with thoughts of surrender, for it seems such surrender requires sacrifices I could never make. I'm not sure I want that depth of faith and I can't imagine being capable of it.

My reverie is interrupted with a request from our driver. Hassan is tall, stooped and big-nosed and he's getting married in the morning. We've known him for two days and he insists we come. He bows and promises, "The best of Kashmir will be on display."

I need to see it.

After a huge breakfast of pancakes and a morning tea of coconut cookies and fudge cake, we are picked up by a friend of the groom and driven to the old part of Srinagar town. Open drains carry human effluent along the narrow lanes. We twist and turn through crooked alleys echoing with the sounds of life lived close; women call from high wooden windows and children chatter as they chase bicycle tires.

We enter a tall wooden home painted green. Atop a dark creaking stairway in a sunlit room, the groom's family surrounds us as special guests and long-lost friends. Hassan's little sister, specially dressed in a blue nylon tutu, sits me down cross-legged on a cushion and squats in front of me to cup her chin in her hands and stare. An embroidered cloth is laid out on the floor and the groom's father washes our hands with water poured from a massive silver teapot. A Pepsi is bought from a shop down the road and placed beside me. I take a tentative sip but as soon as I put it down the little girl picks it up again and pushes it to my lips. The room fills as all the male members of the family gather to eat with us. No surprise at what's on the menu.

Twenty-one types of mutton.

Mutton is to Kashmir what beer is to Australia. To refuse would be a major social faux pas, akin to atheism. I haven't eaten animal product for months as summer in Delhi is not a good time for meat and the health authorities have closed down many of the butchers. But there's no room for vegetarians here—there's not even any room for vegetables. There's mutton on the bone, mutton in gravy, mutton with peas, tandoori mutton, mutton with cream, mutton with spice, mutton kabobs, mutton shanks, mutton intestines, mutton flank, mutton balls and saffron rice with mutton bits. Then there's mutton made in ways I cannot describe, with special spices and softening sauces. Jonathan and I sponge bits of mutton together with our fingers and try to flick them into our mouths—a move the men around us perform with ease. We end up with bits of mutton hanging from our collars, ears and hair. What's worse, our plates are like the magic pudding. Every time we pause for breath the men rush to fill up our load and insist we eat more. The food is incredibly delicious but my belly is bursting with heaviness, my throat tightening in protest.

I stop eating.

The room goes quiet, the men lean back and blink sorrowfully, and the little girl pauses with my Pepsi in midair looking like she will cry. I relent.

"Okay, just a bit."

They grin and pile on another three animals. After four platefuls they can see I'm nearly dying and serve the finale.

"Your full stop to the meal, Sarah. Eat, eat, it's good."

On my plate is a meatball the size of a tennis ball coated in green goo. It's meant to help digestion. I summon a strength of commitment I've never had before, force it into my mouth and sit back in agony.

After a chorus of burps and another hand wash it's time for talk. I'm stuffed silent by food and listen to a lecture by a charming uncle clothed in a beautiful handwoven woolen Kashmir suit and shawl. He lists stories of why Indian security forces are evil and how they must leave Kashmir.

"What do you do?" Jonathan asks, ever the journalist.

"I'm a mechanic for the Indian air force. I work for them in the day and against them after work." He winks and smiles sweetly.

Trying to leave politics aside, I ask some young girls who've sneaked into the room whom they like from the movies. They mention some Indian actors but their deep dark eyes grow soft and their smiles wide as they talk of "the handsome boys of Laiksha e Toiba."

"Who are they, a boy band?"

"No, silly, they are our freedom fighters, so strong and brave they are."

Jonathan and I plead off the wedding ceremony because it won't happen for many hours yet. We thank our hosts and roll back to the houseboat, but there's no time to digest the food or the folklore, for Mr. Bhat is waiting at the gate with a special *salwar kamiz* in purple polyester for me to wear at a dinner with his family.

Four hours later and we are fed the same meal again—all the twenty-one types of mutton in all their glory. I rock and nearly retch at the sight of the stacked silver plates but Jonathan pulls me down with a stern look and I open my mouth like a guppy ready to explode. After a few bites I'm so full that my cheeks are sticking out like a Cabbage Patch doll. Mr. Bhat sees my slack eating performance as a personal affront, so I shove it in, trying to turn my groans into moans of pleasure. Kashmir is killing me softly with food.

And a great deal of love. I've been told "I love you" more times today than at the three o'clock Ecstasy peak at Mardi Gras.

Yet hate triumphs again. The next day the current cease-fire explodes with the bang of a car bomb that kills an Indian journalist and several policemen. Mukhtar lives near the scene and will hear the ringing in his ears for days. I'm relieved to be returning to Delhi, but uneasy about leaving Jonathan in the thick of the danger. I leave laden with sadness about the future of an area racked by religious violence. But before I can escape the politics, on my way to the airport the taxi driver insists on telling me why he would rather Srinagar belong to Muslim Pakistan than secular India.

"We Muslims have given India the wonderful mosques, the beautiful places, the Taj Mahal. India would be nothing without us."

"So why leave?"

"Our past is in India. They don't treat us well. Our future is independence, if we can't have that we must be with Pakistan."

He asks me to describe the Taj Mahal, the tomb of Mogul King Shah Jehan and his wife, Mumtaz, and a glory he has never seen. I edit out my experience of running a gauntlet of the most pernicious sellers in India to share the spectacle with thousands of people imitating Princess Di. I skirt the stench of the dreadful foot odor in the inner sanctum. Instead I rave about the inlay of jewels and the majestic marble that's yellowing from the pollution. He nods happily. I tell him about Shah Jehan's grandfather, Akbar the Great, who built the majestic Fatephur Sikri down the road from the Taj. It's a wonderful palace complex with painted rooms, giant chessboards (where kings used real dancing girls as pawns), massive libraries, mosques and a chamber where Akbar would encourage debates between Muslim, Hindu, Sikh, Christian and Parsi scholars. Akbar, the Mogul Muslim, ruled an India where different religions were respected and tolerated, but my taxi driver is no longer interested in a land of pluralism. He wants to live in a state defined by its religion.

At the airport my body is patted down by three different sets of overexuberant women in curtained booths. All finish the feel-up with a hug and a kiss. In the last security check a large, lumpy woman with jet-black hair and gypsy eyes holds my hand and won't let go.

"I am Leila. Come sit with me, sister."

As I'm the only woman flying out of Srinagar today, Leila is in no hurry. She orders coffee from her assistant and we squat on the floor of her booth, hand in hand. She tells me about her heart troubles, her husband's problems at work and her wish that her two children will leave Srinagar for America. I tell her about Australia, my "husband," why I'm so skinny, my hair disasters, my

Vipassana course and my trouble digesting mutton. After twenty minutes Leila and I are the best of friends. And then we talk about Allah. I tell Leila I'm a Christian by culture but have no God. She lets go of my hand, stands up and shakes me by the shoulders.

"Sarah, my child, you have learned about death, you have learned to be silent, you have learned about Kashmir, but you haven't learned about Allah. What are you doing? He is right here with you right now. You must learn to give control to him."

I stare at her dumbly. She looks as if she will slap me, then softens and sinks to my side; cradling my head in her embrace, she rocks me like a child.

"My friend, can't you already feel your soul yearning and longing? A woman gets lonely even with a husband. You must get to know God. I urge you to save your soul."

I promise I'll try.

Leila takes me to the tarmac and supervises my final body search. She kisses each of my cheeks and my forehead.

"Next time in Kashmir, you stay with me. You my daughter, I love you."

Through the plane window I look down. Three soldiers have let go of their machine guns to wave at me from the tarmac, and Leila is with them, blowing kisses. I'm heavy with heartfelt sadness for Kashmir's future. India will never give up its share of the state; as a secular nation it cannot give in to a religious division of land. Pakistan will never give up trying to get all of Kashmir; as a Muslim nation it feels it should have Muslim areas. As the plane loops around the lake, my wet eyes swell with the sight of the perfect symbol of this country and this valley. The lotus. Out of the slime, out of the shit, out of the crowded, worn land rises exquisite, glorious perfection.

For the first time since summer began I feel a regrowth in my desire to be a perfect being, to rise above my muddy mind, to be an unspoiled spirit that can soar above place and circumstance, to be happy and strong and open and beautiful. Is this God? Or is India indeed fertilizing me, nurturing a new spirit to bloom?

Inshallah.

INTERMISSION | My Wedding Season

November is tourist season. Friends venture back to the Biosphere and I travel with them to Rajasthan. The laughter and the Australian laconic humor revive a lightness of being, and I join them on a road trip to ancient palaces, fort hotels and evocative ruins. In Jaisalmer we take a desert safari of baking sand and cracked skin, of *chapatti*-making around fires and camels farting in our faces.

In December I head home to beautiful brashy Sydney and prepare to make one of the biggest leaps of all.

Marriage.

Thankfully, my hair has grown enough to look slightly glamorous. Just after Christmas in front of our families and friends, Jonathan and I profess undying love and promise to be together forever. Afterward we purge our hotel room of stayers, plot our future and review our past. We give the jingoistic astrologer in Rishikesh good marks. As he predicted, Sonia Gandhi did not win the election and India won the cricket series against Australia. I had faced death and some spiritual truths. And, after a year of ridiculously hard work, Jonathan learned to dance—only hours ago we did the cha-cha to a Barry White song for our wedding waltz. We dismiss the rest of his reading, including his warning of danger for Jonathan. Instead, we plan a year of togetherness, fun and love.

But India will ignore our script.

Our first year of marriage will be a time of separation and struggle. As Mr. Rakesh predicted, Jonathan will suffer great risk for great success, and I will become a karma chameleon.

9 | The Big Pot Festival

Our newlywed travel plans become unstuck in an ungodly traffic jam above the biggest spiritual festival on earth, India's Kumbh Mela. After a fortnight of honeymoon bliss on a beach, Jonathan and I don't feel like being apart just yet. It's January and Delhi is still wrapped in its noxious smog which carries memories of disease and disaster. So we quickly fled the city and set off on a combined work and extended honeymoon trip. And here we now are. Going nowhere.

While Jonathan sits patiently in the car, I'm standing at the railing of the town's bridge beside a giant knot of tinsel-covered trucks, beeping buses, black buffalo, wagons, rickshaws, bicycles and cows with painted horns. There's not a whiff of road rage. Kumbh Mela pilgrims squat beside their vehicles, beckoning boys with steaming glasses of *chai* and touts selling fluffy toys, cotton candy and roasted peanuts in newspaper cones. A train trundles past, a conveyor belt of bulging human cargo; a row of men ride the roof cheering and waving, their faces flashing ecstatic grins.

Far below us on the sandbank of the Ganges is a mass of humanity so large it can be seen from outer space and so strange it seems like a settlement from another world. Stretching to every horizon, a moonscape of gray dust is pockmarked with craters full of rubbish and speckled with beings; the saffron flags of Hinduism fly high from bamboo castles and low from squalid squatter camps. Rivers of the righteous flow across the sands; pilgrims with long wild hair, tattered robes and bright saris walk on cracked feet caked in dust. Cripples and lepers line the paths, their sores weeping with pus, twisted and bleeding stumps for limbs. Camels, horses and Jeeps stir up the fine sand that swirls upward, caking my skin, encrusting my eye sockets and grinding between my teeth. Smells rise: shit and burning onions, incense and urine, sandalwood and spicy sweat, heady hash and burning cowpatties.

As I shut my burning eyes and block my nose to reduce the sensory overload I become fully aware of the noise. The bridge beneath my feet is vibrating with the buzz of a human zoo of millions joined in symphonic song. On percussion, the rumble of trucks and the growling of generators. On brass, the beeping of buses, the duck calls of rickshaws and the tings of bicycle bells. On vocals, a cacophony of chanting, singing, screaming and whistling. Rising even higher is a melody of keyboards, cowbells and sitars. Loudest of all is the constant ranting of lost and found announcements distorted through loudspeakers—a roll call of children and elderly who may never be claimed. Together, this noise could be the hubbub of the three hundred and thirty million gods of Hinduism chatting at a heavenly cocktail party, or perhaps the collective roar of souls in hell.

A young Indian swami in a bright orange robe with his forehead painted yellow joins me at the bridge rail. He mumbles a mantra to the nuclear orange sun, then turns his sparkling eyes to mine. In perfect English he states, "You are living in India but still you are amazed."

I step back from the spectacle to stare at him. Has this holy man read my mind, my future, my very soul?

"How do you know I live here?" I stammer. His bushy beard wobbles as he laughs.

"Your driver told me."

He motions to a huddle of taxi-wallahs squatting and chatting about their passengers. I ask him why he's here.

"Because a Hindu's aim in life is not to have another one."

He shrugs and points to the river below, then tells me a story about how the shallow stinky Ganges came to contain the nectar of salvation.

Once upon a time in a Hindu legend the Devas (the gods of heaven responsible for sun, wind, rain and fire) were weakened by a curse. They cooperated with the demons to stir the cosmic ocean of existence and from the milky depths a pot, or a *kumbh*, containing *amrit*, the nectar of immortality, emerged. The Devas decided they didn't want to share with the demons and a chase across the heavens began. During the battle (equivalent to twelve human years) four drops of nectar fell to earth and at each spot they landed, the Kumbh Mela is celebrated. Allahabad is the most special of places because here the three holy rivers of Hinduism meet—the Ganges, the Yamuna and the mythical Saraswati. So, every twelve years this town hosts the Maha Kumbh Mela, literally translated as "The Big Post Festival." But this current festival is extra special; at this Mela the planets are exactly as they were when the nectar fell from the heavens.

My swami sidekick says I'm extraordinarily privileged to be here as this cosmic lineup is an auspicious, once-in-every-one-hundred-and-forty-four-year event that will generate enough energy to transform these muddy waters into the immortal nectar.

"You must dip. Taking a bath will wash away all your sins, and end your soul's cycle of earthly existence and suffering."

"But I'm not sure I believe in reincarnation."

He laughs and walks away, calling over his shoulder, "The bath is best on certain days. You have time to beat the demons of doubt."

The sun descends into the dancing dust, the thick air grows cold and the traffic suddenly moves. Jonathan shouts, I run back to the car and we lurch off the bridge and travel along sand highways to our camp. A message is waiting. While we've been traveling, a huge earthquake struck the state of Gujarat and thousands are dead. Jonathan leaves immediately to record the devastation and watch people burn the bodies. The romance and the honeymoon are over.

I'm left at the biggest gig on earth with Jonathan's assistant Neeraj and his camera operator Titi. Titi is steady, focused and cool; one of the few camerawomen in India, she shuns convention by wearing jeans and having short hair. Neeraj, as usual, is outfitted in army fatigues but with a new utility belt and vest. He salutes as we split up.

"Meet you at the mess hall at oh-five hundred."

I search the "luxury camp" that is supposedly home to Madonna, Goldie Hawn and Paul McCartney, but the closest thing to celebrities I find is a bunch of docu-makers and Net designers from Channel Four UK TV, trying to out-cool each other with spliff size. While they eat tinned tuna and drive off to buy beer, I sign a form promising I'll abstain from alcohol and meat. I find my tent, wrap myself in a sleeping bag, shove in some earplugs and try to sleep through the unbelievable noise. All night long it rises and falls in massive waves; I toss and turn to the sounds of a sea of souls.

In the morning Neeraj and Titi queue for the media passes they'll need in order to film the mass bathing event to come, while I summon the courage to let myself loose among a crowd as large as the population of Australia. My friend Simi was horrified when I told her I was coming to the Kumbh and regaled me with stories of stampedes, mass drowning and mysterious disappearances. I put her fears down to melodrama but now the sheer scale of the spectacle sobers me. It's also seductive—my fear is weaker than the pull of the party. I walk out the gates and follow a stream of pilgrims across the sands.

In the temporary suburbs of devotion it's ancient India meets *Life of Brian*. Straw-filled stables are jammed with people praying to plastic-doll gods, scrawny men in loincloths stand preaching on corners, small knots of families cook in tiny sandpits and beggars with twisted bones shuffle along. I stumble over the body of a young boy without a head (he's somehow buried it without suffocating), and scream when a teenager drenched in orange paint and sporting a tail jumps at me and demands money. But, such sideshows aside, the Kumbh is mild-mannered and calm. There's no pushing and little sexual leering; pilgrims are here to wash away their bad karma, not attract more.

In the midst of the Mela is a bamboo Las Vegas. Tall, temporary temples are lit by neon signs flashing OM and swirling Hindu swastikas. This is the street of the *sadhu* clubs—a devotional disco alley, with an open door policy. *Sadhu*s are the holy saints of Hinduism. Mourned as dead by their families, they abandon everything to devote their lives to God, reprogramming their body and mind through celibacy, renunciation, religious discipline, meditation, yoga, austerities and secret tantric practices. Well, that's what I've read anyway. It doesn't look like they're doing much of that here—their monastic orders or *akhara*s are set up like stalls at the fair.

The club attracting the biggest crowd is the Juna Akhara. The Juna are *naga baba*s (holy men) or ascetic militant warriors who fought the Mogul invasion of India in the thirteenth century and worship Shiva, the Lord of Destruction. With naked bodies painted blue by ash and long black matted dreadlocks they look like Shiva. But they lack the god's glory. Most lie crumpled in sleep on filthy blankets, some sit and stare, others hobble around in huge wooden chastity belts and a few perform austerities for the crowd to show their body means nothing. One young *sadhu* wraps his penis around a wooden stake and another, who has stood up for two years, leans on a swing showing off his gnarled thick legs. Attracting the biggest crowd is an old dude who's held his hand up in the air for nearly three decades. He's charging foreigners one hundred American dollars for a photo of the atrophied leathery limb with its closed claw of corkscrew nails.

Since the *aghori sadhu* cursed me with pneumonia I've kept well away from India's holy men. Yet this spiritual sideshow alley is hardly threatening—these *sadhus* are more like circus freaks on display. Pilgrims file past pointing, whispering, staring and occasionally touching the feet of the *sadhus*, giving them money or snapping a photo. In return, the hordes are blessed with *prasad* (a gooey sweet) for additional spiritual energy. The Big Pot Festival is literally in full swing in Sadhu Street; the air is thick with hash and red-eyed saints are sloppily stoned. In some pens smug Westerners sit sharing hash chillums with the holy men and a few in the Juna beckon me over. It's high status to have foreigners pay homage in this way, but I'm unwilling to be a *sadhu* trophy and keen to be able to find my way back to camp. I retire to worship Shiva alone with the help of the Channel Four media boys. It's a practical *puja*—the dope helps me sleep through the Kumbh noise and brings on states of bliss. I fall into bed feeling that everything is clear, everything is significant.

The next morning the induced enlightenment has gone and Shiva's favorite weed has made me seedy. I drink *chai* in the kitchen tent with a wealthy plump Indian woman with adorable dimples; her name is Dollie, and she briefs me on the Hindu concept of God.

"There's millions of gods, *beta*, but all represent aspects of three, and all three are really one."

I look confused, so she recites a Julie Andrews–like mantra to make it easier.

"Brahma is the Generator, Vishnu the Organizer and Shiva the Destroyer. Together they are G.O.D. or Brahman. All the millions of Hindu gods are just forms of the one Supreme Being."

Dollie says that Brahman can be worshiped in any aspect and she chooses Shiva, the cosmic destroyer whom she highly recommends.

"You know, dear, now you are married you should pray to Shiva for children. He's very strong and well, um . . ." she breaks off giggling.

"Yes?"

She leans close. "Well, sexual, I'd say, *beta*."

Dollie pats my knee and winks. I suddenly understand why I've seen so many penis-shaped rocks and sculptures in India—these erect *lingams* represent Shiva swollen with the seeds of all creation. He destroys to create anew.

She whispers again, "Shiva is also an easy god. He doesn't care for wealth and royalty and he's rough around the edges."

Dollie is putting it mildly. Shiva ate meat, got stoned, liked to dance, killed the tiger whose skin he sits upon and was unkempt, wild and free. I promise Dollie I'll think of Shiva today. I like the fact that Hindu gods don't have to be perfect to be powerful.

But I end up devoting my day to Vishnu, a calmer, less temperamental god who came to earth in different animal and human forms or avatars. The most popular avatar at the Kumbh is Rama, a prince born about nine hundred years before Christ. His story is told in the Ramayana, and because it's one of the few scriptures translated from Sanskrit into everyday Hindi, it's hugely popular. A television serial of the Ramayana, featuring shaky sets, little action and appalling overacting, stopped the nation when it was shown every Sunday in the late eighties, and reruns still rate. In every sandy street of the Mela the Ramayana is being read. At midday I stumble into the most splendid reading of them all. A massive glass chandelier hangs from the tent's ceiling, thick carpets cover the sand and the walls are hung with silk and red velvet brocaded with gold. Children dressed in sequined costumes stare with stunned expressions down from a stage while the story is sung in squawking Hindi through speakers that distort the sound so much my ears begin to buzz. The children are meant to enhance the performance but they hardly move, let alone act. The epic is excruciatingly long but the crowd is crazy for it.

The Ramayana is *The Wizard of Oz* on a biblical scale. The loyal, good Prince Rama and his child bride, Sita, are exiled in the forest. A demon with ten heads captures Sita and takes her from the forest to his kingdom of Lanka. The monkey god Hanuman helps rescue her in a fierce battle and she throws herself onto a fire to prove her chastity. It's got love and war, honor and horror, courage and killings, duty and devotion. The Bible seems boring compared to Hinduism's wild stories of the supernatural and fantastic. I share the spectacle and some peanuts with a family from a nearby village. Mum is in her best pink sari, Dad sports a fine polyester mustard shirt and puce bell-bottoms, and their tiny daughter, dressed in a starched party dress, somehow sleeps on the lap of the withered grandma. In Hindi and sign language that's way more exuberant than the performances on stage, they tell me they're here to pray for a good monsoon this year. Jumping around using a corncob for a sword, the father tells me Hanuman is his favorite god because he rescues Sita and guards against ghosts.

Vishnu's other most famous avatar is Krishna, a randy cowherd who seduced more than one thousand cowgirls (*gopis*) with his raunchy flute-playing. The bright blue shepherd's games of love are a focus for the more sentimental spiritualists of Hinduism. After regaining my hearing from the Ramayana rave, I find some Krishna lovers in a small filthy tent. I squat on straw as a group of Gujarati men sing love songs about the god and his favorite cowgirl, Radha. Playing tin cans with one string, the musicians' voices soar with love and devotion.

Krishna wasn't just a lover; he was also a fighter. In the great battle of the Mahabharata scripture, the noble prince Arjuna doesn't want to kill his cousins in a battle for his kingdom. Krishna takes the form of a charioteer and gives him a lecture about controlling the mind and senses, about living by noble action and of working to conviction. This chapter of the Mahabharata is called the Bhagavad Gita, and is the tale so loved by the Hare Krishnas, now called the International Society for Krishna Consciousness.

After the love song love-in, I come across a small riot. Men are laughing and pointing, children are giggling and a *sadhu* pulls a small instant camera from his robe. I think perhaps they've found Madonna and push to the front to see about thirty Hare Krishnas ringing bells and clashing cymbals. Indians are used to such parades but not by uncoordinated foreigners so pale they look like they've been stuck down a mine shaft for months. As their shorn heads turn pink, they twirl around drunk on Ecstasy, swaying and stumbling and chanting their mantra.

"*Hare Krishna Krishna Krishna, Hare Rama, Hare Hare . . .*"

I'm swept up in the dance to their camp which sits below two King Kong–sized blowup dolls in saris. The camp is surrounded by a barbed wire fence, and visitors are charged entry and must pass through a metal detector.

Other Westerners prefer to stay with Pilot Baba down the road. He speaks English so I suggest Neeraj and Titi leave the press-pass queue and come to interview him. We arrive at his camp just in time for *darshan*, a process where a holy one transmits his spiritual energy to those who show adoration. Pilot Baba seems to be transmitting his divine nature by sitting on a red and gold velvet throne, slurping his tea, scratching his bum and occasionally giving a devotee an absentminded pat on the head. Potbellied with a chest of silver hair, he teams a red air force beret with a saffron toga. He relishes the camera.

"One day when my plane was about to crash bang into the earth, my guru-master appeared in the cockpit, took over the controlling devices and landed the plane safely to the ground."

The devotees murmur and nod, he slurps and burps. After a tour of duty in Kashmir he decided to give up his wings to work for peace and mass meditation. I curse myself for judging him too quickly, but then Pilot Baba launches into a bizarre conspiracy theory about the United Nations being set on world domination. The devotees' piously peaceful smiles remain intact. We leave.

Travelers to India carry more than one bible in their backpacks.

Autobiography of a Yogi is a spiritual *Lonely Planet* guide that tells the tale of a great yogi and his master; a saint who could appear in two places at once, bring life back to the dead, predict the future and read minds. I'm not unbelieving of the power of the human mind and soul but it seems such yogis are hard to find in this day and age. On my way back to my camp, I almost fall over an Israeli, or should I say what was an Israeli and is now an unwanted child of Mother India. Wild eyes peer out from a face encircled by Medusa-like dreadlocks. His bony body is coated in crud and a filthy ragged caftan. I ask him if he needs help and he mumbles that he's searching for a master. I suspect true masters are more likely to stay in their quiet Himalayan hideouts than come to the melee of the Mela.

The Hindu religion is a guru's gig, where ego is a dirty word and only supplication to a master can kill it. The closest I ever get to understanding the guru thing is my constant ability to fall in love with lead singers and bass players. But I'm down on groupies. Maybe it's my inability to respect authority for authority's sake, maybe it's my Australian independent streak or maybe it's the glazed expression on the devotees' faces, but I'm not willing to touch the feet of any of the *sadhus* I've seen so far. It's hard enough for me to surrender to a faith, let alone a fallible human. While I'm prepared to admit many beings are far more spiritually advanced than I am, the Westerner in me is automatically suspicious of people who claim to be perfect. If I'm to find a god or a sense of grace, I'd rather it be in metaphysical form. It just makes more sense to me to look for the supernatural in something superhuman.

Besides, I'm finding the guru mentality all too manifest in other areas of Indian life. I join Neeraj and Titi at the media tent, where they are still awaiting a press pass for the big bathing day. As we fill out more forms in triplicate, the press information bureau officer sits behind a huge table reveling in his own authority to forbid filming.

"Not that we believe in censorship but we've had to start checking some stories and changing bits."

I try to speak. He shows me the hand.

"Madam, even though it's impossible for us to be offended, because we respect all opinions and criticisms, the Western media has offended us by showing naked *sadhus*."

I can't get a word in to tell the Raja of Red Tape that the local media has featured far more racy bits than the international press. As he speaks, four men watch, drinking in the glory of their Goebbels. They prostrate themselves before him, vigorously nod and fall over with laughter when he tries to be funny. They're unpaid crawlers, men with not enough work and too much time who just love to sit at the feet of someone more successful than themselves. Indians adore authority. To these guys, this middle-ranking official is a Buddha of bureaucracy and a priest of paperwork. To me he's a dickhead of the highest order.

I suspect guru supplication is a cultural and spiritual phenomenon, as much a factor of massive underemployment, the lingering caste system and the legacy of British imperialism as a need to let go of ego for spiritual integrity. But in Hinduism generalizations are dangerous; in some ways this is the least authoritarian religion I've encountered. Almost anyone can become a *sadhu*. The Channel Four crew are filming a freaky dude who calls himself Kali Baba; he wears a bowl in his lip, says in an American accent that he's from the African Masai tribe and beds a different babe every night. I've also heard there's a Swiss stiffie *sadhu* who has a permanent erection, and a Japanese girl has been hailed a saint since living down a pit for days. Hinduism is far more accepting than I am. It accepts gurus of all colors, races and creeds and it has an ingenious way of dealing with its critics. Buddha rejected ancient Hindu teachings and the very existence of God, but Hindus insist that he was another avatar of Vishnu and respect him accordingly. The Dalai Lama has already been at the Kumbh and taken part in a ceremony at the sacred swimming spot.

Most of the *sadhus* at the Maha Kumbh Mela don't have a following. Simi's husband, Vivek, turns up to film and he takes me out for a trip among the thousands of solo saints who shuffle in streams, squat by the sandy roads and sleep in huddled heaps in the open. We film faces etched with hardship and creased with sun, and bow-shaped bodies with bandy legs carrying all their possessions in small shoulder bags. At a dusty windswept dune Vivek helps a solitary *sadhu* put up a tarp for shade. Sharp raven eyes peer beneath an orange turban and a brown and pink jumper clashes with his hemp-stained beard. Carbooterwallah (Pigeon Man) invites us to call him Bum Bum (which is the chant he makes to Shiva when he offers him the first toke of the hash chillum). Bum Bum's worldly goods are a painted tree stump shaped like Shiva's bull Nandi, a trident, a blanket, some tractor oil and a small table decorated with plastic gods, cobras and alarm clocks.

For Bum Bum, India is a sacred land, an enchanted mother, where the divine is present in every mountain, ocean, river, tree and rock. The Ganges is especially sacred, because she's actually a beautiful goddess who crashed to earth from heaven with only Shiva's dreadlocks to break her fall. Pigeon Man coos, "The Ganges is so sacred that even your family in Australia can go to heaven if they just picture the river in their minds."

I don't have the heart to tell him they'd prefer Disney World.

Hinduism is a faith of almost infinite diversity. Yet the broadest, most complicated religion on the planet actually caters brilliantly to the individual. It seems every Hindu is free to create and follow his own unique religion, choosing his own gods and methods of worship. The gods of non-Hindus are respected and Hindu gods are generously shared. A young boy called Anu walks me back to my camp and gives me some options for *puja*. I can look to Hanuman for energy, Varuna (the god of water) if I want rain, Lakshmi (Vishnu's consort, the goddess of wealth) if I need money and Saraswathi (Brahma's consort, the goddess of knowledge) if I have an exam coming up. Ganesh (the elephant god and the child of Shiva and Parvati) can be called on when starting a new journey or venture and Vishnu, Rama or Krishna if I want purity of spirit.

Anu bids me good-bye, saying, "Just be taking your picking, all is for one and one is for all."

Dollie waves me a welcome home, hoping I've chosen Shiva.

There's also infinite variety in the ways of devotion. As the hospital cleaner, Indian Jim, told me a year ago, doing one's duty by living a life still largely dictated by caste is the most common. But at the camp dinner some pilgrims advocate meditation, others ritual fasting and a few the regular chanting of "om" (the first word of the universe and the perfect vibration). One elderly woman, Gayatri, recommends I walk one hundred and eight times around a certain tree to find faith; her daughter suggests I feed a cow for a year. They will take some Ganges water home to place a drop under the tongue of any family members who die. This will guarantee heaven. Yet Gayatri insists heaven can also be found within.

"I like your Jesus and such, and there's no doubt he was a great *sadhu*, most likely trained in India, but you know, he was wrong about God. God is not a judgmental giant sitting up in heaven, it's a force within us all—we are lightbulbs in the electrical system of the universe."

But Hinduism's inclusiveness and its respect for all religions are at risk from extremists. The next day on my morning walk I meet a young disciple of the VHP—the Vishwa Hindu Parishad. This is the World Hindu Council, a body of fundamentalist-leaning Hindus closely aligned to the BJP, which currently dominates India's ruling coalition. This young VHP soldier is keen for me to see his organization's showroom. Inside a tent patrolled by armed guards is a model of a *mandir*, or temple, the VHP wants built on the ruins of the mosque at Ayodhya. The group claims the site is the birthplace of Rama and is unapologetic about its role in the mosque's destruction. The *mandir* model looks like a cross between the Vatican and a Disneyland castle. Its construction would be uglier—undermining India's secular constitution and defying Hinduism's basic belief that any path to God is divine. Until now the mosque's destruction could be dismissed as a mindless act by a mob of minority extremists. But if a temple is constructed, the extremism would seem sanctioned by the government. Extreme Hinduism seems to be an oxymoron but in this country the nonsensical often triumphs.

At other times detachment wins over. Neeraj marches Titi and me to the filthy backwaters of the Ganges to interview some *sadhus* about the state of the holy river. They tell us, "The river is not dirty, your mind is dirty." Only one admits there's a problem: "Yes, the river is dirty, but you must detach from the senses."

I find it hard to ignore the swollen corpses of dead dogs and the occasional bobbing baby (babies are not cremated in India and their disposal in the Ganges guarantees their souls a place in heaven). There are also masses of floating garbage and a stench of sewage. I agree with the Sikhs: *sadhus* can perhaps be too detached from their surroundings.

Yet tonight I cleanse my mind of such thoughts. I sense a spiritual purity in the putrid air. The big bathing day is tomorrow and the crowds are pouring in. The clerks, the farmers, the teachers, the workers and the housewives of northern India are having the times of what may now be the last of their millions of lives. Tonight they will party, for tomorrow will bring salvation. There are balloons, weight-measuring machines, elephant blessings and camel rides. Naked *sadhus* stand stunned as neon robots tell them their future, a motorcycle daredevil zooms around a tin circle of death and couples hold hands as they eat cotton candy.

All night the music and singing and chanting build like a massive rave with dancers fueled by the ecstasy of devotion. At four o'clock it reaches a crescendo as the main DJ, God, takes the stage. The earth begins to tremble as the millions begin the slow march toward the *sangam*, the place where the Ganges and Yamuna rivers meet.

I join Titi and Neeraj (who's now carrying a compass and a canteen) onboard a boat bobbing on the black Ganges. We pass small huddles of floating shapes softly singing to the splashing of oars. The soft first light falls upon a tide of pilgrims patiently and quietly walking along the bank toward the holy spot. Some stop to shave their heads, for every hair shed is ten thousand lives that don't have to be lived. Piles of black hair stain the sand.

The winter season, global warming and water mismanagement mean the rivers meet with a trickle not a bang. Huge sandbars of black mud stick out of the waters, and after Neeraj salutes a huge floating flotilla of policemen, we are allowed to stand on a big spit facing the main riverbank. We shiver in the gray air and look across to a blur of beings chanting for the godly games to begin. *Akhara* bodyguards in white G-strings ensure that the *sadhu*s get to touch the divine waters before the inferior—they form a barrier across the sand and those who try to break it are belted hard on the head. The masses murmur as they feel a slow and steady shaking of the sands.

A trumpet sounds, the crowd cheers and hundreds of *naga baba*s march over the hill like an alien cavalry. The dawn light gives the warriors a ghostly glow and while some seem huge and terrifying as they perform ninja-like moves with sharp tridents and swords, others are as emaciated as supermodels doing heroin chic. Their guru sits on a golden chariot under a brass umbrella surrounded by flag bearers. The press officer has warned us the *sadhu*s are angry, that there's been aggression, breaking of cameras and anti-foreign fury. We're eighty meters from the bank and in the middle of the river, but out of respect and fear I put my camera down; Titi keeps focused with the big Betacam TV camera but looks nervous. As Neeraj checks his watch and calls "oh-five hundred" the *baba*s prance down to the river, throw their garlands of flowers in the water and then squat like racers at the starting line.

A whistle blows and about five hundred *sadhu*s charge into their Ganges goddess splashing, screaming and waving their swords. But they don't stop to wash away their sin, they keep running straight for us. It's as if they are walking on water. The river is only ankle deep and we have nowhere to run and nowhere to hide. A wave washes over us and the sandbank is flooded. They're still coming. I adopt the Hindu fatalism—at least if I die I'm going straight to heaven.

They're here.

Throwing the swords down, the naked blue-black *sadhu*s jump and dance around us and the camera. They are waving, shaking my hand, shivering and doing all too revealing cartwheels. Their faces split into huge grins and their dreadlocks glisten with drops of water. Neeraj stands at attention, Titi films on and I laugh nervously like an adventurer being welcomed to another world. It's a meeting of the primal and the prim, the faithful and the foreign, the devotee and the doubter. I breathe in the rapture and joy on their faces, and for a moment I feel their ecstasy. Together we wade in the waters that form heaven on earth.

After the *sadhus*, the bald initiates dip and then the pilgrims begin to bathe. The women maintain modesty by being diligently dexterous with their saris, while the men put on an exhibition of briefs—high-waisted, saggy, and occasionally leopard-skinned. One family gently leads their blind father, making sure he doesn't slip in the mud. Another celebrates a boy's coming of age, hoisting him up on their shoulders and yelling "Hip Hip Hooray" in the most English of voices. Everyone coats themselves with river mud, rubs themselves free of bad karma and dunks three times. They pour water through their hands, pray, burn incense, sing prayers and then blow snot into the holy nectar. It's a scene of incredible gentleness, patience, purity of spirit and faith.

But I'm in pants, I'm freezing cold and I'm too scared of hepatitis to share the Hindu faith in the Ganges. Neeraj refuses to even let me consider a bath and pulls me toward the boat and breakfast. Before I board, something stops me. Before I even know what I'm doing, I'm kneeling down and splashing a little water on my forehead. It's an impulse that feels right and it pays off. I sense strength and grace; I swoon with a dose of the divine and a feeling that I'm part of a universal force.

I return from the Kumbh on a high, and rave to an earthquake-shaken Jonathan about the crazy party that's made me feel that this country and its many religions have something wonderful to offer me. He needs to hear it; he's been sleeping under a tree for two weeks watching homeless, shattered people search for their dead beneath miles of rubble. Jonathan wants to know that India is not just a land of disaster, that at its best it can show a mass display of patience and joy.

Unfortunately, I then ruin all my good vibes by descending into another downside of the country: its tourist trail. My mum, her friend Val and I travel through Rajasthan. While we stay in divine palaces converted to swanky hotels and our tours are beautiful, fascinating and fun, I become outraged anew at the rip-offs and scams and constant hassle. I vow to stop doing this kind of travel in India; it's too well worn a path with nothing new for me to find. I don't tell my mother I'm heading off on a different track that may get transcendental; I don't want her to worry about my sanity. She's worried enough that I have lost the ability to look after myself; Rachel is on maternity leave after having a beautiful tiny baby-doll girl and I've forgotten how to cook. Mum and Val leave hungry just before Holi: a Hindu festival they would not have enjoyed. Holi is a festival of lust rather than devotion; it hails the end of winter by indulging in spring fever.

Jonathan and I awake to the smell of smoldering bonfires, the sounds of screams and the telephone. Simi and Vivek are calling to invite us around.

"Wear something old and disgusting," Simi warns ominously.

I've never had an Indian tell me not to look nice and I begin to worry. I'm not the only one; Abraham declines an offer of extra pay to drive us to the party. It takes an hour to find a taxi driver who will work and he insists on double the usual fare.

"*Adj Dilli bahoot paagal paan he*," the driver mutters darkly—today Delhi is very crazy.

We nervously drive through streets strangely quiet and devoid of the usual chaos of cars, cows and commuters. The only beings around are strange chameleon alien invaders with green hair, purple faces, pink clothes and red bodies. They stagger and lurch, shooting each other with water pistols. Holi is the day when the authorities turn a blind bloodshot eye to *bung* (marijuana), and the boys with their water toys are off their heads.

Our car pulls up at Simi's flat and is suddenly surrounded by her screaming neighbors. They open the doors and pull us from our seats; a young girl rubs orange powder into my hair, a brash boy paints my cheeks pink with his hands and his mate circles my breasts with red. Screaming blue murder, I run for safety, dodging streams of colored water fired from balconies. I'm not safe yet. Simi opens the door yelling, "Happy Holi," and pours yellow powder down my top, while Vivek rubs purple into my forehead. Jonathan staggers in like a creature from the blue lagoon with his mouth laughing shocking white teeth. We gulp a sweet marijuana milk shake for courage and join in.

Touching, chasing and flirting is normally considered outrageous behavior in India but today sensuality is sanctioned. Even Simi's mother gets into the action, scooping bright green powder down Jonathan's pants and giving him a kiss. The *bung* is deadly. Within half an hour I collapse against the wall laughing hysterically, despite feeling that my head has split open and bugs are crawling out all over my body. It's an even more toxic high than that given by the pot I had at the Kumbh Mela and it gives a blistering *bung* hangover.

As I recover at home the next day, I miss attending mass ceremonies taking place on the Yamuna River. On the TV news we watch as thousands of Hindus quit their faith and convert to Buddhism. It's hard to see what this involves, as the camera gets knocked down in the jostle, but it appears they shave their heads and bow to Buddha. The ceremony is more political than religious; the converts are Dalits (low-caste untouchables) who are making a statement about Hinduism's caste system that puts them at the bottom of society and way down the path of spiritual evolution. While the Buddha was a high-caste Hindu, he rejected the caste system and the Brahman ownership of knowledge to embrace do-it-yourself enlightenment by meditation. While the Mogul invasions wiped out Buddhism in its country of origin, the faith is now making a comeback, largely due to the rise of activism among low-caste Indians and perhaps thanks to its modern-day prince, guru and spiritual leader: a refugee living here called the Dalai Lama.

At the Kumbh Mela I heard that the Dalai Lama is about to give his annual Indian teachings. It's an opportunity just too good to miss. After only a week's recovery time, Jonathan is heading off again—this time back to Afghanistan—and I need an adventure to keep my mind from worrying about his safety.

Upper Dharamsala, or McLeod Gunj, is the spiritual center of exiled Tibetan Buddhism. I'd passed through the town on my way home from Vipassana and I'd found it peaceful and pretty, but as I head back to the tiny settlement perched on a ridge of the Himalayan foothills, I'm shocked to see it bursting at the seams. It takes hours to travel up the packed potholed path on a precipice. Finally my bus splutters over the hill, farts a toxic cloud of black diesel smoke into the air and unloads monks, nuns and tourists. The town no longer looks as it did when I came down from Dharamkot with stars in my eyes and love in my heart. It's developing dramatically to match the exploding Western interest in Buddhism and, at the moment, it's not big enough to cope with the largest influx of spiritual tourists in history.

Waterfalls of plastic bags and bottles cascade down the slopes. Red-arsed mangy monkeys and rabies-ridden dogs graze on huge piles of garbage. Steel pipes snake the paths, and faded prayer flags wrap around barbed wire fences. The thin mountain air is clogged with dust and the stench of sewage; face masks sell alongside silk scarves. Goan trance music, screams of chain saws and the throb of jackhammers drown out the gongs and chants from the monasteries. The sunken faces of squatting lepers plead up at me and the Dalai Lama's face peers down from massive advertising billboards. I have to walk a long way out of town to find a room.

Ladies Venture looks like a sweet and cheap guest house. Inside, a woman wearing a beautiful Tibetan tunic dress with a striped apron shakes her long plaits in a nod at my inquiry and laughs at my relief.

"Hello, lovely lady, there is not much water, and no power at night, you have a great time."

In my bare room that looks up to the snowcapped Himalayas I

have my first existential crisis. There's a centipede in my sink. Buddhists should not kill and in their town I should honor that belief. It takes me half an hour to get the creature onto some paper and out the door; it takes seconds for a monk to walk past and unwittingly stomp on it.

I head out for dinner. The Tibetan shops and restaurants are crowded, and the health-food cafés, chocolate bars, Italian restaurants, Internet centers and video theaters are full. Walls are covered with layers of posters advertising courses. There are reiki, aura reading, Thai massage, yoga, Tibetan cooking, clairvoyance, plant healing, tarot card reading and Jewish mysticism. At the moment, the Dalai Lama's annual lecture course is king. I sit in a café and eavesdrop on raves about His Holiness—one of the few heroes on the planet. A Swedish girl says "HH" speaks the most wonderful wisdom, but a dopey-looking hippie with an incredible cockney accent admits he's having trouble.

"I'm dropping out, man, the three days of emptiness are killing me, just how empty can you pleading be? I'm going to watch *Terminator* in the movie café."

At dawn I'm up as the rain comes pouring down on the wettest town in India. Slipping and sliding along the brown mud path snaking atop the precipice, I join a steady stream of somber devotees. Beneath the black umbrellas and amid the maroon robes flash a pair of purple bell-bottoms, some bright tight T-shirts and bindi-brightened belly buttons. The crowd pools at a defective metal detector below "Little Tibet," the Tsuglagkhang Temple beside the Dalai Lama's palace. Rocks painted with bright yellow mantras purify the earth and huge red-painted barrels spin prayers into the sky. Inside a temple room, young monks are chanting to clashing cymbals and rolling drums. It's a strange sound, resembling a symphony played backward at half speed; the voices are so low, slow and resonant that they vibrate my inner organs.

We enter a huge whitewashed auditorium that's fast filling up. I squeeze onto a corner of a sodden cushion next to one of the Dalai Lama's bodyguards. He offers me butter tea; it's salty, greasy and awful and he laughs at my grimace. I share small talk with those around me—an Irish teacher, a French Buddhist nun, a Swiss grandmother and an American monk with a green tattoo of a dragon snaking around his arm. The Tibetan refugees slouch patiently while Westerners sit ramrod straight, holding tight to their crossed legs like kids on the first day of school.

After an hour of waiting, the crowd twitters. It stands and bends on one huge hinge. But there's not much room for full prostration to the ground; the monastery resembles a giant game of Twister. Breaking the bobbing sea of bent backs, a couple of young guys jump up and wave at HH, giving each other high fives when he looks at them. The Dalai Lama giggles as he shuffles past; looking older in real life than on the telly, he is slightly bent but still sprightly. The serene smile is the same. When HH sits inside the temple and out of sight for most of the huge crowd, there's a groan of disappointment. I tune my transistor for the translation, shake my head free of piercing feedback and settle down for some enlightenment.

There's no doubt the Dalai Lama is a good teacher. Respectful of all religions, he somehow manages to explain the vast complex teachings of his faith relatively simply. He starts with basic human truths and slowly builds up to complicated notions of time and space. Some Taiwanese are crying with the pleasure of his presence, Tibetan monks listen reverently, refugees occasionally nod off and most Westerners seem to be in awe. An emaciated girl behind me is in the lotus position, eyes closed and swaying while attempting a beatific smile; she looks sick and sweaty with fever. The Dalai Lama talks about good living.

"You may think you look beautiful in a meditative state but that's not enough. To generate compassion, you have to get up and live it."

She grins wider, sways more and nods slowly and forcefully in agreement.

I can see why Buddhism appeals to so many Westerners. The

Dalai Lama is a superb ambassador; always calm and smiling, he's untainted by scandals and bad television shows. HH also practices what he preaches—nonviolence, humility and compassion—and he teaches techniques that appeal to Western minds. He even demands doubt, questioning and reasoning. It's exciting to hear a preacher say, "Don't take my word for it. You must question and question."

This is also a good faith for those of us oriented to individualism, as it offers a spiritual psychology of self-development. And its central tenet is the one thing us rich Western kids can't buy—happiness.

The Dalai Lama tells us to stop expecting life to be easy. The first noble truth of Buddhism is that life is full of suffering and is ultimately unsatisfying; the only way to be happy is to want less and to train your mind to penetrate the ultimate reality. That Buddhist reality maintains that there is no God or no soul—we're all just streams of consciousness that have existed since beginningless time in infinite bodies and six different realms. I can barely remember my childhood, let alone past lives. But apparently I have been a demi-god, human, animal, hungry ghost and hell dweller millions of times before. The Buddhist hell sounds as vicious as the Christian version—with torture by molten iron, fire and disembowelment. According to the Buddhist scriptures, hell is located on the other side of the earth on a spot directly opposite Bodhgaya—the town in India where the Buddha became enlightened. According to modern maps, that corresponds to America. The future of Tibetan Buddhism seems most assured in hell—there are more Americans at this lecture than I've seen in the rest of India put together.

Buddhist teachings say that life is a prison and Tibetan Buddhists aim to be our jail breakers. They vow to forsake the pure realm to come back to earth as spiritual superheroes, called *bodhisattvas*, to enlighten others. *Bodhisattvas* are like the Jedi knights in *Star Wars*. They are brave, compassionate and love all creatures equally, while remaining unattached to anyone in particular. They are also extraordinarily powerful in their use of a "force" for good.

At the end of the Dalai Lama's lectures he leads the vow of the *bodhisattvas*. I'm surprised, because I thought *lamas* (teachers), monks and ardent lay devotees would be the only ones allowed to make such a pledge. I can't take the vow—I'm not feeling confident enough of my own spiritual salvation, let alone my ability to enlighten others as a good *bodhisattva* should.

Many young travelers who do take the vow don't seem to realize quite what it means. In a Mexican restaurant I watch a group celebrate their new spiritual status by toasting each other with warm Indian beer that tastes like hops mixed with rubbing alcohol. One guy sporting a FREE TIBET T-shirt and a halo of blond corkscrew curls demands a *bodhisattva* discount on the bill. The waiter seems used to such behavior—he just giggles and walks off.

Tibetan *bodhisattvas* don't drink beer and they don't show off. They're supposed to humbly follow special secret tantric teachings to speed up the process of enlightenment and gain control over rebirth. We ordinary humans have no control over our reincarnations; our consciousness is blown by the winds of our karma to our next parents. In the tradition of Lamaism, dying *lamas* direct their consciousness into another body; that child is recognized as a *tulku* (a reincarnated *lama*) and brought up to continue the work. The Dalai Lama is the most famous *tulku* of our time. Not only is he a *bodhisattva*, he's also believed to be a manifestation of the Buddha's compassionate consciousness. He's Tibet's spiritual savior, superhero, political leader and living Buddha all rolled into one.

As the biggest *bodhisattva* finishes his teachings, the town empties like a drain—buses full to the brim gurgle and belch down the hill and the mountain echoes back the sounds of slamming doors. The locals smile with sighs of relief.

As I sit and sip *chai* and stare at the procession snaking its way down the valley, I hear a whoop and feel a hug. I'm wrapped up in the arms of the girl in my Vipassana course who spent her spare moments hugging trees with a Jesus-like crown of twigs on her head. Katarina still looks a bit like the Messiah with her dirty blonde shoulder-length curls, jet-black eyes and glowing clear skin, but she doesn't look as miserable. In fact, she radiates ecstatic happiness. She'd given up a chance to be an Olympic athlete to come to India and says it's been worth it.

"I've won a gold medal for my heart from the Dalai Lama," she squeals. "I dream about him all the time. Last time I felt this boom of light on me, wham and whack, we started laughing. I just have to see it again. It seems I've been chasing him all my life."

Since I last saw Katarina, she's met the Dalai Lama in two public audiences and traveled to Lhasa to pick him a rose from his former garden.

But Katarina says I can't meet the Divine Leader because he's about to go overseas. Instead, she invites me to come with her to see another famous spiritual superhero, the Karmapa Lama. He is the spiritual head of the Kagyu sect of Tibetan Buddhism and fled to India last year. This high-profile refugee's rejection of Chinese rule greatly embarrassed the Chinese government—it's put great pressure on India to contain the Karmapa Lama and he's now a virtual prisoner in a nearby monastery.

The next morning Katarina and I catch a taxi down the mountain and across the valley to a white and yellow monastery called Gyuto. We wait cross-legged in a huge auditorium with about one hundred people, most of them Western women showing inappropriate amounts of cleavage and wearing lots of red nylon scarves—blessed objects given to them by the Karmapa Lama on previous meetings. The girl next to me has seven and is squirming and squealing with excitement.

"I collect them. He's so gorgeous, I just adore him."

The Karmapa Lama walks into the hall and sits on a wooden throne in front of us. A few women wail and Katarina rocks in rapture. I look up hoping to see the divine soul. Alas, I'm too ignorant to see the *bodhisattva* within—I see a heavyset teenager in the midst of puberty with wide-set eyes and a wide protruding forehead. There's none of the Dalai Lama's panda-like joy and humor;

the Karmapa Lama is serious and somber. We file past him, each gives him a white prayer scarf, and we are given red scarves in return. After the Karmapa Lama leaves, the girls tie their red scarves in Girl Scout style, smile, hug each other and skip from the room. Katarina tells me she winked at him when she bent down for her blessing.

At the photo shop back up the hill, I hug Katarina good-bye and go inside to meet the far more cynical Angus—an Australian who wryly comments that Karmapa Lama photos are now outselling the Dalai Lama two to one.

"It's that whole sexualization of a young pristine monk thing. It's pretty off, actually."

I don't believe Angus, so he tells me to ask for opinions at the Namgyal monastery below the now empty auditorium. There, a slight pale British monk called Tenzin Josh beckons me into his small, cold damp cell and leaves the door open as we talk (his vows forbid him being alone with a woman). In a quiet calm monotone he explains that he left London to find happiness within but believes some other travelers are just here for sensual pleasures and these tourists don't respect his fellow monks.

"They chat them up and touch them, which is strictly forbidden. About twenty monks a year are disrobing, they're listening to Western music which is designed to create attachment, they go to parties, restaurants, they see women in bad clothing."

A fellow student comes to call at Josh's cell and he's just as concerned. Rob reckons it's a bit of a game for Western women who love the idea of breaking a monk.

"They drop them when they've made them violate the vows. But it happens the other way as well; monks who are just monks for a livelihood use the women for sponsorship or for visas and dump them when they get out of India."

That's got to be bad karma. And that's the second noble truth of Buddhism: the cause of the suffering. As in Hinduism, Buddhists believe bad actions fester within our consciousness and are received back in kind in one of our millions of future lives. But purifying karma is hard work in this faith, involving endless education, prostrating, reciting prayers or repeating mantras. According to the Buddhists, my halfhearted dip in the Ganges has done nothing. Josh tells me it's best to start by trying to stop generating more bad karma, and to get rid of my delusions, and the best way to do this is to take the Tushita beginners' course in Buddhism up the hill. It starts tomorrow morning.

The next day I wake early to walk up a steep path past mangy monkeys, piles of garbage and cliff-top hotels. As I reach the top, I feel like I'm entering a heavenly realm—the path is shrouded in a fog that comes in so swiftly it's like Buddha himself has blown a smoke ring. The Tushita center is a sweet collection of Tibetan-style buildings set among damp trees; inside its shrine room, or *gompa*, a massive brass Buddha looks down at twenty Western travelers, and water bowls decorate an altar of photos of past and present teachers. A monk called David takes our class; an Aussie in his former life, he sits pale, shorn and orange-freckled in dark robes. He makes us meditate on the fact that we are going to die. We shut our eyes, David drones.

"We are walking corpses, every breath brings you one closer to the grave. There are earthquakes due here any moment, Indian buses and planes are dangerous. Prepare for your death now, as tomorrow is too late. Your state of mind at death will determine your next rebirth. If you're angry you'll go to hell. It's important to die calm and happy."

Tibetan Buddhists are big on death. It takes many years and possibly many lifetimes of tantric practice to be able to control the process of rebirth, but stage one involves learning to die calmly and with dignity. So, after accepting our death is inevitable, we practice dying. I imagine myself in a lovely bed above the sea with my not yet conceived but now elderly children standing around looking woeful. More experienced Buddhists imagine their flesh rotting and their bones decaying, something I don't feel quite ready for.

Yet, strangely, this death stuff is not depressing, it's kind of liberating. While death is ever-present in India, most Hindus don't talk about it for fear of attracting bad luck. They won't even say the word, preferring "really not very well" for "dying," and "expired" for "been dead for ages." A year ago my brush with mortality made me feel vulnerable and scared and keen to search for answers, but in the peaceful shrine room I calmly accept the inevitable. I figure that if I can find peace in death, then perhaps I can find peace and a sense of grace in life.

We then hear about the importance of loving all beings equally—one of the greatest challenges for Buddhists to face. It is extraordinarily difficult but I can see the need to try. I'm growing weary of the way the tourists here in Dharamsala idealize Tibetans and demonize Indians. I overhear horrible comments about the people who have so generously shared their overcrowded country with the refugees of Tibet. But there's no doubt Tibetans are beautiful-looking and easy to like. One morning I circle the Dalai Lama's palace with some geriatrics. They shuffle bent double, their faces creased into deep smiles, their big hands spinning their prayer wheels. They all stop mumbling their mantras to say hello and laugh at my Tibetan reply of *tashi delek*, the only phrase I know. Their giggles seem to come from a different place than the Australian cynical chuckle; it's as if they are laughing with me and not at me. It's highly contagious and attractive.

However, beneath the smiles Tibetans obviously are not perfect. It's not all loving-kindness here; I see a monk beat a dog, another one smokes and while Buddhist texts forbid meat, the fleshy bodies of sheep hang in roadside butcher boxes attracting swarms of flies and shoppers galore. I've kept up my Kumbh Mela vow not to eat meat—it just feels wrong to me now. I know the Dalai Lama has tried to turn vegetarian but so long as he and other Tibetan Buddhists continue to eat meat, the tinge of hypocrisy will remain. The meat-eating Buddhists do not kill, but it seems unfair that they get Muslims to kill animals for them. While Muslims don't think the killing is sinful, surely the Buddhists must worry about the Muslims bringing bad karma upon themselves for the sake of

Tibetan tummies? What's more disturbing, though, is the violence toward people. A local tells me one of his female staff was being bashed by her husband, but when he reported it to the Tibetan welfare office, they told him it was dangerous to hurt her husband's pride.

"They said if we couldn't cope with looking at her bruised face all the time then to sack her."

He also tells me some young boys got into a knife fight recently and a monk was murdered last year after condemning the worship of a spirit. This is obviously not a community of saints but a population of refugees facing problems of displacement and distress.

I climb down the slippery slope to visit the Tibetan government-in-exile to research an article I'm considering writing about the town. The information secretary, Thubten Samphel, talks about violence, depression and health problems and how he wants Western visitors to be more aware of this reality.

"We want the world to take our struggle seriously and the Shangri-la thing damages us; this is a real political issue with real suffering. We are of this world with the same weaknesses and faults as other people."

As I puff back up the hill pondering his words I let go of my tendency to judge the Western groupies and the Tibetans. Harsh thoughts have always been one of my weaknesses. I've always been too angry, using this emotion as an active alternative to depression and hopelessness. To embrace Buddhism I'll have to transform my fury about injustice, poverty, environmental destruction and negative relationships into detachment and compassion.

Back at Tushita, David explains how the Dalai Lama shows the way—he doesn't get angry at the Chinese, he acknowledges some good things have come out of their invasion and he feels sorry for them because they've created bad karma. I try applying this Buddhist practice. I imagine the stalker who freaked me out during my last year at Triple J and begin to pity him for his problems and the punishment he will receive in some future life. But Buddhism is easier to practice in the mind than in reality. An hour later when a bloke deliberately bumps into my breast to cop a feel, I'm only up to stage one of the rationalization when I spin around, whack him and call him a bastard. I've stuffed it. Now we will both suffer in another life.

The third noble truth is the cessation of suffering: freedom from rebirth, and Buddhahood. The fourth noble truth is the Buddhist path to get there. My reaction to the breast-bumping incident in the street makes me realize I have a long way to go. I've made a start in India along my path to personal transformation and inner peace. The Sikhs have shown me how to be strong, the Vipassana course taught me how to calm my mind, India's Muslims have shown me the meaning of surrender and sacrifice, and the Hindus have illustrated an infinite number of ways to the divine. But right now the Buddhist way of living attracts me most. It complements my society's psychological approach to individual growth and development, my desire to take control and take responsibility for my own happiness, and it advocates a way of living that encourages compassion and care.

Also, Buddhism is proving it can move with the times. For one thing, it's confronting its sexism, largely thanks to one of the first Western women to become a Buddhist nun. Over Christmas I read the book *Cave in the Snow*, which tells the incredible tale of Tenzin Palmo (formerly a British woman, Diane Perry), who spent years meditating in a cave above Manali and now runs a nunnery not far from Dharamsala. I'd love to meet her. Tenzin Palmo's Australian assistant, Monica, agrees to let me visit and I take a teeth-chattering, bone-bashing taxi ride down the mountain, past the Buddhist temples, prayer flags and *stupa*s or shrines, past an abandoned tank and some army barracks, across a small waterfall and into another valley to her nunnery. When Tenzin Palmo met the Dalai Lama she bluntly told him of the difficulties of being a nun in the Tibetan tradition and made him cry; he then supported her work in setting up the nunnery here at Tashi Jong.

The world's second Western Buddhist nun emerges from a small office. Tiny and humble, calm and composed, stooped and steely strong, Tenzin Palmo's shorn scalp has three circular scars caused by candles burned at initiation ceremonies. She sits and patiently tells me her tale over tea, while her students work outside, giggling as they gather water and prepare to make their dinner. These twenty-five nuns are from around India's northeast border—Ladakh, Lahaul, Spiti, Nepal and Bhutan. There, as in Tibet, nuns often became household servants to monks. But Tenzin Palmo speaks without bitterness.

"While there were some nunneries, there was no educational program for nuns, they effectively had no voice. Religious texts were written by monks and so naturally were one-sided. Nowadays this situation is being slowly redeemed as more and more nunneries are being founded and many include a study program, sometimes using the same curriculum as the monasteries. In the next few years we certainly hope to see women study to become teachers. In the meantime, our nuns still believe that monks are naturally more intelligent and pray to be reborn in a male body."

Tenzin Palmo raises money so the nuns can learn Tibetan writing, English, philosophy and debating. It's wonderful and rewarding work but she would rather be shut up in a little cell and meditating. Eventually this nunnery will contain little huts for women from all over the world to do just that. In quiet hills away from cares and worries, it will become a safe space for consciousness-cleansing in long retreats. Maybe when I'm more disciplined I'll return. I can't imagine being able to meditate for months—I still shudder at some of the recollections of my ten days at Vipassana.

Luckily there's no need to hurry with Buddhism; it's going to take aeons for humans to gain freedom. Our delusions are powerful and mushrooming every moment which means most of us will have to return for millions of more lives. Buddhists believe there are one thousand enlightened Buddha beings and Gautama, the Indian founder of the faith in this age, was only the fourth. The next manifestation of Buddhahood in human form, Maitreya (the Buddha of loving-kindness), will appear when humans are stunted, have a ten-year life span, and spend their time killing. Western Buddhists are raising funds to build a one-hundred-and-fifty-two-meter statue of Maitreya in Bodhgaya that they hope will last the thousands of years until he arrives. They also hope it will generate enough great karma for them to be reborn at that time. Three times bigger than the antenna on the Empire State Building, it will certainly put India back on the map as a Buddhist heartland.

It's easy to become entranced by the science fiction quality of Tibetan Buddhism with its visions of endless time, endless universes and endless beings in endless varieties of forms that are as trippy and alien as Hinduism's multiarmed blue beings. But while some travelers love paintings of the web-fingered Buddha with long ears and the scary green wrathful-looking female Buddha, Tara, I'm more interested in Buddhism's inner work. It doesn't seem relevant for me to surround myself with Tibetan art or to bow, prostrate and make offerings to the Buddha when he insisted he never be worshiped or deified. Other spiritual tourists here don't have that problem.

I share a café table one day in Dharamsala with Simon, a lanky, greasy-haired American wearing pajamas. He says when he first saw a Buddha he dropped to his knees and prostrated himself.

"It was just so right, it was all familiar to me. I've obviously been Buddhist in many past lives; you probably haven't."

I must look sad.

"Don't worry." He pats my arm. "Stay cool in this life and you may be born in a Buddhist family next time."

I feel that may be possible, for I'm doing okay at the Buddhist dharma. The Tushita course has another week to go and Jonathan is stuck in Afghanistan battling with Taliban officials, who make his every move almost impossible. I'm not keen to go back to an empty home in polluted Delhi; I'm loving the mountain air, I'm meditating, I'm thinking a lot about death, I'm detaching from fear, I haven't become angry for days and when I hear about major predictions of earthquakes I joke about it.

"I'm staying on. This is a good place to die," I tell Simon.

"Or be reborn," he replies.

"Amen," say I.

11 | Trading Places in the Promised Lands

A few days on and I'm suffering from torturous overkill and emptiness overload. The Buddhist philosophy may be rewarding but it's heavy going. After we spend eight hours in the Tushita course grappling with the concept that everything is intrinsically empty because it cannot exist in its own right, my brain begins to ache. I dodge a class on dying to follow the signs of life to the small town of Dharamkot down the hill.

The sounds of badly played tabla and distorted techno draw me to a restaurant that smells of pot, pizza and patchouli. This is the scent of India's most ubiquitous travelers—Israelis. After hanging around monks for weeks I feel shocked and stirred by the sensuality surrounding me. The scene oozes sex. Israelis are the nubile young gods of the *Lonely Planet* scene—hunks with hazelnut tans and healthy glows, luscious lips and shiny hair, bursting bosoms and big muscles. They're stylishly pierced, bindied, dreadlocked and dressed; with chunky rings on their fingers and toes, they make music wherever they go.

The Indians don't really like the Israelis, for they travel in packs, they're loud and they demand cheap prices (some will bargain for hours over fifty cents). A few hotels here even refuse the backpackers admission. But I'm drawn into the Israeli circle by the pull of passion so absent from my Buddhist being. I am meant to be cultivating detachment from the peaks and troughs of emotion, but showing restraint and being stable can be slightly boring. I miss passion. The Israelis pull me into deeply personal and intense conversations that flow with life.

Within an hour a girl called Moran leans forward to touch my knee and says in a thick Hebrew accent of warm honey, "Sarah, you are knowing we have just met, but I am feeling very powerful, strong, such feelings I cannot express."

I gasp, feeling rather Methodist among all this Jewish hippie hipness. Here everything is about feelings and the favorite feeling is *shanti*.

"You are very *shanti*," "I am very *shanti*," "India is very *shanti*," "the hash is very *shanti*."

Shanti is Hindi for "peace." I find India anything but *shanti*—in fact I find it loud, intrusive, brash, impatient and confronting. But then I'm not stoned most of the time. Baby-faced and beautiful young Irit says it's more than the pot.

"We have to grow up young in Israel. We're in the army before we turn eighteen, there's no time to rebel. This is the place we can rebel. We feel like we're in Wonderland here."

Irit and I define Wonderland differently. To her and her friends, India is a theme park of cheap thrills and easy drugs away from a country constantly at war with itself. India has cost me dearly in terms of health and hair and I'm still a confused Alice-child constantly confronted by creatures beyond my comprehension.

While India makes me feel powerless, it strengthens many young Jews by giving them their first taste of freedom. Two months ago, twenty-two-year-old Avishi loaded up his noisy Enfield motorbike and traveled from Varanasi to Manali then to Rajasthan, and last week to Dharamkot. He's an intense, angry, brooding bloke dressed in black, his beard is twisted into devil peaks and his body is as tight as a spring. He rants and raves at me as his pizza gathers flies.

"Here in India, I feel like I'm king of the world. I'm king at the *chai* shop on the side of the road, I'm king when I drive up to a hotel and I yell and they come running. I say bring me drugs, they do. I can get hash, pot, LSD and Ecstasy. I say bring me food, they do; a bucket, they do. I have total freedom. In Israel I was in the army, the big system, it was fucking with my head. Now I do what I want."

His intensity freaks me out and I decline his invitation to a full-moon rave at the waterfall next weekend. I even decline an offer of free Ecstasy—I'm feeling too purified from the meditation in the *gompa* to cope with chemical highs and pot. Maybe I'm more *shanti* than I thought.

The only words that approach the frequency of the word *shanti* in Israeli conversations are the words "army" and "shit" and they usually go together. Most of the travelers here have just finished their compulsory service (boys do three years, girls do twenty months) and they all seem resentful and angry about a spiritual homeland that trains them to kill.

Michal's *shanti* falls like the ash from her spliff as she spits, "The army is bullshit. You are paid nothing . . . the office work is shit, but if you go to Lebanon you die—we all know someone who has died—and when you finish, they don't give you nothing . . . we are fucked up, that's why we come here, we have hash and here we are *shanti*. When I go home, I might go crazy—three of my friends have ended up in the loony bin."

She takes another deep suck to restore her calm, pats my hand and strokes my leg.

I'm fascinated by the Israeli psychology. I head back toward the Ladies Venture via another restaurant. Only meters away from the

Dalai Lama's palace, perched high on the hill, is the Khanna Nirvana café—another Israeli hangout. I share a table with a charming thirty-six-year-old American who covers his ponytail with a beret rather than a Jewish skullcap. Azriel is actually here to help Israel's ex-soldiers enjoy their Indian R and R without going off the rails. In a soothing drawl with a lisp he tells me that many of the travelers arrive here traumatized by living in a country with a deeply wounded psyche.

"They're brought up with the Holocaust and the phobia is continued. They believe all their neighbors want to wipe them off the face of the earth. There's always a continual crisis facing the country . . . so the young are searching for some relief and escape from that world."

Yet many young Israelis are also escaping a state suffocated by a faith they don't revere. Obviously a lot of the young Jews here are breaking some holy commandments—craven images of idols stretch tight across T-shirts, other gods are adopted and there's a lot of sex happening. Irit walks in and we chat as three. She openly admits she's coveting India's freedom of faith.

"Yes, I'm jealous. Israel is so strict; if you are a bastard or you have tattoos you need to be buried outside the cemetery walls . . . We're not worthy to say God's name; Judaism is full of guilt. In Israel you have to be really religious or not at all. Here you see free faith."

A girl slumped in the corner, so ripped she's almost catatonic, comes alive to comment.

"Religious people sit and pray and get money from the government to wear black. They don't do army, they spit on me on the streets and say I'm not a real Jew because I wear pants and have short hair. In India you can be any religion and no one cares. In my country, Palestine isn't the problem, it's the brothers inside that are."

But what she doesn't know is that some big brothers are here. Azriel's organization, Ohr Olam, is funded from Israel. Azriel doesn't want to spy, but he keeps a loving, watchful eye on fellow Jews. He tolerates the mass worshiping of weed and techno, but tries to bring the travelers back to respecting the sabbath by giving free food to all those who keep it holy. Brought up in a strictly Orthodox family, he was inspired by the way the Dalai Lama updates and translates the ancient wisdom of Buddhism for Westerners. Azriel has set about to rediscover the depths of Judaism with fellow Jews and share it with gentiles like me. I've always felt Judaism rather exclusive, and I'm touched when Azriel invites me to Shabbat on Friday. Besides, my Tushita Buddhist course leaves nights pretty bare and I've always wanted to check out a Jewish feast.

Friday sunset I return to Khanna Nirvana for Azriel's Shabbat ceremony. Shabbat is a family ritual that ushers in the holy day of rest and connection to the Creator. Perched above clouds painted pink by the sunset, a small group of Americans, Australians and a lone Israeli girl (who has just taken the vow of a Buddhist *bodhisattva*) sing, clap and do a group meditation on the gifts of the past week. It's a low-key, friendly sharing of a sacred space. I walk back to my hostel in a peaceful trance, pausing to notice groups of Israelis watching *Chicken Run* and playing pool.

Perhaps they'll be more interested in Passover or Pesach. This is a major event in the Jewish calendar—a spring full-moon festival that celebrates the Hebrews' exodus from Egypt and the beginning of the Jewish nation, Israel. I remember this part of the Bible and I've even climbed Mount Sinai in Egypt where God came to Moses and told him he must free his people from slavery. Egypt didn't let me go without putting the plague of diarrhea on me and clinical depression on my friend, but when it wouldn't let the Jews go, God came to the rescue. He put ten plagues upon the Egyptians; the Jews fled, the Red Sea parted, God's people crossed into the desert and wandered for forty years. At Mount Sinai, God and the Hebrews made a deal. In return for their rescue, and deliverance to the promised land of Israel, Jews would follow only one God and His law as outlined in the Ten Commandments and the Torah (the first five books of the Old Testament).

My Buddhist course is not finished and it shouldn't be mixed with partying, but Passover comes but once a year and I figure I may never be invited to such an event again. Being able to take up such opportunities is one of the great privileges of not working—I love not having plans. In Sydney at our wedding people kept asking me, "What do you do all day in India?" I felt almost embarrassed saying, "Travel," as it's not something valued much in my homeland. But I'm growing increasingly happy with my choice to go with the flow in life. It's liberating and exciting.

It was the Dalai Lama who encouraged the first Passover festival in this town full of exiled Buddhists. In 1990 His Holiness invited a group of Jews here to ask them how they preserved their religion in exile. A bloke called Rodger Kamenetz wrote a book about the event, *The Jew in the Lotus*, and he's now back for Azriel's festival. We meet at the Khanna Nirvana café (which has kind of become my night hang). Rodger looks and sounds like a goofy George Clooney. I ask him what advice the Jews gave HH. He excitedly explains that after exile the Jews democratized their traditions and made the faith practical; Judaism is a religion of "doing," of eating kosher, keeping the sabbath and observing festivals such as this.

"After the Romans destroyed the Jewish temples, our people had to put the elements of worship into everyday life; the home is the temple, the family table is the altar and eating is divine communion."

Eating as worship! Sounds like my kind of faith.

Yet this Passover is essentially a Jewish Reform event and Azriel warns that the two-day communion will also involve lots of "communication." I try not to roll my eyes, for I've always been rather cynical about such group activities and New Age bonding. I steel myself and follow a group of Californian rock and roll synagogue Jews to the community hall. As darkness falls we open the festivities with a drumming workshop. Uncle Steve, a South African with a ponytail, climbs on a chair and pulls faces like Charlie Chaplin as he directs us to bang plastic sticks. It's quite a scene—Californians in stonewashed jeans and cheesecloth shirts, robed Tibetan monks and Israeli freaky ferals unite in a frenzy of beats. This is the cool Kabbalah crowd—Jews who want to reconnect with their more mystical traditions. The Kabbalah is to Judaism what Sufism is to Islam; it's the inner or esoteric counterpart to the outer canonical doctrine of the Torah. It was handed down by word of mouth until the twelfth century and teaches about self-transformation and the spiritual laws of the universe. It was once ruled that no one under forty should study the texts but since Madonna tried it out a couple of years ago it's become rather hip.

Kabbalah aside, the practical laws of the Jewish faith must still be fulfilled. We make the communal kitchen kosher by scrubbing it clean, keeping the milk well away from the veggies on the other side of the room (we're going vegetarian so we don't have to get kosher meat), and the work is inspected by a rabbi. I scrape carrots with a group of girls who are thankful that no one checks about women with periods being near foods (a no-no for some Orthodox Jews). A girl called Donna holds up a carrot and proclaims, "Let's cleanse our truly dirty bits, our psyches."

All the other girls yell as one: "Alright—you go, girl."

Sometimes I love Americans.

Guitar in hand, a big woman with a thick plait, long skirt, bright red lips and big Reebok shoes leads the cleansing. Mimi bubbles with American confidence and Israeli knowledge and radiates the joy of a woman at one with divine love. She leads us in a search for ten pieces of bread that have been placed in different parts of the room. The search doesn't take long; the room is bare and the bread has been unimaginatively placed in corners and on chairs. The slices signify the ten plagues God brought upon Egypt. I've always hated the Old Testament. It starts badly with all that boring begatting business, and the rivers of blood and slaying of children stuff scared me more than *Poltergeist*. I grew up thinking God was a jealous, possessive and vengeful character that I wanted nothing to do with. But Mimi is making me realize I've been taking the Bible way too literally. Jewish Reformers see the Torah section as the story of the soul traveling through hardship toward a relationship with God. So the plagues are not just punishments but physical manifestations of what's inside us. The first, the plague of blood, is anger; we find the bread and consider what sets us off and why. The second is the plague of frogs—about exaggerating and being far too dramatic. By the time the collection is over I'm thinking about my judgment, my wicked thoughts, my arrogance, pride, stinginess, lust and stubbornness. My crash course in

Buddhism has helped me meditate these states away to emptiness, but the Jews try to help me kill them off. I leave feeling lighter.

I'm back early in the morning to help light a fire and throw in the bread or *chametz*. We add our own personal plagues to the flames. I watch my words "fear and doubt" implode, the girl next to me throws in a photo of her ex-boyfriend and hums "burn baby burn" from the song "Disco Inferno." At sunset a huge fat white full moon squats like a bullfrog on the mountain peaks and as it leaps into the sky, we are welcomed into a community hall with a hug and a kiss. Cushions stuffed with newspaper ring tablecloths decorated with candles and plates made of leaves. We are a motley crew of about two hundred sharing our first and our last supper together. The Californians are dressed up in white flowing dresses or saris, the Israelis are wearing glow-in-the-dark rave gear, the Indians in jeans look bemused, the Tibetan monks seem confused and some scrawny Australian backpackers just look hungry for a free feed. We unite in a cheer when Azriel welcomes us with a promise of liberation.

"Tonight, friends, through the story of exodus we will reexperience our own internal slavery and redemption."

Seder—the ritual we are about to share—means order, and the evening must be carried out according to a strict regime; and all the translation from Hebrew to English and the explanations for us non-Jews mean the evening moves rather slowly. The Pesach party begins with prayers, songs and the lighting of the candles. Then there's drinking of fermented grapefruit juice (as close to wine as you're going to get in backpacker India). Our hands are washed and as we dip bitter herbs in salt to represent the tears of the slaves, we're told to make friends with our bitterness and to eat the bitter sprig in life so sweetness can come. The Californians then break out the special matzo bread they've lugged all the way from home. The matzo represents simplicity as the way to freedom; and as we crack it we acknowledge and embrace the brokenness in our lives. Like good children we then sit quietly for some storytelling, and then like good adults we show compassion for our enemy by pouring out some fake wine from our full cups—a drop for each plague brought upon the pharaohs.

Maybe it's the fermented grapefruit juice, the Himalayan air or the full moon, but all of a sudden the Israelis, Californians, locals and even this Australian go crazy. A bloke unveils the massive Torah from its blue velvet cloak and carries it around the room like it's a rugby trophy. We are all given a chance to touch or kiss it. The Jewish Holy Bible is in the middle of a mosh pit. The boys are pogoing and squatting in a Greek chorus line, the girls are dancing in a twisting gypsy conga and the Buddhist monks are standing staring openmouthed at the Jewish joy. Finally, we settle down for some more prayers, more bitter herbs, our second cup of wine and a sweet apple paste that represents the mortar of the bricks the Jewish slaves worked with.

By now it's midnight and there's lots of hugging, massaging and a fair share of tears going down with the feast. I talk about my pneumonia nightmare, a woman shares the sadness about her divorce, and a boy from San Francisco weeps about the trauma of coming out. It sounds tragic but it's actually transcending. My deluded, ignorant, egotistical, empty Buddhist being actually embraces the emotion and the sensual pleasures of song, dance, stories, food and the spiritual power of a shared group ritual. In Buddhist dharma there's no drama. In Jewish faith I'm encouraged to embrace the highs and the lows and show a passion for living—I'm better at that. Rodger gives me a short quiz.

"Do you have deep feelings for nature or do you yearn for detachment? Do you prefer sex or self-control?"

I admit that a stunning mountain vista and a good root can be quite redeeming. Rodger tells me I'm more Jewish than Buddhist. The girl beside me lifts her cup, bangs mine and proclaims me a Jew. I look around the room to embrace my new Israeli brothers and sisters but find they left long ago to smoke hash and prepare for Avishi's full moon dance trance party. Ohr Olam may not have saved their own but they have a new convert. Tonight I'm a Jew and I'm free.

• • •

One week on and I'm kicked off the team. There's a rival Jewish gang in town, and the more Orthodox Chabad Lubavitch group from Israel doesn't want me. I stumble into its house when I'm looking for the Internet center (I now haven't talked to Jonathan for three weeks and I am keen to try to make contact with the Australian Broadcasting Company to check he is okay). A very young, painfully thin rabbi dressed all in black with little plaits beside his ears offers me coffee from a filthy kitchen. His face lights up when he hears my name (Sarah was the wife of Abraham and is considered the matriarch of the Jewish people), but darkens in disappointment when I admit I wasn't born Jewish. He invites me to stay for Chabad's Shabbat but it doesn't really cater to us non-Hebrew-speaking gentiles. I sit silently with Israeli girls while the men stand, rock and pray on the other side of some room-dividing blankets. There's no group meditation, singing without words, dancing or inner journeys to take. I'm not the only one feeling disappointed.

"This is too religious, I just want food," says a beautiful blonde girl as she stomps out in army boots.

Chabad only recognizes as Jews those individuals born of a Jewish mother. Rabbi Dror Moshe Shaul obviously pities me but tells me that there is only a finite number of Jewish people and all are sparks of the souls who were present when God gave the Torah to Moses on Mount Sinai. As his child snorts snot all over me, the rabbi tells me that the spirit of Moses returns to earth in a Jewish body time and time again to save the world from sin. I'm shocked at his beliefs. I didn't think Jews believed in reincarnation, but it seems this group does, if only just for Jews. The rabbi points to the current Moses—a hairy, decrepit, bent old man who peers down from posters all around the room. His name is Lubavitcher Rebbe. I ask where he is.

"Ah, he is dead," states the rabbi.

"Oh." I stumble for words, shocked and more confused than ever.

"Well, no, he's actually not dead, we just can't see him. He is the King of Israel and will bring redemption, in a minute it will be ready. We in Chabad are the messengers. We are all over the world."

The rabbi says the king will come when Jews follow the rules of living as given in the Torah and when gentiles like me follow some simpler steps. I ask the rabbi what he thinks about all the Israelis at Buddhism courses, Vipassana, yoga and the Dalai Lama's lectures. I open a wound. He rocks in pain.

"They are destroying their souls; it looks harmless and good but it is dangerous."

The rabbi is here to teach the Kabbalah and to encourage the Israelis to leave the land of idols and return to the homeland of one God. He cannot rest when one Jew is lost. His mission could be long and impossible. Young Israelis show no sign of wanting to hurry home; in fact most of them seem to want to go to Australia after India. Those I've met are hardly nationalistic.

I fly home to Delhi on a tiny plane and sit next to an Israeli girl with bright green eyes and jet-black hair. She tells me she comes to India every year and hates going home to Tel Aviv and the "religious fuckers of my stoopid country." As we chat about the wonderful nature of Buddhism, she asks me if I'll stick to its teachings. Seeing I can't be a Jew, I begin to say yes. But I stop. We are high above the Himalayas and I've just heard a propeller splutter and stall.

The girl beside me sits stoned, still and unaffected, but my two weeks of Buddhist training practically fall into my pants. I scream. My hands are sweating, my heart is pumping and my mind is clutching at life like a randy dog to a leg. The propeller starts again but I've buried my Buddhist belief. I don't want to die. I like life. I'm completely attached to this body and this realm. I try to stop trembling and meditate. I can't. It's much easier to contemplate your own death in a peaceful *gompa* than ten thousand feet up in a tin can. The emptiness of Buddhism sits heavy in my stomach. I actually find myself praying. For the first time in my life I want to believe there's a God who's in control. I realize I desire salvation more than the prospect of centuries of learning to control my mind. I'm still full of delusions and a long way from taking the vow of the enlightened, let alone getting the *bodhisattva* beer discount in Dharamsala's restaurants.

A phrase from the Dalai Lama's teachings comes back to me: "Some will be drawn to Buddhism but I really think it's best that you try and find truth in the religion of your forebears and ancestors. It is very hard to change religion. I think it's safer not to."

I figure my ancestors are Christian and the Jewish religion is at the root of that faith, so I decide to give Judaism one last go. In Delhi I hear that Jonathan is out of Afghanistan and has flown straight to Mumbai. I'm desperate to see him, and Azriel has told me that the city once called Bombay hosts a population of Indian Jews. I head for a reunion with a lover and a faith.

The Bene Israeli of Bombay balance precariously on the oldest branch of the Jewish evolutionary tree and are fast heading for extinction. Their once thriving traditional Bombay neighborhood near Victoria Gardens echoes with the Muslim call to prayer on the Friday evening Jonathan and I visit. Wandering the bowels of a soon-to-be-demolished ramshackle former synagogue, we find the community's only rabbi atop creaking stairs smothered in dust, in the eaves of a once sacred space.

Joshua Kolet looks more Israeli than Indian. He is twenty-nine, pale and delicate with dark curly hair. Joshua lives here with his aging aunts—tiny gray Indian women wrapped in nylon saris—and his uncle who looks like a brown Woody Allen. Jonathan and I are invited inside for my third Shabbat. The aunts sing shyly through toothless gums and Joshua leads the prayers. Over a dinner of fish, coconut pancakes and curry, he tells us that his ancestors fled Israel after the destruction of the first temple in the fifth century or after the destruction of the second temple by the Romans—no one is really sure. What is known is that they sailed far and were shipwrecked two hundred and nine miles south of the Bombay Islands. Only seven couples survived. They obviously interbred with the locals but maintained their faith for centuries; refusing to work

Saturdays, circumcising their sons on the eighth day after birth, eating meat and making a distinction between clean and unclean fish. When the British came to India most Bene Israeli moved to Bombay to take up jobs in the trade industry; after 1948 they moved again, to Israel en masse. Joshua's parents are there, all his friends have gone and the school in Mumbai where his Auntie once taught doesn't have a single Jewish student now. This soon-to-be-homeless family radiates a sense of loss. Their Shabbat is a bittersweet affair with none of the joy and carefree fun of Azriel's in Dharamsala. I feel I'm at the table of Miss Haversham with her ghosts of better days. I ask the Aunties why they've stayed in lonely Mumbai. They look at each other and shyly shrug.

"India is my Mother."

She must be, for Israel offers huge inducements to attract Jews. Nongovernment organizations give Indians free or cheap airfares and the government provides settlers low-interest loans, assistance for one year, free Hebrew lessons, housing help and a land with greater economic opportunities. The Bene Israeli are believed to be the poorest Jews in the world and Mumbai is getting expensive.

While Jonathan works, Joshua takes me to Worly Hill above the sea where one Jewish building remains; rotting from concrete cancer, it sits small and forlorn among growing numbers of gleaming skyscrapers. Inside is ORT (Organization of Educational Resources and Technical Training), an institute that prepares Indian Jews for emigration to Israel. Its director, Benny Isaac, invites me in with a pat on the back and a couple of jokes. He's a big bloke with a huge heart and, while he just loves his job, he feels sad that he's helping to drain his community dry.

"Most of my school friends have gone, most who come to ORT have gone, most of the staff has gone. They're Jewish, it was their birthright, but mostly they went for economic opportunities. I went to Israel, I loved it, but I love India, I'm loyal to the Mother. India let my ancestors live freely; they . . . were allowed to eat meat, live as they wanted and to be free . . . The Hindus and we have best relations, they have protected us and looked after us. This is the only place Jews have not been persecuted, I can't leave."

I totally understand his decision.

Upstairs, I meet the thick-spectacled and slightly hyperactive Levy Jacob, who's recently returned from Israel and can't stop raving about it. He proudly shows me some freshly killed corpses, the community's kosher chickens he ritually slaughtered this morning.

"We have to be smooth and painless. It's very complicated, the chicken must not know he is going to die."

I tell him the plucked poultry looks peaceful, and he's pleased enough to let me supervise the making of nonalcoholic wine from raisins crushed in sugar.

This Indian community is more lax-conservative than my Jewish Reform friends. Benny Isaac pooh-poohs my story of the Pesach party I attended and frowns when I ask him whether his community studies the ancient teachings of the Kabbalah. Then suddenly he furtively looks around and hunches toward me. In a whispered breath he admits there was one woman who flirted with the mystical side. She wanted to talk to her dead son and enlisted outside help from scholars of the Kabbalah. She contacted her son.

"What did he say?" I eagerly ask.

He shrugs. "He told her not to disturb him."

The experience of Jewish mysticism among the Bene Israeli was dead and buried.

I can't help feeling sad that India is losing a population it has looked after so well to a country where the young suffer so much anger and feelings of rejection. It seems a spiritual homeland does not cure all spiritual ills. In India I've traveled a soul's journey: from hedonism to sickness, from silence to song, from violence to peace, and from learning to die to celebrating life. If I were Jewish, such a story should end with my liberation in the Promised Land. But it's not an option for me because of my birth. I'm glad, for when I reflect on Buddhism's belief that we are all interconnected, the Jewish insistence on being "chosen" and different seems elitist and alienating.

Yet a small flame within me has been lit by what I've shared, a flame that warms me with a realization. India: a land that shares its sacred space, seems a spiritual home worth having.

12 | Birds of a Feather Become Extinct Together

I'm face-to-face with one of the ugliest beasts on earth. Nose to beak with a hunch-shouldered smelly Frankenstein with feathers that could rip my limbs apart, crack open my cranium, munch on my brain and consume every part of me (bar my pelvis and thigh bones) within twenty minutes. If it was alive. But this vulture is dead—formaldehyde floppy and reeking of mothballs.

Mumbai is also dead. The nine o'clock wail of the work-start siren and the hum of millions have been silenced. Today there's a city strike, or *bandh*, called by the ultra-hard-line Hindu Shiv Sena Party. The streets are empty, bar roaming gangs of Sena goons, carrying wooden *lathi* bats above their heads, threatening to hurt anyone they find working.

I'm staying on in Mumbai to spend some time with Jonathan, who is shooting a story for Australian Broadcasting Company TV about a religion, a people and a bird. After driving through the eerie, still streets we scurried between the iron gates of the Natural History Society building. Inside, its director, Asad Ramani, is showing us the vultures; he's breaking the *bandh* because he has little time left to stop the bird of prey from falling off its perch.

Sweating under the hot lights and wiping his glasses constantly, Dr. Ramani tells the camera a story. About five years ago the villagers of Rajasthan started complaining that the vultures were no longer eating their dead dogs, cows and buffalo. No one listened to them, until the bird sanctuaries began noticing that the vulture numbers were down and those few birds that were around were droopy and not eating. Since then the Indian white-backed vulture population has dropped by ninety-seven percent and the bird is now officially listed as "critically endangered." At first, a pesticide was suspected, but Dr. Ramani now believes the birds are dying from some sort of virus that has yet to be isolated, let alone treated.

Jonathan's researcher, Kursheed, listens intently, her head cocked and eyes keenly focused on the Muslim doctor. For her, this is more than a five-minute piece of television. Light-skinned and lighthearted, with dark curly hair and a rather beaked nose, Kursheed is a Parsi. Parsi people depend on the vulture to take them to heaven. Jonathan's story is about this most Western of India's ethnic groups and its relationship to the bird of prey, and Kursheed has promised to get him good access to her people. We're looking forward to meeting some of her flock in a few days' time.

The next morning, with the *bandh* over, Mumbai emerges reenergized from its enforced break. After conservative, staid Delhi the city feels like a cosmopolitan tropical third world New York—its thick gooey pre-monsoon air contains a whiff of energy and excitement. Jonathan and I spend our first weekend together since our honeymoon swapping stories about our adventures. Afghanistan was tough. While he was filming an interview, Taliban officials chopped down a door with an ax and burst in—luckily the ax was so blunt he had time to hide his camera. After experiencing a country suffering from the hardships imposed by a puritanical Islamic regime, a dreadful drought, disease, famine and war, he is depressed about the human condition. I was concerned my stories would seem rather self-indulgent to him, but Jonathan insists he needs them. I am his keyhole to the world of peace and love.

But Mumbai is too exciting to keep us indoors chatting for long. We drive around in yellow cabs that reek of damp skin and onions. We pass giant glittering skyscrapers sitting alongside colonial wrecks stained with pigeon poo. Inside filthy flats, fans swirl above smoking men in singlets painted purple by fluorescent lights. Way past midnight the pavement pumps to the beat of beggars, bar hoppers and cricket matches. Smoky jazz clubs ooze hip, drug dealers peddle in dark corners and coconut sellers squat outside the bookstores.

It's grimy, steamy and bohemian. At a traffic jam we wait beside a motorbike carrying the Indian version of the Two Fat Ladies. One in a spotted sari sits sidesaddle behind her husband, the other in stripes spills out of the sidecar; goggles glued to their faces, saris flapping in the fumes, they chat away oblivious to a goat chewing their shopping and a man selling giraffe-shaped balloons.

Mumbai is a city that dares to be different, a city that worships the Hindu god Ganesh—a cheeky hybrid of baby and elephant that brings luck and new beginnings. But it has the same old poverty. We pass tin suburbs of slums full of flickering televisions and smoldering mountains of methane-charged garbage; high above them, huge billboards cruelly tease with the treasures of household appliances and diamond rings. Slightly seedy and slightly *Blade Runner*, Mumbai smells more of the future than the past—it could well be a Western metropolis in a grimy, greenhouse-effected, post-apocalyptic world. There are already special suburbs for the survivors of the economic evolution of the city. These self-sufficient biospheres have an individual water supply, power generators, tennis courts, shops and landscaped gardens.

If you can make it here, you can make it anywhere. And the Parsis have, by and large, made it.

On Monday morning, Kursheed, Jonathan and I begin the day in our funky hotel restaurant drinking proper coffee and eating pastries that give oral orgasm at first bite. Kursheed fills us in on a little Parsi history. She says many Parsis became rich because they were firm friends with the British, who were attracted to the Parsi liberal way of living, light skin, willingness to eat with other carnivores and their ready embrace of modern education and entrepreneurial spirit. During the days of the Raj, the two groups would get together to drink, ballroom-dance and make megabucks. When the British packed up and returned home, they even invited the Parsis to come with them—British passports all round, old boys! But most of the proud, loyal Parsis stayed in India. In compensation, the Brits gave them huge chunks of Bombay.

Real estate is now hideously expensive here and our first stop for the day is at the home of a Parsi who lives atop some of the most costly land in the world. Malabar Hill features a famous park; rare open space in a city of twenty million. But beside the park is a much larger area of green, and it is private Parsi space.

Smita Crishna's penthouse is style I've rarely seen in Punjabi-dominated, show-off-your-wealth-as-distastefully-as-possible Delhi. With subtle color schemes, beautiful art and sexual sculpture, it's obviously old money. The balcony is a dream. My eyes soar over Mumbai's Miami-like strip of high-rises, palm trees and traffic; they loop over the turgid gray sea and its rust-bucket ships and sweep back over the slums that spread like stains around skyscrapers and crumbling colonial mansions. And then I peer down for a bird's-eye view of death in the scrub below.

The Parsis maintained mystery in their funeral rituals until their church body, or Punchayat, began selling off land here. Apartments like this expose those secrets, for straight below us, behind the extremely thick walls and beneath banyan scrub, are four concrete concentric structures that look like wide dirt-filled wells. The British called them *dakhmas*, "the towers of silence." I have no idea why, as they look nothing like towers. Three are empty, the fourth is not. Inside I can see the shapes of shrunken dead Parsis awaiting their birds of paradise: the white-backed vulture.

The religious beliefs behind this Parsi practice belong to Zoroastrianism. The Zoroastrian religion is one of the most ancient monotheistic faiths and it probably influenced Judaism, Christianity and Islam. Its prophet was Zarathustra, who was born in what's now Iran sometime between 1500 and 600 B.C.E. The prophet's name means "golden shining star" or "rich in camels" or even perhaps "tormentor of camels," depending on the translation. Like Jesus, Buddha and Mohammed, his thirtieth birthday was a turning point for this bloke. Instead of dying his hair pink or taking drugs or going out with someone utterly wrong for him (like I did), he resolved the crisis by taking a sojourn in the desert and meditating on the meaning of life. Zarathustra returned at forty and talked of One God—Ahura Mazda—the omniscient Lord of Wisdom who has no form, shape, beginning or end, but has seven helpers, called Amesha Spentas. These archangels of creation guard and protect humans, animals, plants and the sacred elements, earth, water, fire and air; and Zoroastrians believe these sacred elements must not be polluted by human waste. In the rocky Iranian desert, the faithful were left on mountaintops to be devoured and dried by the sun's rays. In India, Parsi Zoroastrians leave out their dead for vultures believing it's the cleanest, most hygienic way of getting rid of the soul's temporary home.

We have coffee on the balcony and discuss the ugly black and white birds. Smita—a tiny, elegant woman dressed in a white Western suit—understands my horror at the thought of having a vulture rip my body apart.

"It upset me when I was young but my father explained to me, it's the ultimate charity. You are giving food to the vultures—that's what they live on. And the eating doesn't matter to you when you're dead."

I guess so, but it does matter if the vultures aren't there. We try to focus the camera down into the Parsi cemetery. A few black crows hover, mynah birds hop around looking bored, kites ride the coastal currents, pigeons coo and seagulls swoop into the sea. None seem interested in a Parsi lunch. The cameraman thinks he sees a lone vulture, but I can't. Smita says she hasn't seen one for years.

"Bodies just lie there for months on end sometimes, sometimes the whole well is full of bodies, sometimes we get a smell; the apartment next door gets it terribly."

She winces and twitches her delicate little nose.

Only in incredibly tolerant and respectfully religious, overly bureaucratic and corrupt India could bodies be allowed to rot in the open in the midst of a major city. Smita says people used to joke about crows leaving spleens on verandas and livers on their landings but now the laughter is starting to get stuck in certain throats. Her mother just died and was cremated; Smita couldn't cope with the thought that she'd suffer the final indignity of rotting away and polluting the sacred earth and air. Sadly but matter-of-factly, she states, "It was the right decision because it was clean, pure and fast."

Smita's father and her uncle and some of her family friends are also electing to be cremated. But such alternatives seem to be reserved for the rich. Smita's father was the head of the Godrej empire, one of India's most successful industrial manufacturers. Money buys anything in India (apparently it only costs twenty dollars to get someone killed in this city), so rich Parsis can usually pay enough for a priest to buck tradition and conduct ceremonies for a body that's to be cremated. But some priests refuse to help anyone who wants to be cremated. And Parsi religious obstinacy doesn't stop at funeral rites.

Smita hardly looks like a rebel and neither does her equally glamorous friend Meher Rafaat, who arrives for yet more coffee. But Smita and Meher have been ejected from the Parsi nest—Smita for committing the sin of marrying a Hindu, and Meher for marrying a part-Zoroastrian, part-Jewish Iranian who practices the Baha'i faith. One priest even calls them "adulteresses" and graciously told Smita that if she gives up on the idea of cremation he'll do her a special favor and put her in the *dakhma* reserved for prostitutes. Smita takes such threats seriously. In 1990, a young Parsi, Roxanne Shah, died in a car accident; she was married to a Jain. The high priest called her "illegitimate," accused her of "adulterating the race" and refused her corpse entry to any *dakhma*. In response, Smita and Meher founded the Association of Intermarried Zoroastrians (AIMZ).

Meher is furious that a few priests are spoiling the Parsi faith. She politely pouts, "Bombay is the stronghold and the stranglehold of Zoroastrianism. The priesthood is shackling the religion. The prophet appeared to free people of bigotry. He taught us to think, to agonize about our actions . . . and the words of the prophet do not forbid intermarriage."

Smita believes the priests are following certain scriptures that came after the time of Zoroaster, which concern the rituals and not the original teachings of the prophet. I admire her courage for taking on her church but I suspect this whole argument could be about more than religion. Ethnic purity and skin color are probably involved. Skin whiteness is an obsession in Mumbai as much as anywhere else in this brown-skinned land. An ancient Indian proverb says "if the skin is white, it is love at first sight," and the modern roads are lined with massive billboards advertising "fair and lovely" soap and "return to fairness" skin-lightening cream. Whiteness is so jealously guarded, the Parsis probably want to preserve their paleness as much as they want to protect and propagate their vultures.

The Parsi church, the Punchayat, is planning to find fifty pairs of vulture chicks, isolate them, feed them and keep them locked up in an aviary to breed until the population is big enough to be released to feast. It also wants to isolate its children and get them breeding. One in four Parsis marries outside the faith; they also marry late compared to most Indians, and because their women are educated and ambitious they only want one or two kids.

• • •

Before we arrived in Mumbai, Jonathan's producer Tony took a film crew to the wedding of twenty-seven-year-old Behzad and twenty-five-year-old Mazreen Sanga. They came back with pictures of Parsis waltzing away to an Indian-accented great Aussie hit:

I am coming from the larnd down und-eeerrr
Where de women bow and men charmer.

A few days later we visit the newlyweds as they pack up to flee the parental coop and fly north where rents are cheaper. Mazreen is pretty with fair skin, short hair and an outrageously outspoken manner. She matter-of-factly tells the camera she married a Parsi to maintain the freedom of the most liberal culture in India.

"If someone tells me to sit in the kitchen and cook or to take a *burkha* I say NO WAY. It's usual in India that the girl gives up everything for the guy and I was not ready to give all that up, not even for the love of my life; I don't think I can be cooped up anywhere."

In the tiny, stuffy little flat her new husband's parents preen and puff with pride that they have a son married to a Parsi girl. I am shocked to hear an Indian girl be so Bolshevik; she makes Razoo look conservative. She's right, the Parsis are quite liberal. Yet their Western ways only extend so far. For Mazreen to be free of chauvinism in life she'll have to submit to some rigid rules in death.

The next morning we get up at five to join a convoy of Parsis heading north to their holy Vatican. The Iranshah Fire Temple is in Udvada, a tiny fishing town consisting of one dusty street lined by rickety wooden houses. Old men rock and sleep on veranda swings while their wives watch the Parsi parade. Hardly a procession of vim and vigor, it's more like a nursing home's annual outing. The Parsi faithful are shuffling along stooped, potbellied and frail; they clutch each other's arms, shake on walking sticks and plod along with walkers. The spectacled lead those blinded by glaucoma, and the toothless talk for the dumb. Yet the faces show strength, resilience and power. With fierce expressions, hooked beak noses, piercing eyes and white skin, many of the Parsis remind me of Eastern European Jews. The men wear velour skullcaps, while the women pull back their graying hair with scarves and show a bit of rare leg below flowery Western dresses. They're a bossy bunch of cuckoos living in this Indian nest and they're super keen to keep others out of their territory. When we stop at the outside wall of the temple and unload the camera, at least five approach to tell us we can't come in.

We've already got the message. A small door and large sign block the temple entrance: NO INTRUDERS, NO FILMING, NO PHOTOS, NO NON-PARSIS.

Even after being thrown out of Judaism, I'm shocked. I've never seen a sign like it in India. This is an open door country and I've been welcomed into homes, temples, shops, offices and pretty much anywhere I've wanted to go. A year ago, such a sign wouldn't have bothered me at all—of course the sacred spots of different faiths should be respected—but I feel a little put out now. I miss the inclusive, casual nature of Hinduism.

Jonathan is more pragmatic—he sends Kursheed and a Parsi wedding photographer in with a small camera. They disappear behind the tall gate, high walls, white columns and closed shutters to stand beneath a large dome where a birthday celebration is in full swing. Today marks the annual Jashan ritual, and the star of the show is a flame that could light a thousand candles but must never be blown out. Today a fire turns twelve hundred and eighty years old. Its flames have flickered almost as long as the Parsis have been in India.

When Zarathustra came out of the desert he began to preach to try to turn the pagans to his One God. He mustn't have been very good at it—it took him ten years to get his first disciple—but eventually Zoroastrianism caught on well and spread over a large part of Europe and Asia. However, in the seventh and eighth centuries, the Parsi lands of Persia were invaded, their libraries burned and the people forced to convert to Islam. Some fled persecution to Russia, others set sail for India. Soon after the immigrants made India their home, they set about collecting a sacred fire. Flames were taken from the sources representing natural order and the different trades and classes of human society. Flames from a potter, a brick maker, a goldsmith, a tinker, a baker, a brewer, a soldier, a shepherd, a mayor, a priest, a burning corpse and lightning were merged, purified and consecrated over many special days and then carried in a procession to where they burn now. Different temples have been built around the sacred fire, thousands of monsoons have raged around it and generations of priests have served it. Its flames have burned as bright as India's most successful refugee community.

Across the road from the temple, we non-Parsis watch the worshipers walk toward their sacred sanctum sanctorum. Jonathan, his producer Tony and I sit it out on a veranda decorated with beautiful, delicate chalk designs of fish and the words "good luck." An elderly priest shaking with Parkinson's disease sits patting the heads of devotees who come to touch his feet and kiss his hands. In a wobbly whisper he tells us what we're missing. Inside, Parsis are making offerings of sandalwood to the huge fire, which burns in a massive silver urn.

"They pray to the all-purifying elements to take them to a higher plane. The fire represents the divine spark of the soul; the inner light. We worship fire as the Son of God. Today is like thanksgiving. The fire has given so much to this community, we give it back now."

Thankfully we *are* invited to lunch. Under a red tent, along long tables, hundreds of Parsis are hunched over banana-leaf plates engaging in a feeding frenzy. Plates are piled high with huge chunks of chicken, pickle, fish, lamb and eggs.

"We love our food," the lady next to me yells as she sucks on a bone and pulls it from her mouth.

I order vegetarian—the teachings of Hinduism and Buddhism have spoiled the pleasure of the taste of meat and a sense of sin rises from the thought of eating the flesh of a living being killed for my needs. It seems shocking even to watch meat-eaters. As I sit sucking lentils, a group of middle-aged women take me under their wing and cluck in concern over my limpness in the heat. When Jonathan tries to interview one of them, she just stares at the camera and yells, "*We like your wife!*"

There's little small talk between the ladies and me. The caring busybodies all seem to be obsessed with my menstrual cycle. My neighbor Mehru openly inquires, "You don't have your period, do you, dear?"

When I say no, she tells the woman next to her and the information is relayed down the long table with relief. Mehru pats my hand and explains.

"We are very strict peoples, dear, once we couldn't cook for five days when we had them, we couldn't touch certain cupboards, we couldn't touch the prophet, now we cook, but you can't be here with your period, dear."

I feel like I'm in a Woody Allen movie, but it's not funny. I hate crap about women being dirty and long ago tired of the way it taints nearly every religion. Kursheed shows me a Parsi pamphlet from the temple that makes me feel so much better. It explains that women emit "*poisonous dioxins in their impure menstrual blood,*" and when women bleed they become depressed and their aura becomes "*dense, dark and morbid.*" What's more, their "*emanations are poisonous and can kill delicate plants, spoil foodstuff and the very air around her. Even her breath smells foul.*"

"We Parsis are very scientific, dear," explains Mehru as she reads over my shoulder.

The ladies take me to meet their most respected leader. Hunched over a bowl of strawberry ice cream is Professor Dame Mistri Meher Master-Moos. Wearing a traditional Parsi white sari with a pretty border of flowers, a severe expression and bright red lips, she is as verbose as her name. I've come across many mad professors in India—peace experts who support India's nuclear weapons program, feminist critics who touch their husband's feet and eat only his scraps, and science lecturers who don't accept evolution—but Professor Master-Moos takes the cake (and the ice cream). She doesn't believe in a vulture virus and shakes her finger and pecks her head as she tells us her truth in an incredibly posh put-on English accent.

"You see, the Defense Ministry of the U.S.A. found that these high-flying birds got in the way of the multibillion-dollar missiles, rockets and planes and so on. So they wanted to get these birds to fly to lower levels and [they] put in some kind of sound vibration, which prevents the birds from flying at the usual heights . . . It also gives them something like what human beings get, vertigo . . . Their heads and legs droop and they die of starvation, because once the neck gets affected they can't swallow."

As I choke on my ice cream, another man hops up and crows that Hindus are shooting the birds because they want the *dakhma* area for development. Obviously, like most Indians, Parsis love a good gossip and a good conspiracy theory.

A five-minute drive out of town at a rickety rundown holiday home by a boiling beach, the high priest of the Parsis, Dr. Peshotan Homazdir Mirza, is resting after lunching with his family. He wears a light blue outfit like a surgeon's gown made of extremely thin starched cotton, a square matching hat and the thickest glasses I've ever seen. The priest squints intently at the camera, and wrinkles up his nose and bares his teeth as he talks. He's exactly what television loves: a fundamentalist and a great storyteller. Dr. Mirza tells us a legend about why the Parsis are so snobby. When the Parsis first landed on the swampy Gujarati coast, the Hindu King Jadi Rana sent them a bowl of milk full to the brim, signifying that his territory was full of good people and had no room for more. The Parsi high priest put some sugar in the milk and sent it back. The king was impressed; the milk didn't overflow, it was sweetened and enriched. The Parsis promised to do the same to India—to keep a low profile, to breed among themselves and never to stir the pot by trying to convert anyone to their faith. In exchange, they kept their Farsi language, created new sacred places and were left out of the bloodshed when India was divided and Pakistan created. During Partition, Muslims and Hindus killed each other and left the Parsis alone—the Parsis felt their exclusive way of living helped them survive. Dr. Mirza says the Parsis must keep their promise; as birds of a feather they must continue to stick together.

The Parsi priesthood is an inherited right and Dr. Mirza is a twentieth-generation holy man in his family. He feels it's his job to ensure that his religion and race stay as pure as milk without sugar. Dr. Mirza is one of the priests who absolutely refuse to recognize any Parsis who have married out of the faith or any child of that union. Dilution, he says, is death.

"What will happen after the second or third generation? Do you think they will be Zoroastrians? History has proved that it is not so. After the Arab conquest of Iran, it's not that Parsis came only to India, others had the land route to go to Europe and China. All got diluted . . . The only group that kept their identity was the group that came to India."

That may be true but this Parsi extremist seems like a bit of a birdbrain, for his snobbery means the population is aging and shrinking. There are only about seventy-six thousand Parsis remaining in Mumbai. Kursheed shows us the community magazine *Parsiana* which features a table of figures of progeny gained and lost. Birth rates are consistently falling and death rates rising; in the year 2000 there were nine hundred and twenty-two deaths and only one hundred and sixty-four births. The Parsi maternity hospital is now full of Hindu patients—there aren't enough Parsis to fill the beds.

What's more, the genetic stock is weak. As a result of interbreeding there's a high incidence of heart problems, asthma and genetic defects. Dr. Mirza can't see the advantages of new blood; in fact the Parsi high priest can't see much at all. I grow tired of his ranting and join his family on the back porch. The priest's plump, friendly daughter tells me her dad is not just shortsighted—he also has tunnel vision and night blindness. She introduces me to his aunt and uncle sitting so quietly on the couch I hadn't noticed them. They are both blind. She explains in a whisper.

"My grandparents were first cousins, so three of Dad's aunts and uncles are blind. Dad is going blind. I won't be marrying a cousin."

"Are your eyes alright?"

"So far so good and same with my brother. We have no problems."

She points to her little brother playing in the garden. He has Down's syndrome.

The Parsis are facing a dilemma: to populate or perish? If they choose purity they might die out like the dodo. But Dr. Mirza is refusing to compromise. Back inside, Jonathan is still battling with the interview, and the priest is beginning to slam his fist on the furniture.

"If we start losing the faith, if we start being ignorant and arrogant to this, then it's going to be suicide, spiritual and communal."

They discuss the vulture problem. The Parsi leader insists the planned breeding program will work and must work. He shouts an angry argument against cremation on spiritual and scientific grounds.

"If you burn protein, it gives out carcinogenic product, seven percent of all cancers are caused by this."

I point out to him that rotting bodies must be polluting the sacred water, earth and air in Mumbai. He shakes his head and yells, "*No.*" The priest insists the chemical powders being used to break down the bodies are herbal and nonpolluting.

I've now been to about five Parsi homes and I can't help but notice their obsession with purity goes beyond wearing masks for some ceremonies and staying away from menstruating women. Their places are fastidiously clean. Ornaments are kept in glassed cupboards. Televisions, video players and stereos are encased in huge plastic Ziploc bags. It's not that they're suffering genetically inherited obsessive-compulsive disorder, it's more that any kind of pollution and impurity is seen as a manifestation of evil. Yet it seems the pure Parsi faith has been polluted by the Hindu customs of their foster motherland; Parsis wear a sacred thread like Hindu Brahmans, most don't eat beef and they throw flowers into sacred waters. Some, including Professor Master-Moos, even believe in reincarnation. Almost as good as her U.S. conspiracy theory was her bragging that "Souls have evolved from the mineral kingdom, from the plants to the birds and the fish, to the insects and the reptiles and the animals and to the human beings. All souls are in evolution. To belong to the Zoroastrian community means that your soul is spiritually very highly evolved."

Jonathan asked her if that wasn't a wee bit superior and exclusive; she nodded.

"Oh yes, very," she said as she smiled somewhat sorrowfully at us less evolved heathens.

Kursheed grows worried that we are getting a bad view of her kin and gets paranoid the story will be critical. Australian Parsis have power in Mumbai and she doesn't want the community turning against her. She stresses the great things about the Parsis—their generosity in giving to charity, their belief in good words, good thoughts and good deeds. Zarathustra preached love, devotion, selfless service, compassion and respect for freedom, and he didn't preach about vultures. Kursheed seems unfazed by the Parsi problem because she has faith in another winged being that her people revere. Each Zoroastrian has a guardian angel; known as *frvashi*, these winged figures with human heads are always near to observe and help when the righteous are in danger. Kursheed wears a tiny amulet of a *frvashi* around her neck and it comforts her when she's feeling down. Perhaps this explains why the Parsis seem such an optimistic group—everyone we've met thinks their community will somehow survive against the odds.

I think the Parsi sense of humor will see them through these times. While they are not outrageously funny and have little of the Aussie capacity to tell endless self-deprecating jokes, Parsis do tend to make a few cracks about themselves. In their *Parsiana* magazine, cartoons poke fun at the scrawny Parsi physique and a joke column contains witty new words such as "*Dakhmamania*—a mental and physical hyperactivity triggered off by reference to *dakhmas*." Kursheed gives us a parting gag as we say good-bye.

"You know, Parsis love two things. They love good food and they love controversy. If there was just one Parsi left in the world, he would fight with the wind."

I love the Parsi ability to laugh at their lot, I admire the faith's respect for the earth and I'd love a guardian angel. Yet my birth in this life ensures I can't join the flock. If I want to become a Zoroastrian I'll have to migrate to North America where more liberal Parsi immigrants allow for conversion. As the sun sets slowly over the sea I find myself quietly praying to Ahura Mazda for the Parsi survival. May they be able to hatch a scheme to save the vultures and themselves, may they welcome cuckoos into their cozy nest and may they learn to ride the winds of change before their fire is extinguished forever.

13 | Come to Mummy

I've now been immersing myself in India's spiritual smorgasbord for eighteen months. At times I feel god-filled, at other moments slightly spiritualized, but mostly I feel like I'm failing. It's as if, after scrambling to the top of the wall that separates doubt and dharma, I fall Dumpty-down into bad thoughts and bad living. Between faith and faithlessness is a sea full of sharks that pull me down into the depths of doubt, rip any emerging happiness from my heart and spit me back to the surface of cynicism.

The main predators are male.

India is a man's world. As a result of female infanticide, where girl babies are aborted, undernourished or murdered, there are fifty-two men for every forty-eight women. In northern India the ratio seems higher—in the streets of Delhi and Mumbai gangs of guys are out in force, strutting and swaggering hand in hand, smiling and sneering with bravado. It seems no one can adore them as much as they adore themselves; one of the most popular T-shirts stretched over scrawny chests and potbellies this summer declares GOD I'M GOOD.

It's easy to laugh when Jonathan is around but he has flown to Calcutta for another urgent story and I'm stuck in Mumbai alone and extrasensitive to being encircled by giggling idiots and silent stone-faced stares. I'm fed up with having entire busloads stare down at me, of truck drivers motioning cabin mates to cop a look and of being constantly followed. And I'm especially sick of the cocky display of the penis. It seems many Indian men have a chronic urinary tract infection—they piss proudly beside the road, up against buildings and in every park. Those with stronger bladders just seem to love the *lingam*—there are more hands on dicks here than at a hip-hop gig. What's worse are the occasional bastards in a crowd who grab at my crotch or pinch my breasts. It doesn't happen often, but it's infuriating, especially when it's dismissed as "Eve-teasing" by lazy police. Even at home I'm not safe—once a week a mystery sicko calls to try to talk dirty, or just to say, "Hello, howww are yooou, I loooove you." He makes me feel as vulnerable and abused as the Sydney stalker did. The Indian overload of male attention is dehumanizing and debilitating and makes forgiveness, love and understanding of fellow humans almost impossible.

Of course these men are a highly visible minority who are uneducated and powerless in other parts of their life. I also blame the new cable TV channels. *Baywatch* is big here. Perhaps many of the millions of men who watch it believe all we foreign females want is to shove a piece of Lycra up our butts, run toward them without moving our upright nipples and then seduce them on the spot.

I'm still wearing my baggy *salwar* suits, but then again, so do the prostitutes. Apparently the only way to spot a sex worker is to look in her eyes; like a Western woman, she will stare back. I've learned to look down all the time but that only contributes to my dejection. I used to worry about losing my kudos and place in Australian society. Now I fear I'm losing my identity as a human being. When I'm with Jonathan it's common for men to say "hello, sir" and engage him in conversation, while ignoring me completely. It's better than being hassled but at times I feel I don't exist.

I need a shot of female spiritual empowerment.

While I suffer a strong aversion to gurus, I hear of one who might be able to help me deal with India's men. Mata Amritanandamayi sounds like a savior; "The Mother of Immortal Bliss" claims to be the living manifestation of all the divine goddesses of the Hindu pantheon combined. Perhaps if I can get some *shakti* or goddess power I can find a way to stop my blood boiling or at least discover how to get blokes to leave me alone. If not, then at least I get to see an Indian woman who is respected, worshiped and adored by hundreds of thousands of men. There's a rumor that the Mother of Immortal Bliss transmits this power with a hug and a kiss—including to blokes! Barring dark corners of cinemas and under bushes, I've never seen such a thing in India; public displays of affection are confined to male mates. This taboo-breaking religious rebel lives in Kerala—the only state where women outnumber men and where matriarchal tribes once ruled. Kerala was my favorite state when I came to India all those years ago; I decide to return.

I fly from Mumbai and as we land in Kerala I feel I've left India far behind. In the north, Mother Earth chokes in clouds of dust; she's decrepit and worn down by centuries of invasion, plundering, squandering, depletion and desertification. Kerala, in comparison, is a young fecund mother of abundance. Big wide wet rivers snake through acres of fat coconut palms with electric green leaves. Pineapples, mangoes and coconuts are sold under the shade of flame flowers and frangipani. Above is the first big blue sky I've seen for months, and beside the road lurid billboards advertise computer jobs in Australia, gold, jewels and movies starring bosomy babes and men with lipstick. The Keralan people are beautiful, with big round bodies, wide smiles and dark skin. The women wear jasmine flowers in their hair, muumuu dresses and bright saris, and the men, all hail the men! The southern hunks are either ignoring me or smiling to my face. I smile back, safe that their looks aren't sleazy.

Kerala has been a communist state for much of the last half century and since independence has had the highest rate of literacy and best health care in India. Marketing itself as a retreat for stressed Western capitalists, it's importing bodies and exporting a divine soul. The state's Holy Mother has just returned from Europe and Australia, and is about to set out for Japan and the United States. It's May and the southern summer is horribly hot and muggy. It's not the ideal time to visit her ashram, but it's the only chance I may have for a holy hug.

Sweltering in a tin can taxi that bumps along sandy roads, I finally come to the coastal backwater town of Vallikavu. I squat in a small canoe crossing the deep dark lagoon, gliding under fishing nets suspended from bamboo poles like giant spiderwebs waiting for prey. Flies feast on my sweat and mosquitoes spear my slippery skin. Drums begin to beat, becoming louder and faster as we approach the bank. My heart takes up the ominous rhythm. I shut my eyes, fearing I'm being sucked into the heart of darkness.

I open them to see Barbie's world.

Mata Amritanandamayi Math, the main ashram of the Divine Mother, is a candy-colored kingdom. Nearly everything is pink—the phallic fifteen-story-high living-quarters tower, the hospital, the Ayurvedic center, the shops, the canteens and even the temple. Rising up in a series of stories crowned with small domes, the Hindu temple, or *mandir*, looks like a pile of giant cupcakes topped with marshmallows. Spilling out the doors and teeming all around are thousands of devotees. I've arrived on a "*darshan* day"; inside the pink temple of love, Amma (as the Holy Mother is affectionately known) is hugging her disciples.

I leave my bags and let the swarm carry me into the temple's holy hive. Balconies drip with devotees, the floor softly heaves with the brightly colored bodies of hundreds of men, women and children. Up front, Indian white-robed *brahmacharis* (monks and nuns) are chanting holy *bhajan*, or adoration, hymns, and the room vibrates with a drone of harmonium, tabla, clapping, chatting, snoring and singing. It's stinking hot and a sticky cocktail of body odor rises. Amma's face is everywhere, on the clocks, on the walls and on the faces of the goddess statues. But I can't see her. On the stage, two chaotic conga lines of men from the right and women from the left meet in a bulging knot of pushing, pleading pilgrims. Every couple of seconds the bulge engorges, pulsates and then pops out an ecstatic or weeping being. Within the bulge is the Holy Mother.

"You're here for *darshan*? Mother wants Westerners, come," whispers a Western woman at my side.

Suddenly I've joined a queue of five foreigners pushing in to hear the advice of the Holy Mother, ahead of the Indian queue of thousands. Within moments I'm halfway up to the sacred stage. I don't feel like a hug. The humidity is horrific, my thighs are stuck together like two wet slimy flounders, my hair is plastered to my skull, my face is red, blotchy and sticky, and my body is bumpy with an angry heat rash and infected mosquito bites. I also have onion breath from lunch.

"Don't worry," comforts an American gray-eyed, ghostly pale girl in front of me. "Mother loves all without conditions and without limits. She is pure, unconditional, beautiful love."

Western helpers in white saris are on all sides of me. One gently wipes the sweat from my face and then roughly pushes me into the backside of the devotee in front. She rams the woman behind me into my spine. The next helper shoves me forward toward the churning Mother mass. Before I have time to compose myself I'm in the center of the heaving hive. A disciple squatting on the floor yanks me to my knees, grabs my bottom in both hands and pushes it forward. Unseen arms take my hands and put them on either side of Amma's feet, and clawed fingers roughly tilt my head to one side. I'm in the lap of the Holy Mother! Before

I'm tucked into her sweaty armpit I catch a quick glimpse of a short, plump body wrapped in white cotton, a sweet round face with slightly bucked teeth and the glint of a nose ring against dark skin. She looks like my cook Rachel. Amma puts one hand on my shoulder, another behind my neck and babbles in my ear: "mooneemooneemooneemooneemooneeeemooooneeemooonee-mooonee."

I feel a kiss on my cheek, a sweet pressed into my hand and I'm yanked up, pulled away and pushed off the stage. The entire encounter has taken about five seconds.

"Isn't she wonderful?" the woman behind me raves with a rabid look in her eye. I nearly burst into tears of disappointment.

I felt nothing.

Mother, as I'm told to call her, is not the first manifestation of the Divine Goddess in India, but she's definitely the most popular at present. I buy her official biography from the shop and read the story of a spiritual Cinderella. The fourth of thirteen children born into a poor fishing family in 1953, Sudhamani, as she was known then, grew up right here. She was dark blue at birth (like Lord Krishna), laughed as she took her first breath and then promptly sat in the lotus position. When she was six months old she walked and talked and went dark brown. At two she said prayers, at five she composed her own devotional ditties and at seven she began meditating. For some reason, Sudhamani's family didn't see this brilliant development or even the blue skin as anything significant—they thought the girl was ugly, so they pulled her out of school when she was ten and made her the family servant. She worked happily and endured bloody beatings before becoming a teenager obsessed with merging with God. According to the book, "The sounds of Krishna's flute played within her, she danced until God intoxicated and fell on the beach losing consciousness."

At twenty-one Sudhamani manifested the divine moods of Krishna, turned milk into pudding, ate burning camphor and French-kissed a cobra. She foiled murder attempts by her detractors and marriage plans by her parents. Sudhamani died. She resurrected. At twenty-two she "merged with the Omnipresent, the Omniscient and the Omnipotent Being; the Divine Mother."

The foreigners' information center at the ashram gives me a key to a tiny room high in the pink tower and a list of rules. The German boy on duty also recommends I meet Amma's right-hand man, translator and spokesman Swami Amritaswarupananda Puri. I take a cold shower, then travel to the back of the temple where the swami has an office. A rotund, long-haired, bearded dude in an orange caftan opens the door and motions me to sit opposite him. I ask him about when he met his guru. In eloquent English, the swami softly tells me he was a student called Balu when he first came here, and his first hug sounds much more auspicious than mine was.

"She told me she was my mother and I was her child. These words entered deep into my heart. I burst into tears and became enraptured with inexplicable joy. This is what I had been searching for, love in all its purity. Motherhood in its universal essence had assumed a form. I saw the universe of love overflowing with divineness, an experience of complete peace of mind beyond space and time."

"You saw all that in a hug?"

"Yes, I did," he smiles serenely.

Balu had found his guru and his God. Soon he was so in love with Mother's love he became oblivious to the world. He couldn't sleep and had to be near her. Amma initiated him with a meditation mantra, and sent him out of the ashram to earn a master's degree in philosophy that he believes he attained only with her divine intervention. Together they began to initiate other devotees and the ashram grew.

The first Westerners started coming in the early eighties. Swami tells me that one is still here. In a tiny, homely, yet starkly simple flat high up in the pink tower, Sharadumba greets me at the door with a gentle but sickly smile. She doesn't go out much, as her liver almost stopped functioning on a tough tour with Amma last year. Twenty years ago Sharadumba was a Buddhist who meditated on the female manifestation of Buddha energy, Green Tara. When she arrived at the ashram, Amma greeted her on the dock with the words "Green Devi" (Devi is a Hindu goddess). The American saw Tara in human form.

"I left many lifetimes of Buddhism to belong to Amma, who is all-pervasive consciousness, like the Buddha."

Sharadumba swears she saw miracles here and tells me the story of a leper called Dattan.

"He was reptilian, his skin was hanging off, he had missing eyelids and massive lesions on his skin, yet there was a certain dignity about him. He would get *darshan* last. Amma would hug and kiss him—she'd stick her tongue in his pus-filled lesions, put sandalwood on him and dress his wounds. I almost threw up the first time I saw it. Apparently he's cured now."

Sharadumba is a darling and radiates goodness, but I go to my dorm room feeling repulsed and revolted by this story. What kind of a being would lick a leper? Yet as I fall toward sleep, my disgust turns to shame. Even if I don't believe in miracle healing, if this licking story is true, the Mother has performed a miracle of some sort. She must be capable of absolute, indiscriminate love and affection. I resolve to try to open up to the Mother's love.

First, I embrace her ashram's routine. It starts at a quarter to five. In the temple, the first ripples of heat rise with waves of rapid, tongue-twisting Sanskrit. A swami leads the recitation of the one hundred and eight names of Amma—the qualities of the guru. They hail her as the "manifestation of the absolute truth," as a being "whose greatness is unsurpassable" and as "the life and savior of the state of Kerala." Next are the one thousand names of the Supreme Mother (or Devi), each carrying a different shade of philosophical meaning. Such chanting is believed to guarantee the protection of God and ensure our physical and spiritual growth. It puts me to sleep; the rhythms of adoration caress me like a motherly hand stroking my brow.

While Amma might love us without distinction, her ashram is

strictly divided to ensure there's not too much of the wrong kind of loving between the sexes. Men and women have separate rooms, yoga times, temple queues, Mother hugging sides and swimming times. Later in the day I head to the pool, which is like a warm bath and has a cling-guard rather than a lifeguard—a pale, skinny French devotee who checks we are all wearing full leg-covering caftans in the water. The fabric billows out and swirls around like seaweed. We then have to pass an inspection to leave. The cling-guard warns, "Suits stick when wet, do not go sexy."

I laugh and she stares at me, shocked and stern. I wait until my *salwar* is dry enough for a twirl inspection; she grunts and lets me go.

Far more noticeable than the women-men divide is the Western-Indian divide. I am given strict instructions by the "foreigners' registration office" that I must eat at the "foreigner canteen," shop at the "foreigner shop," and I am encouraged to buy the all-white "foreigner uniform." I pay the "foreigner rate" of one hundred and twenty-five rupees a day (about a dollar-twenty-five), while the locals pay thirty. The Indian monks and nuns work hard printing and binding Amma pamphlets but otherwise they live rent-free, while the Western live-in monks and nuns pay eight thousand American dollars for an ashram flat or full price for a VIP travel position with Amma. This doesn't really bother me; Westerners generally can afford more and I'm thankful our cash pays for a smaller *darshan* queue. When I find out the rent also earns me the privilege of doing *seva*, or divine selfless service, I'm happy to participate.

I feel the joy of giving as I build up blisters washing the floor of the massive auditorium. But as I start sweating onto the endless piles of *chapatti* dough my righteousness wears off, for a huge group of Indian visitors has gathered to laugh at how bad our round bread looks. I suggest to the Italian devotee with blonde curls beside me that perhaps the Indians could also do some divine service.

"Don't," she says sharply. "Remember, we Westerners have more ego, we need to do this work to get rid of bad karma and to make

Amma happy. Obedience to a guru destroys the ego that separates us from God."

The reason the devotees meekly obey the Mother in a way they've probably never followed their parents is that they truly believe she orchestrates the minutiae of their lives. An emaciated, balding, middle-aged Mike from Manchester tells me she got him a job and then took it away so he'd come here. Lanky, lithe Bob from Iowa (whom Amma has renamed Hari) saw his savior in a vision where she danced suggestively as Krishna. He then let her decide his fate and at every hug he asks her questions through the translating swami and always obeys her answers.

"I will leave when she wants me to. Until then, I'm hers," he blissfully babbles.

Hari's pale freckled wife Sharona saw Amma in a dream dressed as Kali—the fearsome goddess that wears human skulls as a necklace. Sharona says she succumbed to the divine agent that killed her ego and since then life has become easy. Amma does ninety percent of the internal work on her, bringing about the situations and challenges that will lead to transformation.

"We are completely connected to her, she knows everything about me. I project everything onto her, my love and my dislike, I pray to her, I talk to her, I write to her, I observe her and I know how to be."

This primes me for a second *darshan*. Sharona promises me Amma will give me what I need, and suggests I ask a question in my mind that Amma will hear, understand and answer. I have my fourth shower for the day, wash my hair and brush my teeth but after ten minutes in the hall I'm sweaty, red-faced and blotchy again. Amid the push, shove, knee-crunch and head-yank I concentrate on my question.

"What is my purpose, what does God want from me?"

Again, the flash of the nose ring, the gentle hold of the neck and the whisper in the ear. The answer, my purpose in life is: "rootoongarootoongarootoongarootoongarootoongarootoonga."

My shoulder nearly dislocated by the yank out of the Mother's midst, I wait for a vision. Is the purpose of my life to root?

A five-second flash of nonsensical babble is hardly inspiring faith. I go for a cup of tea and watch Amma's children. The Indian devotees are enjoying the ashram like it's a holiday camp with a divine counselor. The kids spend the day riding the elevators; the women chat and do each other's hair and the men sleep, drink *chai* or play badminton. The Westerners, in contrast, seem pious and precious. Many are sullenly silent, a number are frequently crying and some are very snappy. One yells at me for serving her a small dinner portion and another refuses to let me owe one rupee when I'm a bit short of change. I'm lectured for eating eggs and my jokes are received with stone-faced stares. I see one girl lie to get an extra *darshan* hug and I observe a lot of pettiness, pushiness, jealousy and competitiveness for Mother's closeness and attention. This family seems dysfunctional.

The saintly Sharadumba is one of the few not infuriating me. She agrees that the devotional path is not a pretty process, but says it's essential.

"The jealousies, pettiness and pushiness are the devotees' *vasanas*, their latent tendencies caused by bad karma. Amma encourages the jealousies to purify them all."

Perhaps my impatience and annoyance are caused by my own bad karma and Amma is purifying it while giving me a good laugh at the same time. But could the Mother get annoyed as well? In a little afternoon lecture to the devotees she seems frustrated and talks about small-mindedness. The swami translates.

"I'm trying to give my children time but the situation is changing. As ashramites, we are all in heaven, be brave and not afraid and don't be so glum, you'll give yourselves heart attacks."

I nearly applaud.

Perhaps the saner devotees have all gone. When the inner work is over, Amma's children are sent out to work for certain charities. The Mother still lives in two tiny rooms here and money collected goes to an orphanage, a secondary school, a widows' pension and housing projects for the poor. Her trust also pays for medical dispensaries, a world-class hospital in nearby Cochin, an aged care home, a tribal school, a college for the speech-impaired, industrial training courses, colleges and a computer institute across the river.

What with all their good work and their willingness to help me, I'm feeling guilty for judging the Western devotees. And it seems they show more compassion than their Indian counterparts. At dinner I sit with an Indian girl, Uma, who prefers to hang out in the foreigners' section than with the locals. She came here to study computers when her daddy died but the *brahmacharis* didn't accept her and burned her hand on the cooking pot; she solemnly shows me the scar. Uma says many of the Indian monks and nuns also don't like the paying pilgrims.

"They are believing that you are from a culture that does bad things, they think you are all on drugs."

"Uma, sometimes I think India is just one big drug trip," I answer solemnly.

Before bed are *bhajans*. I join thousands gathered under a massive chandelier in the new auditorium to sing with their saint. Amma finished hugging five thousand devotees only two hours ago, yet she comes out looking fresh in a clean white cotton sari. Backed by a huge rainbow and some dinky Casio keyboard playing with tapping tabla, she transforms into a diva, singing and directing the clapping faster and faster. At a song's peak she leans back and throws both arms up motioning like she's juggling a giant ball or a small world.

"She's calling down the Divine Goddess," the girl beside me gushes.

The Divine Goddess must make Amma happy. She lets loose a guttural sound and a cackling laugh that's amplified by some reverb. We chant the sacred syllable "om" and then some Sanskrit verses. Amma strides off smiling. A small group of pilgrims push and trip over each other to be the closest trailing her every move.

Sunday morning, five o'clock and I look down from the tower roof to see the hive has swelled overnight. A python of pilgrims snakes around the temple, out the gate and down the path. On Sundays Amma does two *darshans*—one as Amma and one as a manifestation of the Divine Devi. People are pacing themselves for a long day. They're sound asleep in the corridors, doorways, gravel heaps and stairways or standing stoically in huge queues for the shop, *chai,* toilet, lifts and, most of all, *darshan* tokens.

Through the heat of the day Amma hugs eight thousand pilgrims at a rate of twenty a minute and twelve hundred an hour. She finishes at three-thirty, and at five is back in the auditorium to sing. The crowd has swelled again. More than fifteen thousand people are here for a hug. Entire families sit clinging to their luggage—women dressed in their best silk saris with fresh flowers in their hair clutch children dressed as Krishna. Old grandmas and cripples stand on the edge of the crowd. The heat and humidity are so incredible that the heat rash has spread all over my body—I haven't been dry for days.

Above us, somehow Amma seems younger, refreshed and blissed out. She gives a lecture in the local language and then leads some songs. As the final "om" rings out, the doors jerk shut on the stage. The crowd is at critical mass. It chants for the costume change that signals the beginning of Devi *darshan.* This is the external manifestation of Amma's oneness with the Supreme where she'll take off two of the veils that separate we mortals from the divine, enabling us to glimpse the ultimate truth of existence. It's like waiting for the opening show at Mardi Gras. The heat rises to hell-like levels; it sits on us like a low cloud and rains sweat smelling of onion and hair oil. The crowd is pushing forward, a sea of ecstatic people drowning in their desire for love.

The doors jerk open. Amma sits under an orange felt umbrella, looking like a small teenage girl playing dress-up. She's in a red and gold sari with a huge silver belt, glittery earrings and a touch of makeup, and sports a tin foil crown on her head. Her swamis prostrate themselves before her. The crowd surges and bows. Then it begins again. The Holy Mother is surrounded and swamped. The sick, the crippled and the love-hungry descend, desperate for a divine hug, a smile and a few words. It's seven-thirty and the queue goes for miles.

I go up onto the stage to give *prasad*—the presentation of a sweet offering. This is an honor reserved for foreigners and strictly timed with a stopwatch to two minutes. I hand Amma little packets containing a bag of sacred ash and a single boiled sweet that she gives to each devotee. Up until this moment I've thought perhaps the Mother was divinely mad, but as I struggle to keep up with her pace, I realize she's too cool to be crazy. Surrounded by shouting, screaming, pushing and pandemonium, she is systematic, disciplined and patient. Each devotee is given the routine hug, kiss and *prasad*. Those who are crying get an extra pat or are invited to sit close by. Amma occasionally looks cranky but is usually smiling. She's highly disciplined love in motion. Apparently she never has a day off and hasn't canceled *darshan* in thirty years.

I find the intensity exhausting and have to go and lie down for a couple of hours. When I come back at four a.m. the music is still going strong, the queue still growing and the hugs still happening. It occurs to me that the only time I've ever felt absolute and unconditional love for everyone and everything was when I was possessed by a chemical goddess. Perhaps Amma's Devi *darshan* will awaken the natural ecstasy within me or at least crack my ego, doubt and bad karma. At five I'm up on stage. The helpers are even pushier than before. I tell one that Amma hasn't told me yet what God wants.

"Ask her for something more superficial then, hurry up, quickly."

I'm knocked to my knees and my head is again in the vice. I don't have time to think. But I'm feeling cheeky.

"*Amma*," I say in my head, "*give me bigger boobs*."

I'm pulled out before I even register the hug, the kiss and the divine ditty.

I push to the middle of the melee, limp with dehydration and disappointment. That's three strikes of the divine and I'm out. Beside me, a shrunken old woman sits whispering to a plastic Amma ring on her finger. Beside her, a young French girl sits rocking, her arms wrapped around an Amma doll in a sari that costs one hundred and eighty American dollars. The girl's head lolls back, then jerks forward, her eyes roll and spin, her mouth flops open and she drools. She's hysterically high on Amma love, drunk on desperation for divinity. An elderly Englishwoman collapses weeping and is virtually carried off the stage.

Can you feel pity for the divine? I'm overcome with sorrow for the Holy Mother surrounded by such grasping, pulling, demanding, desperate people. I need to get out. I walk away to watch the nuclear red sun come up over the canal. Ignoring the music and the mayhem, it kisses the earth from below and blows away the mist snaking through the trees. Fishing boats chug in from the sea. I gain strength for the finale.

At eight in the morning the queue is still getting longer and longer. The flopping doll-hugger is still rocking and salivating, oblivious to the surrounding mosh pit. I try to enter the trance of the true devotee and fall asleep. At nine-thirty I wake up to realize Amma has been going for fourteen hours without a break for water, a wee or a stretch. The *bhajans* are picking up in speed again and at ten the line suddenly stops growing. She gives her last hug, stands up and staggers to the front of the stage. A devotee beside me grabs my arm.

"Trust your heart and not your head. What's your heart saying?"

I tune in. It's beating "bullshit, bullshit, bullshit" in time with the tabla.

Amma throws flower petals. The mass of arms and legs pushes against the stage. Thousands raise their hands and beg for love. The Mother falters and almost falls. She slowly scans the crowd, her exhausted eyes full of absolute patience and love. When she sweeps my face the bullshit beat stops. I feel my heart melt, contract and then explode. A supernova of love sends sparks of pity, compassion, admiration and amazement through my being. If God is the source of pure love then Amma's an avenue. I feel the touch of a pure soul, of a saintly grace.

My suspension of cynicism could be hype or hysteria, momentary madness, the drug of exhaustion or the power of group suggestion. Whatever it is, it fades by lunchtime. I just don't have the good karma, innocence or absence of ego that will allow for the surrender and deep devotion to a guru. Yet I bow before Amma's patience, compassion, strength and the power of her ability to love such annoying groupies. And I hail a saint who tears at taboos, especially ones that restrict physical intimacy. If everything happens according to her grace, she must want the story to end like this: without resolve.

And yet, there is some. By the female *shakti* power invested in me by the Hugging Mother I resolve to give the men of India a better go, for I realize I have been judging them too harshly; they are creatures of habit and conditioning, and if I can treat them with something closer to love than hate, perhaps they will respond and respect me. I buy a kitsch little plastic red ring with Amma's face on it to remind me that love is a powerful tool. I walk out of the ashram faithfully feminine, with my head down but my heart open.

The Mother Hugging Divine Manifestation of the Supreme Goddess has done it. My breasts are getting bigger!

It's a month since I made the wish in her lap and my boobs are blowing up like balloons. Even Rachel notices.

"Sarah, what have you done, your women things are growing? Isn't it?"

Jonathan, who has now been home for a whole week, is rather impressed with my new assets. I know he's planning a surprise party for my birthday so I go shopping for an outfit to show them off. In the wee hours of the morning of the day of my party the phone rings. There's been another South Asian tragedy—the Crown Prince of Nepal has shot his entire family—and Jonathan has to fly to

Kathmandu immediately. The party is canceled. We've now been married for six months and have been together only for about six weeks.

I spend my birthday alone, sulking and, as Indians say, "paining." And I'm literally paining, too, for my breasts are not just growing, they are hurting. The pain builds so much I can't sleep on my side; at times it feels like a hot skewer is piercing through my nipples and I think I can feel major lumps of hardness.

Nearly everyone I know has abandoned the Delhi summer and Jonathan is too busy in Nepal to be of any comfort or help. Mindful of the Indian modesty, the Australian Broadcasting Company's insurance company takes a day or two to find me a female doctor who will touch my breasts. But they can't find one with a bedside manner. She has a quick grope behind a curtain.

"Listen, I don't think it's cancer, but you are old, you have no children and you are Western, that's all very bad. Veeeeerrrrry bad. You have to have mammograms and the like."

The insurance company flies me home to Australia for tests. I spend the trip with my face at the plane window worrying. Again, the reality of mortality is harder to face than the meditation on its inevitability. My parents are grim-faced at the airport. It hurts to hug them. We head straight to a specialist, who orders a mammogram and ultrasound. Three horrible hours later I'm called into his office. The doctor gravely explains he cannot find any cancerous lumps but it appears I've suffered a massive hormone explosion.

"What on earth were you doing a month ago that could have triggered an extreme estrogen flow?"

I can't tell an Australian doctor about Amma and my wish within her holy hug. He may commit me. But what do I tell myself? Did the Divine Mother's powerful presence activate my female hormones? Is she sending me a message to come back to her? Or is she cursing me for my cynicism? I take off my plastic Amma ring; freaked out and frightened, I decide to forget faith in her for a while. The doctor prescribes vitamin B and rest and when my period begins my breasts stop hurting and begin to deflate.

In Sydney I spend days eating sushi, gulping lungs full of fresh air and staring up at endless bright blue skies. I walk through the pristine quiet of the suburban bush, crush its leaves to smell freshness and marvel at the wide empty streets during rush hour. I prickle with pleasure when I see the sea and gasp at the open joy and the jokes and the intimacy between friends. But most of all, I adore the liberty of being ignored! I deliberately buy a pair of skintight jeans just to enjoy walking around in them without attracting a riot. One day when I'm with a friend, a buffed bloke passes, looks us straight in the eyes and drawls, "G'daaaaay, girls." I have to restrain myself from giving him a huge hug. To be acknowledged, to be appreciated by a stranger without feeling like a prostitute is so wonderful, so liberating. Close to the thrill of jumping in the car and going to a supermarket to buy chocolate and a bottle of wine. My Sydney life seems so easy and so picture-perfect.

I fly back to Delhi to find that Razoo has come home from the U.S.A. She rings, highly excited and chattering superfast, her thick Indian accent now tinged with an American twang.

"Hi, it's Aarzoo, I'm back. New York isssso hotttttt, I am telling you . . ."

I interrupt: "Aarzoo? I thought your name was Razoo?"

"No, Sarrrrah, what are you saying? It's Aarzoo."

"Why didn't you tell us it was Aarzoo? We got it wrong for so long."

"Oh, noooooo, I couldn't, that would have been ssso rrrrrrude."

But Aarzoo *is* brasher now she's been in New York for more than a year, more confident and more outspoken. She forgives me for calling her a gambling chip when her name actually means "gift from God," but she's furious when I tell her about my tits.

"Saarrah, you stupid! Such gurus as the Mother are farrrrrrr too powerful for you. Let's parrrty. Us foreigners are all the rage in

America, such a put-down Indian woman they feel I am, so I got great work and great bucks. Let's go for it."

I hesitate to reembrace the life of a material girl living in a material world, but Sydney has teased me with luxury. While India may well have a soft spiritual center, it's also got a hard head for cash, and its middle class (the biggest and fastest-growing in the world) is energetically embracing the products and symbols of Western consumer culture. It may be stiflingly still and steamy but there's still a wind of change blowing through New Delhi and it's impossible not to be ruffled by it. This city has changed more in the last year than in all of the twelve years since I first came here.

When I visited in 1988 India was still in the grips of *swadeshi*, a centrally planned bastardization of Gandhi's love for "homegrown"—soft drinks and other symbols of Western imperialism and decadence were not welcome. Now the Indian economy has started opening up and the top two Bollywood stars are shoving Coke and Pepsi down our throats in ubiquitous advertising. At times I feel like I'm living in America in the fifties. On TV, beautiful housewives sing and dance around new washing machines, airconditioners, refrigerators and ice machines. On the roads, the increasingly rare Ambassadors are struggling to keep up with the new imported zippy sports cars, and tractors trundle behind fleets of Lexus and Mercedes. The old diesel rickshaws have been replaced with new models powered by Compressed Natural Gas and the pollution is slowly beginning to clear. New electronic shops are doing a roaring trade in flat screen TVs, DVD players and boom box stereos.

Our middle-class suburb, Vasant Vihar, is at the heart of the transformation. Up the road at the aptly named Modern Bazaar, cows and beggars graze around McDonald's and Pizza Hut, and shoeshine boys sit on the steps of a delicatessen that sells Australian meat and Italian cheese. The ubiquitous fast-food duo were here when we arrived but they are fast facing competition. Every week a new shop opens and by the end of summer there're Benetton, Nike, Adidas, Levi's, Pepe Jeans, and an American-style bar called Thank God It's Friday where staff wear baseball caps, name tags and rows of badges on elastic suspenders. But the hottest hangout of all is the brand-new Barista coffee shop, part of a chain leading a lust for lattes in this traditional *chai* town. Each café is contemporary cool combined with eighties nostalgia—teenagers sit in jeans and T-shirts and strum guitars while singing along to Billy Joel and John Denver songs. Karaoke is also catching on, with Western songs regularly massacred. The hot favorite is "Hotel California"—almost unrecognizable when screeched in a strong Hindi accent at double decibels.

Aarzoo and her friends don't share my middle-class guilt—they prefer to embrace what money can buy and enjoy it for all it's worth. Most are openly contemptuous of Westerners trying to buy a spiritual fix in India. It's not the cultural appropriation that upsets them, it's more the dress sense—there's a general impression that travelers are dirty, messy and dress like peasants. Aarzoo insists I'm different.

"Sarrrrah, you may not wear enough jewelry but you're clean, your hair is growing, you wear okay clothes; why, you're almost Indian now."

It's the highest possible compliment and right now I need it. For I've slowly but surely been losing my social confidence lately. I'm not respected much in New Delhi as an individual—but as a wife—and Jonathan and I mostly hang out with people he has met through his work. I am the partner who "travels and writes a bit," and while my Buddhist being embraces the eradication of ego that came with being a "Triple J celebrity," I still feel slightly vulnerable so cut adrift from what people once knew to be me. Most Delhi women size up other chicks rather superficially, and among their impeccably groomed lot I feel like a bit of a wallflower. Aarzoo is *my* special friend and hanging out with her gives me credibility and a sense of belonging. She and her friend Billie become my wardrobe consultants, etiquette educators and social swamis.

First, they insist on frequent threading, an Indian hair-removal method, as thin eyebrows are essential this season. Every six weeks a beautician stretches cotton thread between her fingers and teeth and pecks above me like a chicken while she rips hair out by its roots. If it's done well, it's painless; if it's done badly, it's agony. On my first attempt I go to the wrong place and walk out with a ridge of blood blisters that makes me look like Marilyn Manson. The girls don't let me out for a week.

When I'm healed we cruise markets and bargain for new nylon clingy clothes that we hardly dare to wear. Our favorite shopkeeper is the elderly but sprightly Mrs. Sharma, who sells short skirts and halter tops made from old saris. In her tiny shop stacked to the rafters with bright silks, she's making a mint but refuses to even buy new teeth for her toothless gums. Mrs. Sharma giggles and guffaws as she collects and counts the cash.

"Whattthh thhhtto do, hey? I've gothhh you. I'm the only one doing the Indian Westhhhern thing, thooo you pay. I'm nearly ninety and old people can't be argued witthhhhhh, heeeeee hhaaaa."

In the late afternoon (when it's only one hundred °F.) we sometimes stroll around Lodi Gardens, where the former sultan rulers of Delhi are buried. But this walk is not for fitness or to admire majestic tombs, it's a serious Italian-style *passeggiata* with Aarzoo and Billie out to see who is with whom and who is back from America for holidays or marriage meetings.

Aarzoo always warns me not to eat before we go out at night. I always disobey and she scolds me, as food puffs out the stomach and I'm getting rather round. Aarzoo often wears jeans or Western dresses, but Billie, who's far more sedate, wears Indian clothes or conservative long skirts and will only come out when her brother is around to accompany her. The weekly club ritual begins at one of the few discos. Due to licensing laws and a Punjabi prohibitionist attitude to alcohol, most of the places that offer drinking and dancing are in soulless five-star hotels or in the smoky basements of bad restaurants. There's one new nightclub that, apart from having too much exposed brass, is bearable. It always has a competitive queue out front but Aarzoo is a practiced pusher and hustler and we get in relatively easily. Indians always carry their ID—they can get married at the age of fifteen but can't drink in this state until twenty-five. Inside, the decor is bland and the fashion is black. Hundreds and hundreds of young Delhi things in tight black pants and little tops do the *puja* of the pose.

Aarzoo outlines her dogma of the disco with five commandments of clubbing:

1. A chaperone is necessary to keep an eye out for us girls and buy the drinks. Jonathan is always away so Billie's brother, currently on summer break from his American university, is the best.
2. Drink Diet Coke (only cheap girls like me want alcohol all night).
3. Walk with elbows bent, ready to knock the wind out of any slimy men who try to touch.
4. Dance in the middle of the dance floor because fat forty-year-old sleazy business blokes inevitably ring the outside. (I'm having to find a different dance style. I don't know if it's cultural catch-up or just an obsession with soft rock, but Delhi disco-heads love the seventies and eighties. Deep Purple, the Doors, Toto and Bryan Adams are popular, and the city's major anthems are Bon Jovi's "It's My Life," Queen's "We Will Rock You" and, believe it or not, "Living Next Door to Alice" by Smoky. The DJ even stops the record so everyone can scream, "Alice! Who the fuck is Alice?" No one believes I bought the song when I was about seven. When the music gets really bad I stand and practice rule number 5.)
5. Suck in stomach, push out eyeballs and bitch.

Aarzoo and Billie lead the charge.

"Look at her, that's the one he's now marrying after being turned down by my friend. Oh my God! She has the face of a horse."

"Twenty degrees right—she shouldn't be wearing that bra with that top, look at her going jingle jangle jingle jangle."

"Look left—Shanaz Husain just walked in."

(We don't bitch about Shanaz. She's the aging Queen of Delhi; she is to be respected for all the money she makes out of the Ayurvedic beauty goods she sells in leopard-print packages.)

I feel terrible about the cattiness of the conversation. Yet after weeks of being surrounded by women looking me up and down and mouthing off about my belly, my now deflated boobs and my dress, I abandon my Buddhist-inspired compassion, my Sikh desire to stand up for the weak, the tolerance learned at the Hindu Kumbh Mela and the love learned from the Divine Mother. I join a group ritual far less transcending than the Jewish love-fest and the Parsi secret ceremonies. I suck my stomach in and surrender.

"Look at her, she's drrrreadful, and who does he think he is? John Travolta? Trrrrrragic."

I'm still learning the "Hinglish" of middle-class northern urban India. Basically conversations are superfast, high-pitched singsong and, while smattered with Hindi, mostly in English with plosive "Ts" and rolling "Rs." Hindi words are said through the nose, especially "*ha-ji*" (yes), or the equivalent "*hhhaaa*" (yeah). I sit on the phone for hours while Aarzoo talks, replying "*haa, haaa, haaa, haa, haaa*," like Laurie Anderson in the "O Superman" song.

Our favorite sayings, all with dramatic upward inflections, are:

"What are you say-*ing*?"

"Shutt*up*!"

"You're stuuuuppp*id*."

"Ya*ar*."

And, my personal favorite: "I will give you ssssuch a sssssslap."

I see Hari Lal even less frequently these days and usually just to chat, while Aarzoo and her friends teach me the street Hindi words and phrases he so detests. I'm back at being hard on boys, so I shout out the Hindi equivalent of "I will skewer your eyes out with a pitchfork if you don't stop staring" to perverts. Those who pinch or grab me get a punch and a screamed "sister-fucker" the worst possible insult. I'm not so good at the drawl of "man," "dude" and "cooooooooool" that's meant to show you've studied "Stateside," but I make up for it in Indian gesticulation. I wave my arms around, flick my wrists, gesture with my fingers and wobble my head like a dashboard bobble-head doll.

When I'm not out with the girls, I'm inside the Australian Broadcasting Company house enjoying the air-conditioning and the imported cable TV—which is quite a lot at the moment, for the monsoon has finally hit Delhi after a year's absence and the roads are either flooded or steaming. New channels are delivering a steady diet of the early episodes of *Ally McBeal*, *Buffy the Vampire Slayer*, *Angel*, *Seinfeld* and *Friends*. One channel even has *West Wing*, but accidentally plays the episodes back to front so it doesn't make sense. With all this television, Rachel's sublime cooking and the fact that it's far too hot to exercise, I'm rapidly gaining weight. My timing is bad. While I've been slothing and scoffing, India has been turning away from the fat fetish and moving toward the thin look.

I've grown from the post-pneumonia skinniest I've ever been to become fatter than I'd dreamed possible. Aarzoo urges me to give up yoga and go to the gym. In a five-star hotel J-Lo whines from the stereo and we sweat on walking machines. I quit quickly because every time there's a power cut the machines stop with such force that I'm almost catapulted through the window. I refuse to do the Jane Fonda tapes and put the fat belt around my hips to let it wobble. I try swimming but the pool is as hot as a bath and, in places, yellow with kiddie wee.

Aarzoo decides it's time I start driving, and I consider it—having Abraham around is cramping our style and driving with her is terrifying. She careers at top speed in a white, battered dinged bumper car and doesn't obey the road rule of stopping for things bigger. The only thing that stops Aarzoo is a cow—even the beggars avoid her car. One night I have a drink for courage and grab the keys.

"Madam, what are you doing?" cries our guard.

"I'm taking the car, Lakan, out of the way."

Lakan swallows and steps aside, and Abraham and his family look down from their window nervously. I hit the accelerator and race around the block, liberated at last. I'm all brash confidence and after a few dents I'm soon King of the Road.

• • •

When Jonathan finally returns from Nepal I pick him up at the airport. He's shaking by the time we are home; he says driving with me is scarier than being in the Taliban-controlled streets of Kabul.

He's also arrived home on a day when all the men of Delhi are wearing bracelets. Some of the wrist wear is modestly made of string, but this year's extra-showy style is infiltrating an ancient ritual—gold glittering sequins, fluffy pink and bright green wristbands are hot stuff. Once a year, sisters put these *rakhee* around their brothers' wrists to show their affection and to ensure he will look after her and help marry her off. At a nightclub Aarzoo ties a *rakhee* on Jonathan. He's flattered but nervous about this. Aarzoo has called off her engagement to Sunil and this bracelet means Jonathan is now responsible for finding her a new mate. He doesn't know many single guys Aarzoo would possibly want. She's sworn off Indian men altogether.

"They just want a slave. I want a carrrrrrrreeeer, I want to make movies, I can't give it up for a dorrrrrrrk who wants me to make *chai* all day long."

The problem is, she's also dubious about Western men.

"They just want one thing and when they get it, they leave you. Besides, if you marry them, they cheat on you."

"Shutttup, don't be stupid, that's a generalization. An Indian man might cheat," I screech back.

"Yaaar sure, but they don't tell you about it and rrrrrrrrub it in your face and then leave you."

Aarzoo decides to stay single and Jonathan wipes his brow.

Billie is under pressure to get married soon, but she'll accept an arranged match. My feelings on arranged marriages have changed since I've lived here. For months I was righteously furious about what happened to Padma and her mother because they'd dared to look for love. Yet now I've seen that organized matches can often work. Most couples are really very happy. Besides, finding someone in a culture where there's not that much girl-boy mixing can be difficult, if not impossible. Lust doesn't last and couples with things in common do. Billie doesn't have much experience with boys and she trusts her parents to know what she wants and needs.

Besides, Billie says if she becomes an old maid she won't feel like a loser—her parents will take the blame and wear the shame.

Because Billie is an extremely high-caste Brahman, her father will consider only very elite men. Good breeding is not enough; they're culled if they have a relative who is divorced, if they drink, if they have the wrong job or salary or if the parents are showy. I'd been nervous about meeting such a strict man, but I'm welcomed to a family dinner with a warm hug from him and a rowdy romp with the strictly vegetarian Brahman dogs. Billie's dad is an erudite and well-traveled man who makes me feel instantly comfortable. He lists his favorite restaurants in Sydney and the least favorite men he's met so far for his little girl.

"We only want the cream of the crop, we are not Punjabi refugees," he insists while winking at Aarzoo.

She groans. "Stop teasing me, Uncle-*ji*, cheeky man, you are."

We laugh at their ritual ribbing. But Uncle is glossing over a serious problem—so far he's only found a few "suitable" boys and Billie dismissed them quickly. One because he wanted to talk to her alone and the other because she didn't like his parents.

"Sarrrrrrah, I just want someone who is from a pleasant family, yaar? I'm not getting married to him, I'm getting married to his family. They have to be nice."

Aarzoo agrees but rolls her eyes.

"Billllllllieeeeeee, you are going to become a spinssssster. I'm a rough refugee spoiling your reputation and I'm going to hug you, here I come."

Billie screams—she cannot stand being touched.

She and Aarzoo are the Oscar and Felix of the Indian X generation.

Aarzoo is turning twenty-eight and wants a groovy party with alcohol where she can wear a shortish skirt. That leaves out her house and the homes of all her friends as they still live with their parents. It's time to call in a favor from her *rakhee* brother, but

Jonathan has turned around and gone again, this time to Pakistan. As the good sister-in-law, I let her party at my house.

In some ways it's all very Indian. The bootleg alcohol arrives at nine, Aarzoo at ten and her guests at eleven, Billie's parents drop her off and pick her up two hours later, young married couples talk about their sons and one man insists I run up and down the stairs and bring him warm water all night. In other ways it's all very Western. Lots of girls get changed into tight jeans and T-shirts in their cars and the boys spend the night screaming into their mobile phones. Most drink bourbon and Coke and couples French-kiss in the corners. They keep screaming and fighting over the music until four o'clock, and when they eventually blow up the stereo, they abandon for home. I feel like I'm back at my graduation party.

Indian society forces its middle class to live an extended adolescence; most married couples usually live with one set of parents and unmarried ones must lie, sneak around and borrow bedrooms to fulfill their sexual desires. The Australian Broadcasting Company house becomes a bit of a fuck pad for a few young lovers in the next months and it's something I don't feel entirely comfortable about.

This crowd is where the West meets South Asia head-on. Most of them work with Aarzoo on the first Indian reality TV show. It's loosely based on a mixture of *Survivor* and *Temptation Island* but drastically altered for Indian tastes and sensibilities. The American shows are seen as materialistic, individualistic, immoral and tacky—everything that this country hates about the West. Aarzoo finds *Temptation Island* especially excruciating.

"It is absolutely disgusting to an average Indian. They are not wearing any clothes and what is the concept? It's tough enough in life to stay together, here you are spending millions of dollars trying to pull them apart. It's bizarre."

"What do you think would happen if they tried to do an Indian one?" I wonder out loud.

"There would be rrrrrrrrrriots."

Shot in Ladakh, her show is called *RAAH*: Romance Adventure *Aap aur Hum* (You and Us). Aarzoo and her mates force young married couples to ride bikes, rappel down mountains, trek, cross rivers and (shock horror) cook their own food. They all freak out, especially when they break a nail or lose a blue contact lens. I love it.

Aarzoo's generation believes it will be able to adapt consumer culture without its destructive downfalls. But her parents' generation is beginning to worry that things are going too fast. The city's first rave is held at a farmhouse and soon after there's the first big cocaine bust. Television discussions and newspaper articles rant about pernicious Western habits, "revealing, loincloth clothes and strange techno-music." I don't think they need to worry too much: Indian culture may just be strong enough to take what it wants from American cultural imperialism and reject what it doesn't.

India's one billion people simply refuse to play by the new Raj rules, and their rich traditions and absorbent, flexible Hindu faith may well survive the global onslaught. Aarzoo and her friends will party all night and get up at six to go on a pilgrimage to a temple, and Billie will definitely marry a man her parents choose. The top films of this summer are all Hindi musicals and most Hollywood hits are still not showing in Delhi. About seventy-five percent of the film clips on Channel V and MTV are Indian songs, and local literature is booming. India has changed the food Goliaths to suit her tastes; McDonald's has taken the beef out of the beef burger and Pizza Hut adds spice and chili. The funky new crowd is just as likely to wear a *salwar* suit and a sari as jeans. India is too nationalistic to give in to the cultural cringe. The new cars carry the same old stickers that brag INDIA IS GREAT.

I'm sure Hinduism will also ultimately absorb the New Age philosophies of the West that are beginning to infiltrate the New Delhi scene, many of which are based on Hindu truths anyway. Hinduism is like a sponge—it's already an amalgam of thousands of local beliefs and faiths and I believe it will continue to move with the times and with the people.

I begin to meet people a bit older than Aarzoo who are attending New Age courses. Groups meet weekly to discuss ideas about modern marriages, workshops on career fulfillment are common and eight-week courses concentrate on individual growth and the transformation to prosperity. Non Resident Indians (NRIs) are lapping them up, and are usually cashed up enough to pay the huge fees (most of the courses cost more than one hundred American dollars and some are even charged in that currency). I'm cynical about any teachings that charge vast amounts of money but there's a unique seminar in town that I'm willing to pay for.

The seminar involves studying the transmissions of an alien called Kryon. Kryon is as big as a house, has eleven spinning sides, hovers in the orbit of Jupiter and communicates telepathically with nine chosen earthlings. Brought up on a steady diet of *Star Wars*, *Star Trek* and *The X-Files*, I do believe we are not alone in the universe. I like the idea of ET existentialism and I'm still feeling slightly nervous about Hindu gurus and intense religious study. I decide learning about Kryon could be fun and also perhaps give me some insight into how India is changing spiritually as well as economically and culturally. I've also learned to suspend my disbelief over the last year or so and outrageous beliefs such as alien transmissions no longer seem that bizarre to me.

The course reading is *The End Times*, a bright orange fluorescent bible of bizarre psychobabble. Kryon channeled its teachings to California baby-boomer businessman Lee Carroll in 1992 after jumping into his thoughts while he took a shower. The entity begins each chapter with "Greetings! I am Kryon of magnetic service." He then goes on to reveal he is the technician that designed us and that we too are from a different dimension. Kryon says we humans volunteered to come to earth in human form to fulfill a special mission or "lesson." Unfortunately we have forgotten what that is and are marooned here with no purpose. The "Who Am I" course will help me rediscover my mission, and I need to hurry. Kryon is here to raise the vibration of the planet and the last two times he did that he had to terminate humanity. There was a plan to get rid of us all in the year 2000 but at the last moment we humans earned the right to stay and control our destiny well into this century.

The course is held in an "NRI Complex." Perhaps because there are a billion Indians they like to put themselves into categories. Most will identify themselves as being from a certain state and associated culture such as Punjabi or Keralan or Bengali. But, of course, occupation and caste also divide groups, and Non Resident Indians are now a caste of their own. Their Complex is a set of massive towers of flats that have been bought with American dollars by Indians living offshore or Indians who spend a lot of time overseas. It looks like a high-rise space station. Skyscrapers loom around a courtyard dominated by a tall obelisk like the pillar in *2001: A Space Odyssey*. Behind the pod bay doors is a self-sufficient suburb of luxury, with apartment towers, a swimming pool, restaurant and kindergarten. It's a bizarre bubble of cleanliness and uniformity. Foyers are decorated with Greek columns and Roman busts and porthole windows.

On the top floor of one building I am welcomed by the course assistant, whose name is J, and an incredibly fit and farty Doberman called Sweetie. The course chamber is a private home but its walls are bare bar a poster of a fat white child puckering up with the words "kiss me quick" printed above her. Before we start the course I promise I won't reveal the names or the journeys of my fellow inner space travelers. What follows is a starship log of my own personal voyage.

We start the trip by staring into a mirror for twenty minutes for inner secrets. All I see are puffy eyes, tiredness and the need for makeup. J sees sorrow, an issue about money and rebelliousness in my face. Maybe my mirror is faulty, maybe he's right, but then again, maybe he's guessing. After all the ego-reducing of Vipassana and the Buddhist course I'm finding it hard to concentrate on myself so intensely. I'm worried self-analysis will lead to spiritual paralysis. In the hours that follow, the only thing we have to think about more than ourselves is our parents. I begin to slump, drowsy in the moist air that's rank with Sweetie's breath. The thick atmosphere is making my limbs wet and heavy, I feel I'm breathing water and my mind is soggy. Luckily we are allowed to disobey Kryon by turning on the fan (he says appliances have magnetic fields that disturb our magnetic makeup). I stand under it, splash myself with water and try and get back to the mission of finding my mission.

At eleven, S walks in wearing her pajamas, a creased bed face and sleepy eyes. She and her partner, R, are the humans Kryon chooses to communicate with when he wants to talk to India. I don't know how the alien gets a word in. A tiny, wide-eyed attractive woman in her late thirties, S starts talking and doesn't stop. I brace myself against the wall, shrinking from a ballistic spray of stories about her life, her son's life and Sweetie the dog's life. The tales are fired at machine-gun rapidity in scratchy screechy Hinglish and every sentence ends with an exclamation and a penetrating stare. All I catch is: "there are three things in the world: sex, money and power, my dear" and "all enlightenment is an accident, isn't it?" and "Sweetie is an important guide."

That perks me up. One of the course objectives is to put us in contact with the guides Kryon promises will help our mission. Previous participants have sworn that the smelly Sweetie is their spiritual savior. When S finally shuts up, we try to make contact with our guides by imagining we are standing on the edge of a cliff with a big black cloud in front of us. With our eyes closed and arms outstretched we ask our guides to come out from "beyond the veil." S says when our hands start tingling that means our guide is holding them. My hands tingle. For some reason I think of Mira Sorvino from *Romy and Michelle's High School Reunion*. S sees Mahatma Gandhi, and one girl feels the tender touch of Sweetie's paw.

The actress and the dog are supposed to help us escape our past karma, astrological influences and the Kryon implants that stop us from understanding the true nature of time, space and our mission on earth. I'm intellectually attracted to the whole alien thing, I'm happy to accept that God is a universal force, but it seems a bit egocentric to believe I am one of the few chosen to know my mission. Why me? Perhaps it's a mistake and I'll sabotage the grand plan. Maybe I'm Kryon's Zachary Smith from *Lost in Space*.

After a break, we do another exercise that's the antithesis of my previous Buddhist and Hindu training. Instead of imagining death we engage in a rough rebirthing. Breathing our way back into the womb via humming and rapid hyperventilating, we imagine ourselves as fetuses and attempt to relive the pain of birth. We then watch ourselves grow and try to remember our childhood, stopping to share our first sexual abuse. The book *Bitter Chocolate* by Pinki Virani estimates that at least twenty percent of Indian children are abused within their extended families, so our teachers seem disbelieving and disappointed when none of us cough up or break down. Tissues are placed before us and we're encouraged to cry at any childhood pain. I feel a big pressure to perform but unfortunately I've no repressed tears to shed. I was a happy child and I'm a calm adult—my expressive past is making me look like a failure in the New Age present.

I also fail when we are told to remember past lives. Kryon receivers S and R recognize each other from hundreds of past incarnations, including one as prisoner and guard in a Nazi death camp. S's teenage son remembers losing his legs in the 1971 Indian-Pakistan war, and another girl recalls being a famous singer. I crumble with performance anxiety and invent a story. I tell the group I'm seeing myself in a past life as a man in a dinner suit at a roaring twenties party on New Year's Eve in New York City. It always amuses me that people see themselves somewhere interesting and never as a slave, a prostitute, a builder or a housewife—I make my invention the conductor of an orchestra.

The course finishes with some *chakra* cleaning, pop psychology and self-indulgent crap. I think back to the British Buddhist nun Tenzin Palmo's concern that psychotherapy can become overfocused on empty dilemmas, and I have to smile. I feel empty, trained for a mission I don't believe in. When Kryon does raise the cosmic vibrations of the planet, I'm not sure I'll be able to vibrate in time.

Ground Control to Kryon. Get me out of this New Age nightmare. I'm going back to my guru girlfriend. Aarzoo may not know the secrets of the universe but she helps me enjoy India to the hilt.

We have only six months left here before Jonathan's contract expires and I want to enjoy it all I can. Of course I'm still interested in higher truths but I'd like to wait until the end of summer before I attempt to access them again.

15 | Face-to-Face with God

A man with a mullet and three thumbs, wearing a white Simon Le Bon suit and a pink pastel sweater around his shoulders, is jumping over vicious crocodiles to rescue a girl. She has big eyes, a big nose and huge tits, and has fainted up a tree. He carries her to his boat but the motor is dead, so he puts the rope between his teeth and swims—dragging her across the ocean to a hospital. Moments before, she'd won an international bike race and he'd donned Rambo gear, multiplied into one hundred clones and danced with a small army of himself on the beach. Later, in a palace, he'll pelvic-thrust while wearing a slashed tank top, leather pants, a fringed suede jacket and a bandanna. Her mother will be killed by a car, her father will sing a song to a can of Coca-Cola and she will fall in love with the man with three thumbs in front of a wind machine, while jumping from planet to planet in a Jackson Five–inspired intergalactic song. After four hours, eight songs, seven dances, one interval and a couple of million dollars, they'll all live happily ever after.

I walk out of the movie *Yaardein* (Memories) on a high. In India, going to the movies is a spiritual act, as transforming as going to a temple and just as entertaining. The monsoon is heavy; moving is like swimming and breathing like sucking on bubbles; every afternoon the rain buckets down drowning the city in mud and mayhem. It's safer inside the local modern multiplex watching high-pitched, high-volume Hindi films alongside chatting women, screaming babies, girls talking on mobile phones and boys imitating fight scenes in the aisles.

India's melodramatic "masala movies" are a spicy recipe of action, violence, music, dance, slapstick humor, moralizing and, most of all, romance. There must be a love story, a death, a birth, a marriage, a battle between good and evil and eight song-and-dance routines before good will triumph and tradition be upheld. Heroes with fluffy hair, ball-crushing jeans and rubber hips get the girl, the chaste virginal light-skinned chick obeys her elders and the cute niece or nephew will be rescued from danger. The cigarette-smoking vamp will die of a terrible disease, the bad man with the big mustache will be shot and his sidekicks or a trio of corrupt cops will be locked up. The rubber-faced funny guy and simpering servants will smile happily and the good, religiously righteous mother may die and come back as a ghost in a shimmering chiffon sari.

I've always loved a song-and-dance flick. Indians are great groovers specializing in pelvic thrusts, head wobbles, shoulder shimmies, knee slides, moonwalks, jumps, turns, spins and the Punjabi arm-flicking lightbulb dance. In happy songs, entire street mobs move as one. In love songs, doe-eyed men and dreamy-eyed girls with trembling lips will run toward each other so that he can play with her *dupatta* in front of spectacular scenery. This year's popular backgrounds are the Swiss snowfields, New Zealand waterfalls, Thai beaches and Australia's Parliament House. I don't get most of the lyrics but Aarzoo translates some lines as she passes popcorn.

"These Romeos are ruinous. No! We're playful paramours."

"Open the doors of your heart and let the thief in. In bondage let us fly together like kite and string."

"The whole world admires my beauty, I could bewitch the world."

"I've pined for all these years, I've sought you in my prayers to God. No one has longed as much as me. You have taught my heart to beat, my love."

"You have plundered my soul, tell me and I will even leave this world for you."

It's as if Indians put all their repressed longing and love into their movies. As someone who hasn't had much romance in my long-distance marriage, I understand the need. I also enjoy the innocence. When I watch an Indian movie I am thirteen again, dreaming that one day a handsome prince will run to me over fields of flowers and, while my long hair flies back in the wind, he will get down on one knee and profess undying love until the end of the world. The soppy lyrics and high passion are all rather adolescent, full of frottage and foreplay. A man and woman may get so close a piece of paper wouldn't fit between them, but they shall never kiss, let alone have sex. Indians would be too offended and actresses would lose their reputations. The women lose their careers soon enough—after they marry, most find it hard to get roles because Indian men don't want to see them on screen lest they lust after another man's wife.

With its crocodiles, interplanetary love and Rambo cloning, today's flick, *Yaardein*, is a sign of how mainstream Hindi movies are changing while still staying the same. It's targeted at NRIs in America, Britain, the Gulf and Australia who provide sixty-five percent of a film's income in today's market. Indian sensibilities remain strong; *Yaardein*'s heroine may sing sexily in sheets but she and her sisters are happy to leave London for India to have arranged marriages. The Western influence is confined to the prominent Coca-Cola product placement, the girls' skinnier bodies, cheerleader outfits and glittered baseball caps and the boys' camp eighties Wham look. Plus the occasional English phrase:

"Hey, babe, I'm a superman," "Geez, man, how you doing, man, cool, man" and "I'm in love" are splattered among the dialogue.

For me, though, the best thing about *Yaardein* is its star. The heart-thump hunk of the moment, Hrithik Roshan, is a freak. He has green eyes, an angular face, a chunky torso, skinny legs, rubber hips, a brilliant moonwalk and an extra thumb on his right hand. He won't get the digit cut off, as he believes it brings him luck. His father, Rakesh, is a famous director who insists all his movies have titles starting with the letter "K."

One night I meet some Westerners who share my love of Hindi films. Ruth is a petite, laid-back Australian married to a local (Indre), and Jeni is a tall, jumpy redhead from America volunteering on Women's Poverty Programs. They don't live the life of diplomats so I invite them to enjoy the Biosphere for all it's worth. They turn up the air-conditioning, raid my CDs, eat pasta and down two bottles of wine. Then Ruth drops a bombshell.

"You know, Indre and I are good friends of Preity Zinta's."

"Shutttttttup," I scream.

Preity is the Julia Roberts of India, a huge star. I yell again when Ruth tells me she once traveled to Switzerland with Preity on a shoot and got a ten-second part in *Chorie Chorie Chupke Chupke* (Quietly, Stealthily). It's a great film. Preity plays a rough prostitute with a heart of gold who has a child for a rich woman who'd lost the ability to conceive when she fell down trying to catch a cricket ball. It was a gutsy role for Preity to do, despite the fact that in the prostitute scenes she wears a taffeta gown to her knees.

"When she's next in town I'll give you a call, we'll go out," Ruth teases.

"Shuuuuuuuttup, what are you saying?" Jeni and I yell in unison.

Two weeks later, Ruth, Jeni and I sit in the suite of a five-star hotel watching Preity do interviews with starstruck journalists asking questions like "Oh God, you're so cool, and so great. It must have been so amazing to work with Aamir, isn't it?"

Preity puffs on a cigarette, asks them not to print that she smokes and giggles gorgeously. She is twenty-six and more beautiful in real life than on film, with dimples, pouting lips, flawless skin and a hot bod. Jeni is dumbstruck and I try and chat while looking casual. Then Aamir Khan walks in. Aamir is hot. Short, stocky, with a little goatee and big brown bedroom eyes, he produced and stars in this year's huge hit, *Lagaan*. I gulp, more starstruck than when I met Salman Rushdie, Courtney Love, Mike Myers and Shirley Manson. Aamir asks me if I've seen *Lagaan*; I stammer no, and Jeni jumps up and jumps in.

"Hi, yeah, I have and I liked it, even though I'm American, it was about boring cricket, it was three and a half hours long and it was in that bizarre Hindi Rajasthani dialect, so I couldn't understand a word."

He looks at her, cocks an eyebrow and drawls, "Thanks. I think."

Aamir walks out. Jeni crumbles to the sofa and screams, "Shiiiiiiiiit, I can't believe I said that."

Nonetheless we are invited to a special preview of Preity and Aamir's new film *Dil Chahta Hai* (What the Heart Wants). We bolt through a gaggle of kids wanting autographs and somehow in the chaos I end up in a tinted black Mercedes with Preity and Aamir. I sit stunned in the front seat while they chat about their upcoming tour of the United States in the back. They plan the movie hits they will mime and dance to get all those thousands of NRIs screaming in the aisles. I make a suggestion for the opening act.

"Preity, why don't you come down from the ceiling on a mirror ball like Madonna on her last tour?"

The Indian superstars stare at me blankly. I turn back to the front, grimace and shut the hell up until we pull up at the theater.

We walk down the red carpet through an honor guard of starstruck soldiers who drop their mouths and weapons and wonder who the hell I am. Beyond the machine guns and metal detectors, a party is in full swing. It's an all-star cast. I recognize two of India's most internationally famous actresses, Shabana Azmi and Nandita Das (from *Fire* and *Earth*), Jeni spots fashion designer

Ritu Beri and Ruth points out other directors, producers, hunks and starlets from movies and TV. We wait for an hour until Home Minister L. K. Advani suspends parliament to attend. The lights dim and a new kind of Indian mainstream movie is born.

Written and directed by twenty-seven-year-old Farhan Akhtar, *Dil Chahta Hai* is about the year between college and marriage—the one brief moment most middle-class Indians have to be free. Three male friends spend the time hanging out, going to Goa and falling in love—one with an older divorced alcoholic, one with lots of girls, and Aamir's character with Preity's character, who is already betrothed. Of course the older woman dies, the flirt falls in love with an arranged match, Preity's character gets permission to marry Aamir's character and no one even kisses. But otherwise it's radical. The movie uses real sound (not badly dubbed, overly dramatic studio sound), they dance to a trance beat in leather and silver pants and take the postmodern piss out of Indian film culture with a song featuring a woman's sari being blown tight against her body while she dances on a hill. (The blowing sari is ubiquitous in Indian cinema—it clings in a sensual way signifying passion and abandon, but its status as the traditional dress also signifies goodness and tradition. The character's honor is preserved even though you can see the outline of her bosoms and hips.) *Dil Chahta Hai* is cheeky and irreverent but not too rude. The best jokes are against Westerners—an Australian drunken tramp and a Swiss slutty thief provide slapstick while subtly showing that India is the best country and foreigners are loose and immoral. For the first time I find myself laughing with a Hindi flick and not at it. Until the action moves to Sydney. Then I nearly cry with longing as Preity and Aamir dance around the trees in Hyde Park, flirt on the Luna Park roller coaster, run to catch a train at Homebush and cry in my favorite place in the world, Waverley Cemetery.

The night ends with Jeni, Ruth and I joining the Bollywood Brat Pack at Shabana Azmi and Javed Akhtar's bungalow. We sit watching Preity entertain with stories of fame, including one about a mob of NRIs knocking Angelina Jolie aside while pushing to get Preity's autograph at JFK airport.

When Preity drops me home, I walk over to Lakan and whisper, "Preity Zinta is in that car." He nearly faints.

When I get up at eleven the next day, Lakan has told Rachel and she has told everyone in the compound. I have breakfast to the sound of Rachel on the phone telling everyone she knows about my adventure. To me it sounds like: "Tamil, Tamil, Tamil, Tamil, madam, Tamil Tamil, Preity Zinta, Aamir Khan, Shabana Azmi, ha ha, ha, ha."

When I call Aarzoo and Billie they scream for an hour.

"Shuuuuuuuuttup, what are you saying?"

Dil Chahta Hai becomes the soundtrack of summer played at every party. Jeni and I now have status in Delhi and we don't want to lose it by dancing badly, so we decide to learn some Bollywood moves. Along with Rebecca, a Melbourne traveler staying with diplomat friends who live nearby, we head off to the neighborhood teacher. We watch a class of ten-year-olds mix some hardcore dance styles—wriggling their hips and making some sensual eye movements. Then it's our turn. The teacher, Reshna, is in her mid-twenties, with gorgeous big eyes that betray she is dubious about our desire to dance. Still, she shrugs, leads us in a bow to Shiva and shows us some moves. Within half an hour we are wet with sweat and tears of laughter and our backs are aching. The dancing is like liturgical gone luscious, involving acting out every word sung. We point to our eyes and flick our hips as we sing "look at our pretty eyes." We shake our heads and wag our fingers as we say "don't you tease me." We open and close our imaginary *dupattas*, walk with water jugs and learn to head-jerk, hip-roll and shoulder-shimmy. Rebecca is fantastic, especially at the shoulder moves, Jeni likes the jumps, while my favorite action involves slapping my hands together and twisting them. (Reshna says this means "I will say bad words at you.")

Driving back from Old Delhi the next day, Rebecca and I look up from our chat to see a car full of lads staring at us. I try out the hand twist. The lads scream, shout and fall about laughing hysterically.

Later, I ask Aarzoo what I did wrong and show her the action. She screams.

"Sarrrrrrah, you stuuuuuupid, you told them you were a eunuch."

We give up on lessons, not because of the eunuch mistake, but because we just can't manage the coy, flirtatious, bug-eyed innocence that Indian girls pull off while moving their bodies like bawdy babes from a bordello.

But I'm not dismissing the celluloid scene yet. There's one more actor I want to meet. More than an actor, he is India's hero, a man worshiped as a god, a man with three temples dedicated to him, a man who stopped the nation when he lay at death's door, a man who inspired a character in *The Satanic Verses* and stands waxed in Madame Tussaud's. The man the Indians call the "Big B."

Amitabh Bachchan.

The Big B was the angry young man of the seventies who went on to star in more than one hundred films, including the classic Western *Sholay* that ran for six years in Bombay. Then he was lanky and big-lipped and wore tight white denim bell-bottoms. Now, at sixty, his beard may be silver but his hair is jet-black, thick and big. I'll be lynched if I call it a wig, so I won't. With a deep resonant voice, a commanding presence and a not bad shoulder shimmy, Amitabh Bachchan is worshiped as the classiest Indian in the world. Jonathan is finally home from his latest travels and I convince him to do an interview with the superstar who once refused to talk to the media for seventeen years after a bad review. For Mr. Bachchan is talking now. The megastar owes millions in taxes and has had to take a day job for Rupert Murdoch. The Big B is the host of the Indian version of *Who Wants to Be a Millionaire*, or *Kown Banega Crorepati*. With an audience of up to twenty-eight million, *KBC* is the most popular show on television (barring the soap with a title that translates as "Mothers-in-law were daughters-in-law too one day").

• • •

Jonathan and I fly to Mumbai together and drive straight to nearby Bollywood, the dream factory of India. The approach to Film City is hardly a boulevard of glamour. The road is awash with mud and mashed rubbish, potholes and sodden slums. Elephants and pigs, cows and crows, rats and cats and kids forage the filth, and mosquitoes rise with the rich smell of rotting garbage. Slick sarongs cling to scrawny legs and women lift up their saris to walk through the black oily mud. Beyond the iron gates of the studio a fiberglass temple rots in the lantana. Up on the hill stands a building I've seen many times before—the ubiquitous mock-Tudor mansion used in all the main movies.

The director and producers of *KBC* bustle around in matching blue T-shirts herding the starstruck contestants into makeup and controlling the crowd bussed in from Mumbai. They tell us that the Big B is the most professional and punctual man in the business but then admit he will be late today. The three hundred–strong audience will wait, so will the contestants, the two hundred and thirty crew and Jonathan.

I hate to wait so I head to a studio down the hill where a film shoot is in progress. The director, Harry Baweja, is woken from a nap in his car and is happy to let me watch. Harry looks like Fred Flintstone; rumpled, square-headed, big-grinned and relaxed, despite the fact that his film has no name, no script, no storyboard and no cast, barring the hero, Ajay. Harry screams "break over," pounds a *chai* and gives me the pitch in a bizarre Indian-American twang.

"It's in Rajasthan, roooight? Where women are in purdah, got it? No school cos of purdah, so in this small town, the mother wants some education for daughter, goart it? So a tutor teaches from behind a screen and they fall in love. She becomes a rebel, the dad finds out and forces an organized marriage with another man and the hero teacher gets arrested and roughed up. That's the scene what we're doing now."

Ajay's face is caked in orange makeup and his thin hairy chest pokes through a ripped white pirate shirt as ropes are stretched out from his arms. Harry screams "actiooon" and six actors dressed as cops begin to beat the star with floppy foam *lathi*s, thin wooden bats similar to billy clubs. Over and over and over again. Shots are taken from every conceivable angle while Ajay grimaces, flinches and slowly twists to look resolutely, righteously and revengefully at the tracking camera. Like most Indian industries, it's labor intensive. Four men lift the cameras, five push the shooter chair and three shoot. Two makeup artists apply pancake and redraw police mustaches, ten men move heavy smoking lights, eight sit up in the ceiling watching and four turn on the portable air-conditioners as soon as Harry says "cut" and off when he says "ready." There's one man who turns on the smoke machine, two who flap the steam across the set and about twenty who make *chai*. The only woman on the set takes notes for continuity. The black background screen is scratched with "I love Azma," the lights are antique and an old-fashioned electronic box of sizzling sockets looks frayed and flammable. I retreat nervously outside, where I'm approached by a slimy man with bad acne scars.

"Hello, madam, you are actress, yaar?"

"No."

"Yaar, but you are good. Do you want to come on a fifteen-day cruise to Singapore and Saudi, we will film, you can be extra. You can wear bikini. Yaar?"

Somehow I refuse this chance for a big break and walk back to the safety of the *KBC* studio to wait for the Big B.

Two hours later we are invited to the star's dressing room—a pinewood Swiss chalet that's a shrine to himself. Above the massive bed and on every wall are life-sized posters of Amitabh shooting, swaggering and sexing it up. I'm searching for his less glamorous new Coke and car ads when the real thing swivels around in his makeup chair. He stands, dismisses his butler, gives Jonathan a firm handshake and nods gruffly at me.

I am face-to-face with the screen God of India.

God is chewing gum, he is incredibly tall with a potbelly and elegantly dressed in a white *kurta*, the popular loose cotton suit with a long shirt and baggy pants. He has slightly googly eyes, wrinkles, a large nose and a deep voice that's even more resonant and rich than it sounds on television. God is guarded, reserved and looks serious, fastidious, cool and disinterested. Yet he can act. When we turn on the camera he plays down his fame and turns up his humility. When Jonathan asks the secret of his success he says, "You'd better ask the person upstairs that. Things have just happened to me. I didn't try too hard, things just flowed. I find it very embarrassing to be seen as a god, sometimes shocking. In India people have a more emotional attachment to their heroes, a unique way of showing affection."

The Big B tells us he likes meeting the common people but when he walks onto the set he seems utterly uncomfortable. Until filming begins. Then he is transformed, and turns on the charm; smiling, laughing and using his rich rumbling voice, he encourages the starstruck contestants with his stage presence—"sure?" "confident?" and "okay, computer-*ji*, lock it in."

The audience titters and the contestants are so overawed that the director has to reshoot scenes because one of them freezes completely. Another gives Bachchan a poem, a third (a bloke) smiles when he loses and says, "Hug me and I won't care."

My favorite contestant is a Sikh in a pink taffeta turban; he stutters, "Cccccan I ttttell you a secret?"

"Yees," says Amitabh.

"I'm madly in love with you."

Amitabh grins modestly. They leave it in the show. At the end, a woman walking out in tears turns to me and sniffs, "A demigod stepping down from a plane to relate to us."

There's only one man Indians are more likely to worship than the Big B. But this bloke admits he is indeed God in human form. His name is Sai Baba.

At the Amma ashram I'd met a middle-aged Australian from the Gold Coast called Krishini and her tall, eccentric English girlfriend Shivani Ma. Shivani Ma spun me a fantastic tale about finding the Divine Master that began when she was in her twenties and her mother was dying.

"A huge light filled the room, it started speaking through me to my mother. I didn't understand most of what I was saying, lots of things about an orange robe came out, Mum started filling with light and I was in a state of bliss. Two years later I was in my art gallery and a guy turned up, he showed me a photo of Sai Baba and I yelled, 'That's him, that's God!' I understood all the orange robe stuff. I said I have to go to him."

In 1996 God called up Shivani Ma in England by dialing in on her karmic plane.

"I lost my job, my flat, he sent a man who'd abused me in my childhood back into my life. Then Sai Baba came to me in a meditation and called me to India."

Shivani Ma told me when she first saw the form of Sathya Sai Baba he became a ball of light and merged into a rainbow. She bought an ashram flat with her inheritance and still lives there. Shivani Ma and Krishini made me promise that one day I would come and see Sai Baba, and now the opportunity arises.

Jonathan has to fly from Mumbai to Bangalore to film an Internet technology story, and since God's ashram is only a quick trip from Bangalore I decide to hitch a lift and see what all the fuss is about.

Sai Baba says he is a *purna avatar*—a manifestation of God in human form and a coming predicted in the Bhagavad Gita, a Muslim Hadith and the Bible. He claims to be a modern Christ, Krishna and Buddha in one, capable of manifesting in many places and bodies at once and of bending time. Devotees believe they've seen him resurrect the dead, take the moon from the sky, cure AIDS, stop tornadoes, hold back floods, regurgitate *lingams*, materialize watches and pour *vibhooti* (sacred ash) from his hand.

But God is here to do more than tricks. Sai Baba says he's come to save the world and he will not fail.

I love Bangalore instantly. It sits on the top of a plateau and must be at least ten degrees cooler than Mumbai. Its air is also clearer, with a touch of bright Sydney light. The Internet technology capital of India has drum and bass clubs, shiny new computer centers, great south Indian food and even a sushi bar. Jonathan and I indulge in some raw fish and copious amounts of alcohol before getting to bed rather late.

In the morning I suffer by the pool while Jonathan does some interviews, and after lunch we catch a taxi ride to Sai Baba's ashram at Whitefield, an hour up the road from the city. While Jonathan has been dealing with the facts and reality of modern India, I have been indulging in the boundaries of belief and the unbelievable; he's keen to catch a glimpse of my world. The adventure begins below a giant billboard of a freaky dude with an Afro and a rainbow falling from his hand. We are in Sai Baba World. There's Sai Travels, Sai Cyberspace, Sai restaurants, Sai music shops and a Sai Market which sells Sai books, Sai CDs, Sai tapes and photos. There are photos of Sai Baba on Perspex pyramids, lockets, bracelets, pens, rings, watches, clocks, postcards and prints. Salesmen and beggars hail us with "Sai Ram," the swami mantra, and then hit us for cash.

The ashram is a sanctuary from the dirty, dusty town, but it's stark and sterile compared to the chaos of Amma's World. With buildings painted pink for girls and blue for boys, it's ringed with signs forbidding handbags, pagers, water bottles and mobile phones. Devotees are allowed to carry only fans, cushions and specially approved Sai Baba chairs. Most pilgrims wear Indian dress teamed with a Western scarf tied around their necks in a Boy Scout knot (swami likes group consciousness, so different colored scarves signify groups by nationality or spiritual association). I feel naked without a neckerchief and begin to have flashbacks to the childhood nightmare of not wearing knickers to school. What's more, Jonathan is not up on ashram etiquette and walks in the girls' gate. He is pulled up and lectured; he laughs. I feel upset, awkward and suddenly rather nauseous.

"Good," snaps an American girl in the canteen as she hands me a well-needed water. "That's the swami getting rid of your bad karma, already. This is a hothouse for clearing bad karma—it speeds up the process. Sai Baba says when you are dripping from every orifice thank him."

Jonathan laughs loudly again and looks surprised when I don't giggle. I've become used to such talk.

Thankfully I don't drip and I'm well enough to queue on the women's side for one of Sai Baba's daily appearances. Jonathan disappears into the crowd of men and I see the swami's first miracle—hundreds of Indians are waiting in ordered queues in total silence. The only people who talk are dressed primly in white with special blue scarves and big gold badges imprinted with the symbols of the major faiths (Islam's moon, the Zoroastrian fire, the Hindu om, the wheel of the Buddhist dharma, the Christian cross and the Jewish star). These are the ashram prefects—scouts in saris who keep strict order. They let the person at the front of each line pull a number denoting the position in the hall for that queue. My group is about the tenth to move. I stand up and nearly get knocked over in a silent stampede to the metal detector. We whip past the fashion police and trot toward the floor. Everyone wants to be close to the stage that Sai Baba sits upon for his afternoon *darshan*.

On the platform Sai's red velvet chair is sprayed with disinfectant, towels are placed on its arms and a statue of Ganesh is garlanded with flowers. The *bhajan*s begin softly and the band plays Muzak versions of holy Hindi hymns. No one in the crowd utters a word. Right on schedule a door swings open like magic and God steps onto the stage. He doesn't look holy—he seems small, rickety and has a bit of a stoop. But his hair is cosmic. It's a blue-black Afro—Jimi Hendrix meets the Jackson Five. Sai Baba's eyebrows slant strangely, his double chin quivers and his nose is reminiscent of Michael Jackson's pre-surgery (and aged sixty years). His hands are strangely compelling. Delicate, long and almost ash-blue, they flit below the orange robe like butterflies, opening to hold the palms up, pointing and twisting, keeping time with the music and writing on the wind. He sits on his throne for twenty-five minutes, then shuffles off. The crowd stays—stunned, crying, ecstatic, mesmerized and meditating. I quietly head for the exit.

Jonathan runs toward me yelling, "Christ, what a weirdo. I don't reckon he's going to make it much longer, he looks a bit sick, yeah?"

Except for sensing the hostile glances at my husband, I don't get a transmission of anything from Sai Baba or his ashram. So in the morning I get up early and return alone for the *darshan* where the swami actually moves among his disciples. At six, the queue is already long. The devotees are immaculately groomed and dressed in their very best chiffon saris and white *kurta*s. All want to attract God's attention and earn an interview after the *darshan*, but thousands will be disappointed. Again the lineup, the queue lottery (apparently controlled by him) and the hushed hurry to flank the red carpet he will walk upon. I get close; I must have good karma. Then God performs another miracle. Sai Baba is the first Indian I've ever seen arrive early. He shuffles along the carpet as the crowd ripples and does a wave of *namaste* moves, touching their hands together in the prayer position.

The living God is like a moon pulling the tide—wherever he walks the crowd reaches to touch his feet, plead for an interview and whisper wants. His hands have more color this morning and do more than write in the air. Swami receives hundreds of letters, pats people on the head, chats to some, points to the lucky ones earning an interview and motions for others to come and kiss his feet. At one stage he jerks his arm, circles his hand and drips a stream of sacred ash into an ecstatic devotee's outstretched hands. Sai Baba then stretches his hands upward as if to say "nothing up my sleeves" and moves on. He spends most of the time on the male side, chooses mostly blokes for interviews and then slowly shuffles out.

His divinity has not been revealed to me, but Sai Baba has been charged with revealing much more to other Westerners. Foreign male devotees have accused him of massaging their genitals, demanding a head job and kissing them on their lips. But in India, Sai Baba seems beyond reproach. He has twenty-five million followers, including chief justices, an army chief of staff, ex–prime ministers, senior politicians and cricketers Sunil Gavaskar and Sachin Tendulkar. A court has already ruled his gold comes from

God and it seems there aren't any Indian investigations into the sexual allegations. Most followers even believe these matters are all part of God's plan. Shivani Ma laughed when I raised the subject with her at Amma's ashram.

"He is just a mirror, showing us the number-one issue in the world at the moment is abuse—sexual, physical and mental. He paid those making the allegations to say it."

Yet if she was here, Shivani Ma would be disappointed in me—I see no ball of light, no rainbow and no dancing Ganesh. She had told me that if I didn't see God in human form, then she'd pray for me to be around for his next earthly incarnation. Sai Baba has said he will die in 2020. Eight years later he's promised to be reborn as Prema (love) in Gunaparthy, Karnataka, but says he won't have anything to do with this ashram. I'm glad. Whitefield feels too sterile and ordered; I dislike its uniforms, its patter of passwords, its fastidiousness and the cold, humorless sanctimoniousness of his devotees.

I sit in a corner and read Sai Baba's message. He says all religions should be honored as pathways to God, that meditation is a way to the divine, that community work is good and that we should all try to be free from sin. As I prepare to leave, I tell a Swedish devotee that I like Sai Baba's words but I'm going without seeing his divinity. She tells me it's not too late, that the great one comes to those who ask. She holds my hands and makes me repeat after her.

"Oh swami-*ji*."

"*Oh swami*-ji."

"Please come to me tonight in my dreams."

"*Please come to me tonight in my dreams.*"

"Let me see you."

"*Let me see you.*"

"Go now, sister, see him."

I return to the hotel in Bangalore. In the middle of the night I wake up from a dream in a warm sweat with a racing heart.

Coming to me across the waters is an Australian god of TV. Max from a show called *Sea Change* in a wet suit.

16 | Hail Mary and Good-bye God

Back in Delhi it seems a few of the Australian Broadcasting Company staff are upset with me. Abraham hardly talks on the way home from the airport, Rachel doesn't make my favorite juice and Peter seems unimpressed by my Sai Baba stories. I ask Neeraj to find out what's up with the troops. He reports back with a click of his heels and a salute.

"The Christians are cranky, skipper. You keep going to Hindu saints and Parsi people and Buddhist retreats but you're ignoring your own faith."

The Christians have a point. I've avoided their God like the plague because I've always been hypercritical of my own culture's dominant belief system. We always judge those things closest to us the most harshly, and I'm no different. As a child I appreciated the way Jesus loved everyone but as I grew up I became increasingly appalled by the behavior of the major Christian institutions. Their hypocrisy and sexism, their vast accumulation of wealth and the egocentrism, anthropocentrism and superiority complex contained within their teachings upset me most. I couldn't cope with the insistence that those who didn't turn to Jesus would rot in hell; I didn't like the belief that humans were given the earth to do with what we liked; and I was sickened by the notion of missionaries spreading the word. I couldn't understand why a religion so suited to ancient times in the desert was relevant today and I perceived Christianity was presently dying a slow, painful death. But in India I've already begun to see the religion differently. For it gives people with so little so much. Rachel, Peter, Mary and Abraham adore their faith and their weekly trips to church. I can see the comfort and happiness the love of Jesus stirs in their hearts, and admire their ability to love the teachings without shooting the messenger. Christianity survives here and this two percent of the Indian population proudly wears its religion on its collective sleeve. Our office manager Peter is named after a saint, Rachel wears a cross around her neck, Abraham has a giant Jesus poster on his wall and Mary mutters prayers as she cleans. They all meet up at church every Sunday and we give them Easter and Christmas (as well as Hindu) holidays.

I confess my sin to them and ask for forgiveness and suggestions of where I should go to see Christian India. They smile sweetly and answer as one.

"To Our Lady of Velangani."

Christianity first came to India in C.E. 52 when Saint Thomas the Apostle arrived in Kerala. Its beginnings were peaceful—while the Romans were feeding Christians to the lions, Keralan converts were building churches. The faith spread farther via the Portuguese who arrived in Goa in the fifteenth century. Here the church was not so compassionate—some of the ancestors of modern-day Indian Catholics were forced to adopt the faith or risk being burned to death during the days of the Inquisition. Others eagerly embraced the Christian concept of equality, its social projects for the poor and its quality education. Aarzoo and many of her friends even went to a Catholic school and loved the "sweetie nuns," who never tried to convert them. I've already seen God's army on display in Kerala. I remember a Godzilla-sized Jesus weeping down from a billboard, glass tubes containing life-sized Saint Anthony mannequins, tiny Mary dolls in the nooks and crannies of marketplaces and the scene from the stable on many a dashboard. I've never heard of Velangani. It's not in the travel books but India's Christians see it as the Rome of their country.

Jonathan is back in Kabul—some Australian and German aid workers have been accused of trying to convert Afghans to Christianity and he is covering their Taliban-run trial. My former Sydney flatmate Emma and her husband, Matt, have just arrived in Delhi and I convince them to travel with me to Velangani on the southeast coast of India in the state of Tamil Nadu. Emma and I make as odd a couple as Aarzoo and Billie. She is a midwife and everything I am not—calm, composed, practical, beautiful and content. Matt is an ER doctor—tall, intelligent and guarded. Emma is Catholic, Matt an atheist, while Rebecca, my dancing friend, just loves Christian kitsch—she's also in for the trip. Our timing is perfect; on September 5 it will be the Virgin Mary's birthday and the anniversary of one of her visits to earth.

We set up a mobile home on a second-class sleeper for a forty-hour journey south to Chennai. It has dirty blue bunk beds, cream paisley curtains and a table for our Tupperware which Rachel has filled with goodies. As we eat and play cards we are constantly interrupted by a parade of men carrying trays filled with deep-fried goodies. They scream: "Miloooooooo, chhaaaaaiiieee, carfeeeeeeee, *parattttthha*, somossaaaaa, vegeeeeeetable cuttttttttlllllllllet, omeeeeeelllllllettte. You like, yes?"

The word gets out that a very tall man with three wives is in the carriage and a queue forms to file past us. I feel like I'm giving *dar-*

shan but the passengers seem particularly entranced with Rebecca's red hair, pale skin and green eyes. There's no room to perform our Indian dancing, so Rebecca and I sing a medley of ABBA songs to keep the crowd entertained. Matt and Emma are humiliated but the fellow passengers smile and hum along nicely. On the first night we rock to sleep to a soundtrack of snores, farts and burps. But we wake in fright in the early hours when the carriage fills with a bloodcurdling cry.

"Ahhhhhhhhhhhhhh HHHHHheeeeeeeeeeeeeee!"

I sit bolt upright and bang my head on the ceiling; in the bunk opposite, Rebecca is rocking with laughter. Below me, a new passenger is screaming in his sleep. He's an elderly man wearing his hair back in a John McEnroe headband and it appears he's playing dream tennis and losing. He doesn't wake up when we hit him.

As the sun rises and the train trundles south, the dusty fields give way to long strong corn, which gives way to wet rice and finally electric green lantana with fat fleshy leaves. Tiled villas with slated peaks and thatched huts replace the concrete bunker homes of the north. The people beside the tracks become smaller, and darker. Men's pants are replaced by *lunghi*s, long checked sarongs or miniskirts that they constantly fold and refold. Some of the women do not wear the sari tops; their breasts hang like empty wine sacks and floppy babies drip from their hips. Buffalo become bigger, their horns bend in to form love hearts with bells tingling on their tips. The train fills with a southern smell—heavier and darker than the sweat of the north, it's a combination of jasmine, coconut, hair oil and damp skin.

At Chennai we hire an Ambassador taxi to drive to Velangani, about four hundred kilometers south. Its velour bench seat sinks in the middle, its springs are shot, its cabin is full of exhaust fumes and it has no air-conditioning. It's about one hundred °F. and ninety-nine percent humidity and we melt, sweat and swear along the goat track of a highway. The landscape is drier and flatter than the southwest coast of Kerala and life seems harder. Yet I realize how used to India I have become.

Matt and Emma sit staring out the window with their mouths

agape, much as I did nearly two years ago in the taxi to Rishikesh. They're aghast at the putrid-smelling monkeys beside the road, the bamboo huts, the psychedelic movie posters, the scarecrows keeping crows off partially built buildings, the tough female road workers shoveling bitumen, the matted hair of the street children and the towns with more temples than Chinese takeaways. They scream "fuck" and flinch every time the car swerves to narrowly avoid head-on collisions with trucks, cars and slow-moving tractors. They take photos of the chilies drying on the road and the people stacking hay. They attempt to plug their ears to the blast of the horns and endlessly politely repeat "no thank you" to the people who push and invade their space every time we stop and get out of the car. By the end of the first day they look limp and filthy, exhausted and like they could kill me.

On the second day the road is worse, the drive more dangerous and we all get splitting headaches. Yet we feel we are about to arrive somewhere special, for along the road shuffles an endless ragtag ribbon of bandy-legged men in orange robes and skinny women in fluorescent silk saris. All have heavy loads—babies on hips, bundles of belongings on heads, and occasionally a huge statue of the Virgin Mary rocks on a sea of staggering shoulders. They are pilgrims walking up to five hundred kilometers to join the Christian Kumbh Mela.

Velangani is a tiny village with a huge history. In 1560 a shepherd boy saw a lovely lady appear in the sky; she asked him for milk to quench the thirst of her baby Jesus and his pitcher kept filling forevermore. A small thatched chapel was built at the site of the miracle. At the end of the sixteenth century the Virgin Mary materialized in front of a lame boy, and he regained the use of his limbs. Another church was built. Then on September 8, 1869, a Portuguese ship sailing from Macao to Goa got caught in a massive storm in the Indian Ocean. The sailors prayed to the Virgin Mary to rescue them; she promptly appeared in the sky, calmed the storm and deposited their wrecked ship on the shores of Velangani. The sailors built a basilica and now every year at this very place their survival is celebrated along with Mary's birthday three days earlier. The site is renowned for its miracles—Our Lady of Health has cured the sick and the lame, the infertile and the insane here.

At first glance the festival looks like a fun fair in a dust bowl. Last week Peter insisted on ringing the local priest here and telling him that his memsahib would be coming and to please look after me. Peter, Rachel, Mary and Abraham are all from Chennai, and this is their favorite place on earth, so they are desperate that I enjoy it and am comfortable. When Peter told me he'd made the call I felt embarrassed, but now I'm unbelievably grateful, for the crowds are huge and the dirt is bumpy with the bodies of people sleeping out in the open. Rebecca and I set out to find Peter's priest, leaving Emma and Matt melting by the overheated Ambassador. Emma's stricken with shock and Matt stands beside her, his face set in a grimace; infuriated by the bedlam, he curses "Jesus Christ" as we abandon them. I turn and tell them not to worry and that we'll be alright, but I'm not sure they believe me.

Behind the Ferris wheels and roller coasters, Rebecca and I enter a market of Mary. Her sweet, sad face and sari-clad body appear on sunglasses, thongs, clocks, rings, necklaces, umbrellas, rubber balls and cassettes. There are posters and three-dimensional plastic bubble art of her floating above the sea and tiny little flashing dashboard altars featuring Jesus with a sheep. There are banners proclaiming JESUS IS KING OF THE EARTH, plastic flowers, inflatable toys, cricket sets, gumball machines and piles of bright purple and green candy. Lost in a sea of kitsch, we look up to get our bearings. Rising above us is a massive gleaming basilica with spires like the masts of ships. The church is so white and clean it looks like a marzipan model or a Disney castle complete with flashing red disco lights and a neon cross. Nearby is a pink ten-foot-high Mary in a sari.

In a small room beyond the basilica, screeching nuns and devotees surround Father Arun Irudyara. He spots our red-blotched Western faces through the crowd, yells us a "welcome" and throws me a key to a church lodging. The crowd suddenly goes quiet, for all know there's no room at the inn—this tiny town is absolutely jam-packed with people and we have just been given a true blessing. Rebecca and I cheer Peter and his priest as we battle our way back through the wet air and the swarm of thousands and thousands of south Indians. The scale and density of the crowd are extraordinary and things are far less organized and controlled than at the Kumbh Mela. In a way, the scene is also more alien. Bobbing above the sea of blue, green, pink and purple silk saris are bright orange bald heads. Men, women, children and babies have shaved their skulls and then painted them with a thick paste of sandalwood. The sight of women without hair is more shocking to me than a *sadhu* with a penis sword; for an Indian woman, giving her hair to God is an act of incredible devotion and commitment. Rebecca and I take photos of the grinning baldies and they pose proudly in front of giant altars they've carried for miles. Saint Anthony stares from a jungle setting, Saint Francis of Assisi is painted pink and blue, the angel Gabriel is decorated with tinsel and Saint Sebastian stands surrounded by flowers. The basilica's saints are also lined up ready to be carried to the sea for Mary's birthday party. Endless queues of people wait to kiss statues' feet and put jasmine around laden necks.

Those not pushing into or out of the church, or lining up to kiss a saint, are squatting, shopping, cooking or sleeping. The dusty ground is dense with families exhausted from the journey—children and parents sleep soundly, spooning their few possessions with their bodies. The smell of sweat, hair oil, jasmine, petrol, incense, urine and religious fervor is stifling and nauseating. A massive generator chugs black smoke and loudspeakers blast a blancmange of Tamil, Hindi and English sermons about chastity and goodness.

By the time we find Emma and Matt, they are pressed against the car—limp, ragged, sweaty and speechless. We push them through the crowds and help them climb over rag doll babies and floppy families to get to our cell room at the church building. When we open the creaking door and turn on the single lightbulb, the floor moves as cockroaches scatter. It's then that I realize I've made a huge mistake. Rebecca and I are used to India, and are almost unshockable, but for Emma and Matt this is all too much too soon. Matt is concerned about the filth, the lack of sanitation and the chance of disease. While they were waiting for us a "public health officer" had sprayed them in a cloud of DDT to prevent malaria; it did not make Matt feel any safer. Emma is suffering chemical poisoning, overheating, dehydration and sensory overload—she also has a bad cold and is covered in a film of sticky black dirt. She shakes with fury as I did after the Rishikesh earthquake.

"What the fuck are they doing? They're worshiping the Virgin like she's another god. She's the bloody mother of Jesus. And why have they shaved their heads? There's nothing in the Bible about giving God your hair. Christ, this is just berserk, it's too bizarre."

She begins to sob. I've hardly ever seen Emma get upset about anything. I feel terrible.

Rebecca washes Emma's feet in cold water, I place a wet towel over her forehead and lay her down on the bed high above the cockroaches while Matt hovers over her hesitantly. Rebecca and I decide to give them some space. We exit and Rebecca heads straight for the Mary market. She is enjoying herself like she's at a spiritual festival and can't get enough photos of the pilgrims and the merchandise. We come back carrying cartloads of kitsch including statues of Our Lady emerging from a pink lotus. She looks like the Hindu goddess Lakshmi but has paler skin and fewer arms; Mary's sari is golden and she holds a mini-Jesus. Emma groans but agrees to come out for the procession.

Hundreds of men swirl and stink, haul and heave, scream and stagger as they carry the plaster statues to the sea. Screeching generators rock on a sea of backs behind each saint. Our Lady of Velangani towers high into the night. Dressed in a red and gold sari, she is crowned with green and red flashing lights. We join the priests on the balcony of the church office building. Below us the crowd swirls like a whirlpool. Waves of heat rise and swarms of mosquitoes descend as the fireworks explode overhead. Emma is handed a dehydrated baby and as she cradles it and talks to the mother in sign language she looks slightly less shell-shocked. But she still wants to "get the hell out of the madness." I reluctantly agree to leave in the morning.

We wake up to Tamil hymns and the shouts of "alayloolya alay-looolya" through distorted speakers. An endless spiral of seekers is entering and leaving the basilica and a fat queue of pilgrims reaches to the sea and down the coast. Each squashed, sweating saint-seeker carries an offering—palm leaves or flowers or co-conuts or candles shaped to look like whatever body part they want cured. There are red hearts for those with cardiac complica-tions, yellow wax livers for jaundice and green lungs for tubercu-losis. The pilgrims will walk to the shrine in the basilica on their knees and place their candles at the Virgin's feet. If she heals them they will then return to Velangani to present the church with a thank-you—in the form of a solid silver replica of the part that has been cured. We can't get close enough to see Mary, let alone be cured.

Rebecca and I return to the church building to bid farewell to our savior Father Arun. If he hadn't given us the room I don't know how I would have coped, much less Emma. Tall, gray and handsome in his white robe, Father Arun is listening and nodding as three women try to one-up each other on Mary sightings.

"I pray, Father, then last night I saw her, Father, she told me my son is good in the Gulf, all is well in the Gulf and today he rings," singsongs a plump Goan in a pink silk sari.

"I saw her, Father, she came to me to tell me I shall have no more money problems," adds a woman in purple.

"I saw her too, Father," nods her friend.

"And me," pipes up a younger woman not wanting to be out-done.

Father Arun nods calmly. He is used to tales of divine visita-tions; they happen here all the time. He doesn't even mind that the

Vatican doesn't take his flock seriously enough to investigate. Nor does he care that most of the people here are Hindus who seem to be worshiping Mary like she is just another goddess.

"Hinduism's cultural bindings don't change our religion. Externally these people are Hindus but internally they are Christians. They are not prepared to accept Jesus alone as God like I do, but God is not going to condemn them," he says with a beatific smile. I like his style.

"Do you think there are real miracles?" I ask.

"There are so many miracles and so many graces. A boy falling between the train and the track near here reported a lady rescuing him. A nut farmer who follows Sai Baba prayed in America to win a court case and, after a lady appeared in the courtroom, he did. He flew straight to Chennai and came here saying it was divine intervention. I don't give credit to apparitions but something has happened. I don't know how God works."

God is working better here than in the West. Father Arun shyly and slyly reminds me that India is now exporting priests to cover shortfalls in Australia and America. Perhaps the future for Christianity lies here in a church that has had more faithful visits in a day than the average Sydney chapel would see in a year.

We bid farewell to the priest; Emma and Matt leave in relief, Rebecca looks back laughing and I'm quietly impressed. The Indian reinterpretation of Christianity has made the Jesus and Mary gang more attractive to me. For the first time I can see that Christianity can be a dynamic, living faith that can evolve and spread without interference from a human hierarchy. Here in Velangani, Christianity is at its best—sharing, ritualistic, democratic, forgiving and female. Seeing half a million people visit a large porcelain doll in a sari is strangely uplifting. Perhaps Christianity has got something to give the world apart from Easter eggs, the Osmonds and guilt. For the first time I see the faith, divinity and goodness in the faith of my forefathers.

I spend the sweaty, backbreaking, terrifying return taxi ride grinning inanely. As the roadside sellers slash a coconut and give me a straw, I toast my future with the warm sweet liquid. By absolving my anger about Christianity I have cleared the last obstacle that stood blocking my readiness for faith. I realize I don't have to be a Christian who follows the church, or a Buddhist nun in robes, or a convert to Judaism or Islam or Sikhism. I can be a believer in something bigger than what I can touch. I can make a leap of faith to a higher power in a way that's appropriate to my culture but not be imprisoned by it.

We drive north to Pondicherry, a small coastal town that's a former French colony. The whitewashed homes are stained, the bougainvillea binds to crumbled walls and the charm of the past is for sale in the antique shops. We find a sanctuary by the sea—a guest house that's run by followers of another saintly mother. The Mother of Pondicherry was a Russian born in Paris who came to India in the fifties and became a follower of Sri Aurobindo—a freedom fighter turned holy man. When he lapsed into a *samadhi* (the state of blissful silence and awareness), Mother took over the ashram until she died in the seventies. Images of the holy duo stare down at us from every wall—an Indian man with kind eyes and a long silver beard, and a stern, regal-looking woman wearing heavy kohl eyeliner and wonderful shawls. This Mother of Pondicherry was an aesthetic ascetic who believed art and style could manifest the beauty of living and the universe. Rebecca, an artist herself, is captivated by this idea; she loves the sculptures of gods and goddesses, the clean lines of the architecture, the simplicity of the buildings and the lack of clutter. We share a room that looks out over a gray sea and a beautiful garden with palms, ponds and stone statues garlanded with deep red hibiscus and pink frangipani. A mongoose runs around in the lengthening shadows, frogs croak and ducks crisscross the paths. As the sea and the sky turn pink, other guests run along raised concrete beams, jump from raised rock ledges and leap small ponds of floating lotus flowers as they take the ashram exercise course. This place has style and grace—it's a sanctuary for our frazzled souls.

We spend a few days playing cards, staring at the sea, reading and resting. Then we are finally ready to go back into the real world. One morning we find a French café with checked tablecloths, a thatched palm roof and slow lazy fans. The four of us squeal with joy at the menus and order croissants and chocolate pastries, baguettes and proper coffee. Emma and Matt smile happily, Rebecca declares she is "loving it." We feel a sense of unity now because of our shared hardship in Velangani and are buoyed by the familiar luxuries and the space and light around the sea. The world seems shiny and new and beautiful. I feel the touch of grace. But delivered to the table with our delicacies is a devastating weapon of misery. The waiter throws down an English-language newspaper with a shaky shot of two buildings burning like matchsticks.

"Look what those filthy Muslims have done now, we Hindus told you they couldn't be trusted."

It's September 12.

I feel the buds of belief and faith leave my body in the exhalation of swearwords. Shock and then fury take their place. If God exists, he's dead to me. As we read, rigid and silent, I feel the return of familiar cynicism and a new depth of hopelessness. I take off the plastic Virgin Mary necklace I'd bought as a tribute to my new respect for Christianity, feeling foolish for wearing the trinket and believing in goodness. My flimsy faith was too small and too weak to withstand this battering. How could Yahweh create such dreadful beings as we? How could Allah let murderers into heaven as martyrs? What kind of bad karma meant people could deserve to die like that? Where was the Sikhs' spiritual strength to withstand hatred? The Buddhist focus on nonviolence and happiness seems naive, the Parsis' push for survival useless. If Sai Baba could take the moon from the sky, why didn't he stop this? Where was the love of the Holy Mothers? The human race seems headed for self-destruction.

But as we stumble through the day, stunned, set-faced and grim, I realize I feel differently about the attacks on the World Trade Center and the Pentagon than I did about equally stupid and tragic events of the past such as Tiananmen Square, Rwanda, Bosnia and the Gulf War. Then, anger, righteousness and hatred swelled in bitter bile, consuming and paralyzing me with hopelessness. Today, the knot of anger moves slowly down from my heart to sit in the pit of my stomach. Now sadness swells in my chest. I've always seen anger as strong and sadness as weak, but now sorrow seems stronger than fury. It's less likely to spread the energy of hate, an energy that must have consumed those terrorists. If I can be strong enough to use my Buddhist training by not giving in to anger, then I become less like them; I can help stop the cycle of hatred and violence. I realize life is precious and tenuous and I need to focus on what I do believe in and what sustains me: my family, my husband, my friends and the lotus people—those who grow tall and beautiful above the muck and mud of humanity.

Emma, Matt, Rebecca and I now feel the world has changed forever. But India seems not to have noticed. Indians live in a land that's always been outside the bubble of safety that has now burst in the West. In a land used to death, disaster and disease life goes on as normal. Black-skinned beggars still watch us with white weeping eyes, women still sit outside our hotel to wail as we walk out, the rickshaw drivers still beep and beg us to get in. The relentless search for food, shelter and survival goes on. It's so surreal we begin to lose our grip.

In the evening we are walking home and a leper stumbles from the shadows and makes a strange yelping sound. We quicken our pace and he limps behind us trailing a stump where his foot once was; a slipper around the raw flesh slaps against the pavement and he groans as it hits. Somehow he gains ground. We quicken our pace again. I look back at the sounds of the slap, stumble and groan—he has stumps for arms, one eye is falling out and he has no tongue. I mutter, "I feel like I'm in Michael Jackson's *Thriller* film clip." Matt recalls the Monty Python scene where the legless, armless knight keeps pushing for a fight. Suddenly we all start laughing. It sounds cruel and crass, and it is, but we are not laughing with joy, we are all cried out and nothing seems real. Within seconds Rebecca stops. She yells "fuuuuuuuck" at the world and the beggar and at us. She wheels, turns and tries to give the man some money. He has no hands so she shoves it in his pocket.

In the morning we awake sadder than before, older than yesterday and exhausted by living. We want to stop the world and get off. And for once we can. Up the road and inland from Pondicherry is an alternative world—Auroville—a community created under the Mother of Pondicherry's guidance in the sixties as a peaceful and harmonious space where people could be free to fulfill their artistic or practical potential. Fifteen hundred people from twenty-two nationalities now live together there without dogma, rules or ritual, just the desire to understand consciousness. A friend of a Sydney friend grew up there and I ring his dad, Johnny, who invites us to his home.

Johnny races up on a trail bike to meet us at the *mandir*, or temple. Dressed in a filthy orange *lungi*, he wears a rag around his long silver hair. His face is hard, weathered and friendly, and he has a dry sardonic Australian wit and drawl.

"If Mother could see this place today, she'd laugh, I reckon. She was a bit of an odd witch and very strict but she had a sense of humor."

The community is divided into zones and Johnny is not in the inner architecturally beautiful swirl of homes; he's out among the trees in the camp. Small cabins on termite-proof concrete piles sit in a circle below eucalypt and jarrah trees that stretch high and wide creating a dense canopy. Dark ferns and shrubs cover the ground, and small black statues ring tree-stump stools. When Johnny left his mates to come here, he lived with his three kids on the beach for a year while helping plant two million trees in the red dust. He now lives below the fruits of his labor which make this haven at least ten degrees cooler than Pondicherry. The camp has fat content cows, meaty chickens, a brilliant black bullock and fields of millet, corn and fruit.

Johnny makes us tea, offers millet biscuits and shakes his head when we talk about the twin towers of the World Trade Center. As I swat mosquitoes and survey his hard but simple life, I feel like asking him if I can move into the spare hut. When I was young my favorite Dr. Seuss book was about a character looking to travel to Solah Saloo "where there were never any problems, at least very few." When the fuzzy bear thing finally gets to the special place, there's a problem with the keyhole. Johnny is the Auroville gatekeeper. He lets me down gently.

"You know, you can't change human nature. There's no money here and more freedom, but as more people come, there are more personality clashes and we even have people who want to be bureaucrats. Can you imagine, that's your creative goal?" he guffaws.

Back in Pondicherry at an Internet café above a New Age bookshop I eventually manage to log on to the Australian Broadcasting Company website. I think Jonathan is in Pakistan and I want to e-mail him; we haven't talked for weeks and I need to send and receive words of love and discuss the different world we now live in. Up comes the news that the United States is blaming outlawed Saudi magnate and al Qaeda front man Osama bin Laden for the suicide attacks, and Afghanistan, the country that harbors bin Laden, is steadying itself for swift retribution. As I feared, there won't be any forgiveness or compassion, there will be more death and another cycle of hate. Experts warn that military action could begin any moment. The Australian Broadcasting Company site states that Jonathan is in Kabul.

As I sit in shock, a new report flashes up—Kabul is under attack. I download an audio file of Jonathan talking on a crackled phone line as bombs explode in the background. He reports that it's not known who is bombing the city but he believes it's the Northern Alliance taking retribution on the Taliban for the recent killing of its leader, General Massoud.

The self-cherishing mind of pre-Vipassana leaps back into action. My sadness for the victims of terrorism is submerged by self-interest. My compassion is annihilated by fear. I sob and feel sick. I then disgrace myself by ringing Jonathan's boss, hysterically weeping and demanding he be flown out of Kabul this minute. Matt, Emma and Rebecca gently lead me out of the Internet café and we stumble to the Ganesh temple across the road. A baby elephant with his face painted pink lifts his trunk to touch our heads in blessing. Rebecca suggests we buy some of the ready-packed baskets containing a coconut, a pink lotus flower and a banana as offerings and take them into the temple. We find ourselves standing in front of a disco Ganesh made entirely of slivers of mirror ball glass and handsomely attired in a party dress of coconut palms and garlanded with lotus flowers. My friends wish for new beginnings. I pray there's no new ending. I pray to preserve my husband's life.

17 | War and Inner Peace

Be steadfast for Allah in equity and let not hatred of any people seduce you that you deal not justly. Deal justly, that is nearer to your duty.

The Koran

Over two long nights on the train to Delhi I rock on a rack of fear, for this terrorism attack and inevitable war against Afghanistan just got personal. I may have learned to accept the inevitability of my own death but I've never thought about a life without Jonathan. I'm no longer able to see all beings as equally precious, or my psychological state as empty, or to put my trust in a higher plan. By night I cry softly into the stained pillow through dreams in which I see myself standing under the burning towers trying to catch the people jumping to their deaths. By day I stare out the train window trying to retrieve my lost belief in a greater good.

Back in Delhi, there's news. Jonathan got the last seat on the last U.N. flight out of Kabul. He is safe in Pakistan. But he wants to go back to Afghanistan as soon as he can. I cannot understand why. Padma calls from New York; her husband, Surinder, was at the base of the World Trade Center when the first plane hit; he survived.

"I tell you, Sarah, that was divine luck. We've escaped all of our bad karma and my mother's curse—it's over. I know our life will be happy now."

I tell her about Jonathan's future plans to cover the war. She gasps. "Sarah, get out of India, it's the land of bad karma, it's a hothouse where it all happens."

Matt and Emma do get out—they cut their trip short and head home for Sydney. At such a devastating and terrifying time they want to be with the people they cherish. I understand and envy them, for I also want to turn to relationships that prove the redeeming power of love.

My love calls on crackling phone lines with echoes, cut-outs and the occasional soft breathing of a Pakistani intelligence officer. Jonathan is exhausted, depleted and distant and we don't communicate well. We are living in different worlds. He is pumping with adrenaline, high on the story of his career, the thrill of an important job and the companionship of people at the center of a seismic shift in human history. I'm sent low with fear, insecurity, sadness and self-pity. I have no right to force my feelings on him and he has no time or space to deal with them.

I begin to mourn a marriage of absence. In the nine months since our wedding day Jonathan and I have been together less than nine weeks. The upcoming war in Afghanistan may be a unique situation requiring special sacrifices but it comes as a last straw after a haystack of letdowns. Our relationship has had to come second to natural disasters, cricket matches, famines, shootings, scandals and insurrections. I've been clinging to the knowledge that we were to be heading home in three months to be together in a country that will give us time for each other. But the Australian Broadcasting Company asks Jonathan to stay on until the story is over, and the work is too exciting for him to refuse. The light at the end of the tunnel of long-distance love is getting dimmer and is in danger of going out.

I may have got fat like a good Indian wife but my teary self-pity is not pukka according to the good women of Delhi. Aarzoo visits, sees my red eyes and puts her hands on her hips.

"Sarah, sssssttop it. You have to support your husband, his fate is out of your hands. Besides, when the war is over he will have to give you a diamond for all this."

Aarzoo is being subtle. In the park I run into Mrs. Dutt and admit my fears; she sets me straight.

"What are you doing? This is your lot, now cope and be cheerful, a woman's life is about surrender to a husband's will, he is your god, look after him, not yourself."

But as I try to keep the home fires burning, the flames of anger rise phoenix-like from within. I become angry with the Taliban, the terrorists, bin Laden, George W. Bush and with the Australian Broadcasting Company and Jonathan. I'm angry I've given up a career, an identity and a safe, secure life to be here all alone with my future plans at the mercy of madmen, fundamentalists and a gung-ho American cowboy president. I'm furious that the upcoming war will kill people already tortured by the Taliban and the world's neglect. But most of my rage is reserved for myself: how can I expect the world to change while I stay the same? After nearly two years traveling India's spiritual supermarket I'm still a self-occupied, selfish, pathetic, pessimistic bitch who's dropped any faith at the first sign that things aren't going well.

My friends on the phone from Sydney become my rock. Jonathan is being replaced as a confidant, comforter and best friend, and that increases the distance between us. I'm becoming jealous of other relationships and cry in the *Friends* episode where Monica and Chandler get married—I'm losing the plot. I try to worry less, but then I find myself traveling down a familiar road—pulling back, hardening my heart and then not caring. In the past that path has inevitably led to the dead end of a relationship. It's not an option when you are married and still deeply in love.

I ring Yogesh and he prescribes a yoga lesson for conquering fear. First he suggests drinking warm salty water until I vomit up my pain. I decline. He then orders gargling of lemon water and a round of throat clearing and spitting. I remind him of my sputum deficiency. I do agree to hum like a hummingbird, buzz like a bee, pant like a dog and scream like a banshee, and I do feel better. The knot of anxiety in my stomach softens and I realize my histrionics are those of an Indian wife who believes she is nothing without her husband. I stop watching Hindi films and decide to face my fears and join Jonathan in Pakistan.

Just before I go, I'm invited to a party. Neeraj has won a scholarship to a London university and is going to celebrate at the house of his best friend (an eccentric Irish diplomat who rides around in his own cycle-rickshaw). Neeraj insists I attend.

"Sarah, I order you to come. You must keep the morale up, it's good for the skipper to know you are happy, especially when he is confined to barracks in Pakistan."

But the party does little for my morale—I spend the night being called a traitor to India for wanting to head north of the border. Young, educated gangs of men spray me with bullets of bile about their Pakistani neighbors—enemies that were compatriots when their parents were young.

"They are all inbred and marry their cousins."

"They are dirty."

"They have more than one wife and they breed like sheep."

"Strict purdah they keep, women are locked up."

"Disgusting fellows, you know they eat cows?"

None of the gang have even been to Pakistan or met anyone from the country. I grow nervous about the trip—not because I believe the slander but because of the obvious animosity between my adopted country and my destination.

I enter enemy territory on New Delhi's Shanti Path (Peace Road) through the gates of the heavily fortified purple and white marble

Pakistan High Commission. The elegant and fashionable diplomat there offers me some mutton kabobs straight from his lunch box and hands me one of only two visas issued this week. Australia has closed its embassy in Islamabad and most foreign citizens and nonessential workers are being evacuated. He sighs as he bids me farewell.

"Enjoy my country. You are an honored guest, I only wish it was not at such a hard time."

Pakistan is between a rock and a hard place. It has close ties to the Taliban but it would be suicide to defy the U.S.A., especially when its archenemy India is getting so chummy with the American administration. Pakistan's President Pervez Musharraf says he will support the war on terror but hard-line Islamic groups are threatening civil strife. These groups hate one thing more than America—India.

Thankfully I'll be traveling with something that will pave with gold the road between the two nuclear enemies—luggage that causes citizens in both countries to go weak at the knees. Kids.

At the airport I join Phoebe, the wife of the U.K. *Guardian* correspondent. She is a young strawberry-blonde Englishwoman, and has two children—four-year-old Tilly, who has big blue eyes and blonde ringlets, and one-year-old Ruskin, with green eyes and a gregarious manner. Ruskin was born in India and he knows that as a boy child he can get away with anything. He runs into security zones and X-ray machines, jumps on the pilot as he prays to Mecca under the stairwell, takes away a mullah's walking stick and nearly knocks over a fish tank. The Indian ground staff and Pakistani passengers watch adoringly, occasionally picking him up and giving him a hug and a kiss. On the Pakistan Airlines plane we take off with a wing and a prayer to Allah, and Ruskin is passed close to the cockpit to meet the captain. The events of September 11 have tarnished the Muslim world, but so far our greatest danger is not fanaticism but overfriendliness—Ruskin's chubby cheeks are constantly pinched adoringly by the captain, the crew and the passengers. By the time we get to Lahore he has red marks. Tilly remains relatively unscathed, though, because she holds up her hand when anyone gets close and yells, "*Neh. Bus.*"—No. Stop.

En route to Islamabad we fly over a landscape of fifty types of brown that swirls up soil to the plane's belly. On landing, Ruskin (whose cheeks are now turning purple and who is still running around like a Duracell toy) bolts straight out of the terminal and into the arms of his dad.

Pakistan is strangely similar to yet oddly different from India. We join an endless queue for forms, dodge pushy porters wanting money and ignore stony stares. The men are larger here and, compared to the small, slight average Indian males, seem like big bears with their bushy beards and broad shoulders. Most wear *kurta* shirts with baggy pants in dusty brown. The women wear the Indian *salwar* suits in polyester with baggy cuts—none swirl a sari and some are veiled. When the eyes of a veiled woman look at me I smile, but it's an awkward transaction because it's impossible to know if she is smiling back. Within moments, I notice a different smell, the spicy vegetarian sweat of India is replaced with a stronger, denser meaty smell of a nation that loves its flesh (bar pork, of course).

Jonathan and I have a tearful reunion. It's overwhelming to see him again after such a long and stressful time apart. I want to kill him for being in such danger and cherish him for surviving. We hug so hard it hurts us both. For a few minutes I can't look at his face—I feel shy and ecstatic and furious and excited. He's exhausted and elated but shamefaced and sad about the stress his job has put the relationship through.

After a few more long hugs and strange incomplete conversations, we decide we need to relax with a drink. We head straight to the U.N. club—one of the few places that serves alcohol in this Muslim nation. The doorman demands strict security and confiscates my bag, but as he takes it, he drops it. My compact breaks and Jonathan jokes, "We'll have to charge you for that, I'm afraid."

Quick as a flash the guy quips, "Just send me the invoice, sir."

I'm too taken aback to laugh. India's humor is predominantly slapstick but it seems Pakistan understands cynicism and dry wit.

Perhaps because, like Australia, it feels it's an underdog—a condition that so often breeds wry humor as a way of dealing with the world.

After the club, we attend a party in a front-yard marquee warmed with braziers of hot coal and gorgeous silk carpets. Here, elegantly clothed and stylish women, wearing beautiful shawls and huge precious stone jewelry, and pale, large-nosed men are desperate to know what Indians think of them. I edit the reality and remark that my friends Aarzoo and Billie think Pakistani women are beautiful, the men are handsome and they would love to come here to shop. They seem surprised, impressed and flattered, but pretend they don't care. I feel like I've traveled between two divorced parents who are trying to outdo each other.

Yet at the moment, the Pakistanis are more annoyed with the Americans than the Indians. This party crowd is the jet set that travels to the United States frequently for business or to visit relatives. In the last month the FBI has questioned quite a lot of them.

"Do they think all Muslims are terrorists? They really have no idea, my dear; it's just outrageous. They are paranoid and scared," whines a woman with an American twang. Her friends all murmur in agreement.

On the way home we encounter our own grilling. Two policemen, bent with cold, their faces hidden behind woolen shawls, stop our car, demand we pull down our window and then ask to smell Jonathan's breath. They accuse us of having *sharab*, or alcohol. We argue. They point at me. We say wife. Eventually they grow bored and let us go.

Pakistanis joke that Islamabad is forty kilometers up the road from Pakistan. It's a bubble of diplomatic suburbia with little in common with the surrounding cities, villages and tribal zones. The Australian Broadcasting Company has hired a house near the bucolic bushland where the air is clean and fresh and cold; Jonathan and I sit on the veranda above a wide, black and, in comparison to Delhi, wonderful road curving beneath a green mountain range dotted with sedate mansions. We watch the trucks pass—all intricately painted with bright scenes of sunsets, mountains, grapes and festivals—and I can't help noticing there's not a cow, a pig or any human waste in the streets. Islamabad is deadly quiet and cool; the Indian summer has sucked me dry and I feel instantly revived. Jonathan and I try to talk about all we've been through, but the words are too heavy and loaded and strange. We've spent too much time apart to bridge the distance instantly and we both realize we must start rebuilding slowly.

In the morning I take my first exercise in months—walking through green trees and blue air feels so wonderful that it hurts my lungs. The Marriott Hotel breakfast bar is our next port of call. The awkwardness and angst between Jonathan and me is easing and we eat together happily holding hands across the table. But I soon feel self-conscious; all around us men and boys sit separately from tables of women and girls. In most regions of Pakistan, women seen chatting to men who are not in their family are risking their husband's or father's reputation. A woman here is not only partly responsible for men's sexuality (she must dress modestly but elegantly so as not to be too arousing), but she is also burdened with upholding men's honor. The separation of space makes things easier. But what men may gain in terms of respect they lose in friendship. All around India, Pakistan and Afghanistan, Jonathan has shocked men by telling them he has female friends and I have male mates. He believes most are not appalled, but rather intrigued to know that not all communication ends in sex or scandal. Some admit that they'd like to have female friends. But here, as in India, keeping up appearances is all-important. I put my head down once again, drop Jonathan's hand and resolve not to smile at another man. There's little chance of eye contact anyway. As in India, when Jonathan is around, men here do not meet my gaze.

Pakistan averts its gaze from many things. We make friends with Nigit, a stunning, slim and elegant woman with wheat-colored skin, deep brown kohl-ringed eyes, a thick mane of hair and an astoundingly posh English accent. Nigit and her husband Imran were living in London during the eighties and came home to try to spread the word about HIV/AIDS. Their progress is slow. Nigit writes pamphlets and runs workshops but can't mention sex, homosexuality, condoms, prostitutes (who are called "dancers" here) or pedophilia. She has to pierce through the widespread belief that Muslims don't get AIDS by constantly arguing that good Muslims can't control the behavior of bad Muslims. And, of course, there are some bad Muslims in Pakistan—men pay one dollar to have sex with street boys, apprentices serve their masters sexually, there's cheap Afghani heroin but not many needles, and close male friendships often become sexual. The Koran forbids homosexuality but Nigit worries that "the men don't see it as sex, they see it as fun. So there's a huge state of denial here. It's just so difficult."

Sexual looks, touching and, of course, kissing are also denied on television. For safety's sake I'm told to stay inside the house under the mountains. In my self-imposed purdah I grow bored and brainless watching a lot of terrible TV, while Jonathan works twenty-hour days. Pakistan's movies and song clips make Indian popular culture look raunchy. Goofy guys with beards, tight black jeans and Cuban heels skip clumsily between tall trees and morph into Mujahadeen fighters brandishing knives or guns. (Former Dictator General Zia banned dance, so there's a lot of catching up to do before Pakistan can match the Indian disco moves.) Women dreadfully dressed in polyester suits and shoulder pads look on with downcast, adoring eyes but don't even seem to touch the heroes. When an American movie gets too rude, a yellow censorship sign saying MOVIE MAGIC comes up over a pair of red curtains.

MTV, which I access by cable, is not so funny. It's ninety percent American, so nearly every film clip features girls gyrating in bras and writhing in G-strings below big black guys in gold jewelry. No wonder Pakistani people accuse Westerners of sexual immorality. I see the Islamic perspective—these women are playthings out to please men. It's a concept just as offensive as the top-to-toe *burkha* that reduces women to blue blobs. The houseboy

Mustafa often cleans behind me so he can watch the TV over my shoulder. One day as Shaggy dances with sixty near-naked babes he giggles.

"Do you like the American movie, with the girls so shameful in nakedness?"

"Not really," I answer, wondering where this will lead.

"That is how women will be in paradise for men. It is sign of what is to come."

In Allah's heaven men will be surrounded by succulent, scantily clad virgins who will have eyes as adoring as American lap dancers.

"Where do good women go in heaven, Mustafa?" I ask hopefully, wondering whether there will be sweet boy-toy orgies for us. He bites his lip and stammers, "Women? I-I-I-I dddon't know."

At least Mohammed did advocate giving wives sexual pleasure in the Koran; in India there is no Hindi word for female orgasm. But in Islam sexuality is to be secluded from all but husbands. An ex-diplomat friend warned me before I left Delhi that I mustn't get a bikini wax here because the beautician will take all the hair off. Women aren't going for the "Brazilian" to be trendy—in Islam it's recommended for women to remove all body hair every twenty days or so to stay clean and attractive for their husbands. Many men here also shave their genitals—which possibly explains a lot of the scratching going on.

One day I catch Mustafa and the cook looking at a *Vogue* magazine belonging to a Canadian journalist. They stare confused and quizzical at scrawny women in lacy underwear with their legs open, lips loose and eyes saying "fuck me, stupid" who are advertising a bag that costs an average Pakistani's yearly salary. From here the Western worship of sex and consumption seems shameful. As does America's apparent willingness to engage in a war with powerful religious overtones. When George W. Bush talks of a "crusade" and "infinite justice" he only further alienates people already suspicious and resentful toward his country.

• • •

The bombing of Afghanistan begins.

Pakistan becomes jumpy and tense. There are riots in the hard-line heartland cities of Quetta and Peshawar. The trouble is stirred up by Islamic ideologues, Afghan refugees and Pakistani Pashtuns, who are bound by bloodlines to Afghanistan's dominant ethnic group who form the bulwark of the Taliban. It's an ugly minority but I willingly submit to staying indoors even more. Outside, emotions are unpredictable and enflamed with rumors. Pakistani *chai* stalls are awash with the conspiracy theory that the Israeli secret service—and not Osama bin Laden—masterminded the twin towers attack. Many are convinced that thousands of Manhattan Jews knew it was coming and didn't turn up to work that day. Another theory states that the United States is dropping food packets to lure Afghan civilians into the open so that they can shoot them. But the hard-liners' protests against the American bombing are small in Islamabad and they die down quickly.

At the Marriott Hotel the journalists are ecstatic that they finally have a story—for weeks they've been chewing their nails waiting for bombs to drop. The hotel roof is a mass of satellite dishes, director's chairs and steaming lights. A halo of hair spray sits in the chilly air. The restaurant is full of (mostly male) Spanish, German, Italian, Arabic, Japanese, English and—loudest of all—American accents. The lobby is packed with ponytailed cameramen and journalists dressed in brand-new equipment vests looking like frustrated fishermen who have yet to get their feet wet. In this five-star foyer the only sign we are in Pakistan is a bronze statue of Allah's name mounted on a big black marble block. To many of the cameramen, it's a handy place to park their arses unaware of the offense it causes. It's a five-star front line complete with poolside analysis—legs jiggle with stress, excitement fills the air, egos clash, war stories and hangover comparisons are exchanged.

I am too bored to sit still any longer and the journalist lurking within me dislikes missing the story of the decade. I ring Triple J and Radio National and begin some interviews and stories; Radio New Zealand calls Jonathan and he hands the phone to me. It's fun to be on air again but I feel distant from the thrill and the adrenaline. I have lost the hunger for the chase and have stopped seeing the world as a story; as something I can package, explain, reveal and talk about as if it's distant and different from myself. It occurs to me perhaps that's why I feel so sad and depressed—as a journalist and a broadcaster I was so busy regurgitating information and analyzing words and events I didn't make the emotional space to truly process them and let them sit still with my soul. Now I am a citizen again and I'm viewing the current war as an ordinary human watching my species fail. I don't want to go to war, to learn missile names or to be part of the action in a bubble of bravado. I feel more vulnerable to sorrow but more connected to humanity.

I now feel slightly ashamed of my fear for Jonathan's safety. Afghans have begun to die—nameless, faceless and out of the way of the world's media, they will never be mourned by many. My concerns for one man seem petty and cruel—yet I'm thankful he's stuck in Pakistan waiting for permission to enter Afghanistan. I miss our simple life in Australia so sharply it hurts. But I'm realizing my long-distance love affair with my country has been blinkered by nostalgia and distance. Australia is supporting the war against Afghanistan but is refusing to accept Afghan refugees; it's at the end of an election campaign fought over a boatload turned away, while poor crowded Pakistan somehow struggles with two million Afghan refugees. What I've missed most about Australia is its low density, its space and its capacity for solitude. I understand my compatriots want to preserve this space but such a pursuit seems selfish here. This war has shattered my Great Australian Dream—the fantasy that I could be part of the world community with all its benefits but isolated enough to be safe and separate from its violence and brutality.

The morning John Howard wins the election I sit in the garden of our house and interview the bravest woman I've ever met. "Rafat" may be too scared to tell me her real name but she's forthright about what she wants. With a sweet open face, a scarf around her head and a black cloak around her body, she kisses me on both cheeks and tells me about life in Afghanistan. She escaped during the days of the post-Soviet Mujahadeen when warlords ruled, which she says were not much different from the days of the Taliban that followed. She couldn't go to school, appear unveiled or feel safe. She talks of wanting a role in a future government and then leans forward to touch my knee.

"Why do the people of Australia hate us so much?"

"I'm not sure they hate Afghans. I think they are more scared of you," I mumble, shamed and embarrassed.

"How can you be scared of people who have nothing?"

I don't know what to tell her, for the hospitality in this part of the world is overwhelming. Goodness to guests is a God-ordered duty of a good Muslim. We are invited to countless homes, including that of Jonathan's Pakistan fixer, Irshad, where we sit with his wife, their dimpled daughter and strong sons and are fed kabobs and love. After dinner we are presented with a pile of presents up to our chins—a pair of earrings, a necklace, a bangle, shawls, bags, cushion covers and a beautiful toy truck. I'm so overwhelmed I begin to cry.

Of all the things I've learned on my Indian pilgrimage, the lesson that makes the most sense to me now is that concerning the redeeming power of love. I have come here to save a personal love but at such a time in the world's history I realize the importance of finding the love in Islam. I have read some Sufi poetry that talks of love and longing among Muslims. Jonathan recalls he has met some Afghan Sufis living in Pakistan and heard them talk of a "Muslim purveyor of love." He makes some calls and discovers that this purveyor of love is a Sufi saint and refugee living in Peshawar near the border with Afghanistan.

The following morning a taxi speeds me through Mad Max territory. Over pale brown rubble and dirt and under a weary sky, stone homes squat around whitewashed mosques; long lines of cattle stand under the sun on their way to the slaughterhouse. At the meeting of the dirty Kabul River and the glacial ice-blue Indus, the fort of Akbar the Great stands grand and stark. Beside the road, men's suits match the dust, and black veils give way to big blue *burkha* tents. Peshawar is a frontier town on the modern Silk Road. There's not much silk for sale but you can get cars, heroin, electronics, household appliances and weapons duty-free and dusty after their trip through Afghanistan.

In the family section of Chiefs, the local hamburger chain restaurant, I meet up with Hamid Iqbal, who has helped Jonathan set up stories here before. Hamid doesn't live in this smugglers' paradise because he wants cheap household appliances. He's an Afghan and a Sufi who came here to educate his daughter; Sufis follow a softer form of Islam that is less concerned with the outer laws of the faith, which are often interpreted as nonsupportive of women's education and involvement in society outside the home. About a year ago, in a local Peshawar market, Hamid felt the nearby presence of a "pure soul." He followed the feeling to the man who now helps him find heaven within—his Sufi saint. Well-educated and urbane, Hamid speaks softly with an American-Arabic accent and in a romantic, poetic manner.

"Jonathan is my brother; here you are my honored sister. I will take you to meet the man who makes music within my soul."

We travel down dusty lanes to a large house set around a courtyard. Inside a room seventeen men sit on cushions smoking strong cigarettes and drinking weak green tea. They are Sufis engaging in a form of worship that is illegal under the Taliban. All Muslims believe that they are on the pathway to God, but most feel they will become close to Allah after death and the final judgment in paradise. However, Sufis believe it is possible to experience this closeness while alive. They follow a mystical, inner, esoteric psychospiritual dimension of the faith where they aim to access inner consciousness and spread love, peace and kindness across the world. Sufis feel a fervent love of Allah, and their saints, or *pir*s, are like the Hindu *sadhus*—pure souls who can help followers find God. The Taliban follow a hard-core version of Islam; they deem Sufis un-Islamic, arguing no man can be a conduit for Allah, and restrict some Sufi practices. In Pakistan, Sufism is still practiced freely, so these refugees now feel free to worship; they meet regularly to speak in their own language and share common hardships.

The Afghan refugees nod their heads in greeting as I cover my hair and sit to listen to them reading poetry. They bow before the wisdom of an unlikely-looking saint. Asana Seer is a South Asian Robert De Niro with a short beard, a mole on his strong chin and a seventies-style leather jacket hanging on his angular limbs. The poetry stops and they begin an activity subversive in Taliban Afghanistan.

Singing.

I listen to songs that last for hours—steady drums and soaring melodies that swirl and loop; tunes that begin mournful and whirl toward ecstasy. The men sing or clap or close their eyes and smile with the joyful passion for inner harmonies. They are not playing my song but I understand their rapture. I've been apart from good music too long and my soul is missing tunes of transcendence. Prior to India, my church was a party, club or floor between two speakers, and Delhi's nightclubs just don't stack up. I travel with the Sufis to that place of bliss and true love for all.

We return with the shadows to the cooling earth as the call to prayer wafts across the suburb. Some of the men go to face Mecca and repeatedly touch their heads to the ground in prayer, but most stay to listen in on my chat with their saint. He agrees to an interview for Radio National but mystics are not good at simple radio spots; Asana Seer talks in rambling poems and Hamid has trouble translating. Basically, he tells me he facilitates pilgrims' relations to God by communicating with the Sufi saints of the past in prayer—this magnifies the power of Allah, whose miracles are everywhere.

Suddenly an elderly man with a white beard and bad gout begins to scream at me in great excitement, throwing his stick in the air. Hamid softly translates his rant.

"A week ago I lost the power of my left leg and arm. Doctors could do nothing. I had that crutch over there. I came and touched the master and his pure soul; look, now I'm perfect."

He hobbles painfully and slowly across the room to show me; he laughs with a lopsided smile on his face. It appears he's recovering from a stroke.

Asana Seer tells me he won't answer any more questions, and says, "Why are you asking me this? You have the answers, you spend time alone with self. You know it deep inside, I know you do. What are you doing in India?"

"I'm learning about different faiths," I answer.

"What have you learned?" he demands.

I stammer, "I-I-I-I'm learning different things from all—from Buddhism about controlling my mind, from Hinduism respecting other paths, from Islam the power of surrender."

The saint stares hard and unflinching while Hamid translates my words. Suddenly there's a mini-riot. The men begin screaming at each other, motioning toward me and throwing their arms up in the air and then banging them on the floor. Increasingly nervous, I ask Hamid what they are fighting about.

"Some of them are saying as Muslims we have a duty to try to convert you to Islam, as you should not follow these atheist faiths like Buddhism and look upon the false idols of the Indians. Others say, no, we are Sufis, we show her with love that we respect all paths. She must find her own inner journey."

My head is reeling from the strong smoke, the deafening debate, the mystic music and the passion. The saint is impassive. He dismisses me curtly.

"You have the answer. Follow your path, it will lead to peace and love."

I'm driven back to Islamabad reeking of cigarettes and feeling more cancerized than purified, but I do feel strangely peaceful. It's a state not shattered by saying good-bye to Jonathan when he tells me he's off to Afghanistan. Spending this week with him has been tense, fraught and rushed, but at least we have been together. I have been buoyed by the Sufi belief in the power of passion. Of course I'm nervous about Jonathan returning to Afghanistan but I attempt to abandon myself to love without fear.

I fly to Delhi as Kabul falls and Jonathan drives across the border from Peshawar toward the Afghan capital. He stops in Jalalabad, where he plans to join a morning convoy heading through the lawless war zone. At the last minute he gets impatient and sets off alone on a risky race with dusk. The next day I hear on the BBC that an Australian man has been killed on that road. The Australian Broadcasting Company doesn't ring me and the name is not released. My imagination begins to run rampant—I think perhaps my mother is flying over to tell me I'm a widow.

For two days I wait for news.

I turn to music for solace, for songs are like religions; they mean different things to people at different times of their lives because they speak directly to the heart and soul. My favorite song, U2's "One," means something more than a breakup tune now. It's a song I've returned to time and time again to ease or indulge in heartbreak but now I listen with a willingness to love another beyond togetherness and beyond death.

I let go of the hurt, the need, the fear and I trust in love, the greatest power of all. The BBC announces the name of the dead. A wonderful, much-loved cameraman, Harry Burton, and his companions had been held up, taken over a mountain pass and shot. It was the group with which Jonathan was supposed to travel.

18 | Land of the Gods

When the relief and the sorrow settle, my heart feels at home back in Wonderland. Yet leaving brown Pakistan for India's kaleidoscope of Technicolor has made me feel less like Alice and more like Dorothy in the land of Oz. A yellow brick road of marigold petals paves the local shopping center. My smiling guard Lakan salutes me and volunteers he's feeling "one hundred percent excellent first class." Bright golden saris flutter on mopeds, and pink bougainvillea and blooming frangipani paint and perfume my house. India's organized chaos has exuberance and optimism, a pride and a strong celebration of life. I truly love it. There's no place like this home.

Quite a few people and their many gods are taking credit for Jonathan's survival.

Aarzoo says her Hanuman prayer book created a protective aura around him, my favorite shopkeeper Mrs. Sharma believes her mantra at the Ganesh temple worked and the Australian Broadcasting Company Christians prayed to the baby Jesus, mother Mary and daddy God. Jonathan puts it down to luck. I set out for Old Delhi to thank Allah.

The Jamma Masjid is one of the most important mosques in the world. It was built in the Golden Age of Mogul power when Shah Jehan ruled over most of India, all of Pakistan and great chunks of Afghanistan. Every Friday the emperor would leave his palace of pleasure and his huge harem to ride a grand elephant to this mosque. Three hundred and fifty years later I scurry along the same route—now filled with bleating goats, cages of chickens, flurries of feathers, fly-encrusted animal corpses and lepers reaching for alms. The huge red sandstone floor of the mosque is red-hot under my pale feet and the shady corner crunches with pigeon droppings. Below the stunning red and white onion dome and between the two crumbling minarets I softly give thanks. In this temple to God of magnificent proportions my desires feel insignificant, but my relief is real. I don't care what spared Jonathan, I just feel blessed that it did.

And right now it's time to celebrate. Old Delhi may look the same but New Delhi is in the midst of the most important Hindu festival of the year. Summer is over, and November ushers in Dushera and Divali—the anniversary and celebration of the battle in the Ramayana when the god-king Rama and his devoted servant, the monkey-god Hanuman, fought the demon King Ravan and rescued Rama's wife, Sita. But before the fasting, rituals and *puja* period, the festival focuses on gambling and giving. The Australian Broadcasting Company spends a fortune on Divali gifts for officials and bureaucrats—the telephone man tells our office manager what size suit he takes, the electric company wallah gets cash, the deliveryman prefers sweets and staff are paid a month's bonus.

This is India's Christmas. Children emerge into the autumn light, pale and blinking from too much study and tutoring. Cashed-up workers hit the crowded shops for the sales. The pavements are packed with stalls selling televisions, refrigerators, stereos and sickly sweets made from sugar and boiled milk. Aamar, our most devout Hindu guard, decorates the house with tinsel and HAPPY DIVALI banners. I display new painted plaster statues of Ganesh and Lakshmi. Local parks feature pink papier-mâché Ravans with ten heads that tower over slides for children flanked by models of his two demon brothers painted bright green with big black mustaches. Aarzoo's family adopts me for the holiday.

"A woman should not be alone at this time," commands Auntie-*ji* as she shows me to the spare room.

On the anniversary of the battle for Sita, Aarzoo and I flit from house to house, sitting on friend's beds, gossiping about boys and stuffing our faces with gooey sweets. At dusk we push our way through the crowds to enter the local park and bluff our way into the VIP area. Tiny children dressed as Rama, Hanuman and Ravan clash with paper swords and papier-mâché mallets. They duel, then stand in a huddle to chat up the next move. The boys wipe their dripping pancake makeup, touch up their fake mustaches, pull up their sequined suits and lunge for the kill again. On the loud-speakers a distorted drone of the Ramayana reading rises in volume as Ravan's army starts to fall. One imp spends ten minutes sinking to the dust clutching his side in a death scene he's copied from a classic Amitabh Bachchan movie. He then sits straight back up and yells at me, "Good, hey, Auntie? Photo please, what is your good name?"

When the pantomime is over, the dead jump from the dust and hug the victors, who punch the air with performance pride. The child playing Rama leaves the dust stadium on the shoulders of his monkey army. It's now dark enough to really celebrate. The local pyrotechnicians (who happen to be Muslim) get the honor of lighting the fireworks that will destroy evil and celebrate the triumph of good. Catherine wheels fly from bending bamboo poles, the bangers blast with more bang than beauty and rockets shoot straight toward nearby buildings. The electricity wire straight above the fireworks glows dangerously hot. The air grows thick with smoke and the crowd begins to chant and scream their support for Rama like he's their favorite football player. The ten-foot-high demon-king Ravan and his brothers begin to burn, exposing the bamboo skeletons stuffed with fireworks. The bangers explode horizontally toward the crowd. A tree catches on fire, a firework hits a car, the electricity wire begins to spark, my eyebrows are singed and the crowd chants, "Rama, Rama, Rama." As the Muslim men stomp out the flames and Hindu mothers herd up their children, we drive through streets of smoke and sulfur, happy that good has triumphed once again.

A week on, we celebrate the anniversary of Rama and Sita's triumphant return to their kingdom. I light cotton wicks in clay lamps saturated with heavy oil, and Aamar and I wind tiny little red and yellow flashing fairy lights around the roof. Moolchand claps happily—our mixed Christian-Hindu household has one of the best displays in the suburb. I then head back to my adopted family home, where Aarzoo and I dress up in silk saris and drip with her mother's jewels. We sit cross-legged at the family altar, which is covered with cards containing Sanskrit mantras for Shiva, Krishna and Ganesh and, in a typically inclusive Hindu manner, a Christian prayer. But tonight we restrict our offerings to the goddess Lakshmi. Aarzoo and her mum and dad chant while I ring the bell that supposedly brings our minds in tune with the divine. It's confiscated when I don't ring in the proper rhythm, but at least I impress by joining in one mantra I remember from the Amma ashram. After a few mantras, Aarzoo and her mum begin to mumble and pause and then collapse into laughter when they forget the words altogether. We give up and bow in silent prayer. I wish for peace in Afghanistan, but when I tell Auntie, she admonishes me.

"No, silly, you should pray to Lakshmi for money, this is the money time."

I pray again for cash. Sacred thread is wrapped around our wrists and red powder smudged onto our foreheads. We touch up our makeup, check our jewels and set out for more ceremonies.

The streets are like a holy war zone. Entire crumbling apartment blocks are blacked out, the air is thick with smoke and bangers explode on roofs and roads. Aarzoo's uncle and grandparents open their door with smiles, hugs and gifts of coins and cash. After another *puja* we sip Coke, stuff ourselves with fatty foods and light more fireworks. The air is so thick with smoke, our eyes are soon streaming and few of the explosions of color can be seen. We get home at midnight, our stomachs popping, our eyes scratched with sulfur, our lungs aching. Aarzoo and I chat long into the wee hours in the spare room double bed like schoolgirls.

Mornings at Aarzoo's house always make me homesick. Like my family, Aarzoo's people have a habit of refusing to talk to each other while in the same room. Instead, they scream from one end of the house to the other.

"Mummeee, look at my broken beeeeeellllie ring, it's rubbing on my stomach—so sore it is, what kind of mother are you not getting me a new one."

"Look at you, my daughter, so pretty with kohl on your eyes from the night before—if only a husband could see you like this, I could die happy."

It's all playacting in the land of drama queens and soon we are laughing, drinking *chai* and snacking on sweets on Mummy's bed (all the goodies are in the bedroom locked up in cupboards away from the servant).

With Jonathan still war-bound I move in to Aarzoo's for the winter wedding season with its ostentatious display of wealth and beauty. Through the long nights on the dance floor (where my Bollywood lessons finally pay off), the eating around open fires and tripping over saris, I think of all the things I love about India and will miss the most. The drama, the dharma, the innocent exuberance of the festivals, the intensity of living, the piety in playfulness and the embrace of living day by day.

It is time to prepare to go. The war may not be over but the West is getting sick of seeing the death and destruction and the rebuilding, and the Australian Broadcasting Company is nearly broke.

• • •

Jonathan returns home to Delhi for Christmas and we begin again to try to bridge the distance imposed by the months spent apart leading very different lives. But true intimacy is impossible when his life is not his own and work always comes first. We decide to leave India as soon as the Australian Broadcasting Company can find a replacement, for we realize at this stage in our marriage we cannot continue to spend so much time apart. Aarzoo takes him for a walk to talk about the damage done.

"My brother, I have to tell you, you have failed in your first year of marriage, you are way beyond a one-carat diamond now, you are up to a ruby and an emerald. I will take you shopping."

But the smoggy winter day we plan to have a look at some jewelry, Jonathan has to file a story and Aarzoo is sent to Rajasthan to shoot a new television series. I set out alone for our favorite jeweler in Old Delhi. Dodging rickshaws, and the flying sweat from the singlets of cyclists, I follow Wedding Street to Kinari bazaar. Turning left at an indescribably odorous urinal, I enter Naujhra Lane. It's a sanctuary of calm and beauty, with small wooden homes painted white with bright yellow and blue trimmings. This is the street where about a dozen Jain families live; they have been here for centuries. Jains follow a religion that's often described as an extreme form of Buddhism—it's a small sect and members tend to stick together and clump in certain professions they see as low impact on the planet and their karma. In this street a young Jain jeweler, who preciously calls himself Prince, made our wedding rings (brilliantly copied from *Vanity Fair* but made in the wrong sizes).

Prince now runs green, blue and black stones through his fingers and drapes silver and gold around my neck. They grow dull before my eyes. I don't want payback from Jonathan. And precious stones don't buy precious lives lost by the war. Prince—a proud Jain and a pacifist—sees my disinterest and seems to understand. He offers to take me to a hidden treasure.

At the end of the alley behind ugly concrete walls is a beautiful ancient Jain temple. Prince and I step onto a huge chessboard marble floor surrounded by sixteen carved marble pillars and then climb up a steep staircase to a glass-tiled atrium. Vivid ancient murals, tapestries made with small pieces of mirror, and stunning statues serenely stare through the centuries. They depict the twenty-four gods of Jainism; they include a gleaming silver statue with a shining black stone face, a pearly white being with a gold crown, a beautiful tall man in a tranquil trance and a bizarre, shapeless, bright orange blob.

Suddenly the silence is broken by a gasp, a crash and running footsteps. A large woman with wild red curls pants past me to stumble down the steep stairs, her face stricken by shock. I follow to find her standing in the middle of the alley, staring back at the temple and shaking. She's about forty and her mass of hair clashes with a hideous lumpy blue parka and a fluorescent-pink Indian *salwar* suit. She grabs me like a woman drowning.

"I'm Rita, can you get me out of here?"

I've become quite used to strange tourists who freak out in the intensity of India. There's a look on Rita's face that reminds me of my own shock after the shaking at Rishikesh two long years ago. I feel a special kinship and responsibility for this woman and figure she needs some air, some familiarity and some calm.

I bid farewell to a bemused Prince and drag Rita along Chandni Chowk, the main street of Old Delhi. Built by Emperor Shah Jehan's favorite daughter, this street, with the name that translates as "Moon Square," was once lined with pools of water which reflected the lunar light. It's now a highway of hassle, a freeway of filth and fury. Above, dreadlock knots of power lines spark dangerously. Below, pickpocketing dwarfs skip and stumble as they're slapped away, while hawkers sell plastic spiders, horrible hats, useless miniature water pumps and Indian flags. The black smog and the blast of car horns and pings of cycle-rickshaws fill the air, and every rickshaw wallah stops beside or in front of us to insist we take a ride. By the time we are at my car, Rita is almost hyperventilating with hysteria.

Abraham drives us to Lodi Gardens, where Rita flops onto the faded grass and groans. She recovers enough to tell me she is from New York and has been at the ashram of the Rajneeshies in Poona. The Rajneeshies are the followers of the now dead bearded dude called Osho, whom they adore as God but whom Westerners would best remember for his multitude of Rolls-Royce cars and tax problems. The Indian ashram is still a popular tourist destination infamous for its sexual freedom and its "crazy dancing" sessions where followers rock in their socks. Rita liked the liberation of wild dancing but when the music stopped she felt fleeced by the flock.

"It was a Club Meditation. The courses cost hundreds of dollars, I had to pay for the maroon robes, an AIDS test, the use of the pool, classes, only the sex was free."

Rita played with many of the pilgrims but now says she feels contaminated by their vibrations. She left in late September disillusioned and guilt-ridden over bonking her brains out while her city's tallest buildings burned.

"I'm a good person, ya know, I love metaphysics, philosophy, I'm a greenie, but the Rajneesh is too much about dancing and drinking and fucking and buying and I can't handle it anymore."

"So what are you doing in Delhi?"

"I was in the temple to check out becoming a Jain."

She pants and pats her heart beneath her parka.

"So what happened?"

"I was overwhelmed by it. The vibrations of perfection were too strong for me. I'm not yet ready, but it spoke to me."

Despite her histrionics, Rita is actually onto a good thing. Prince has told me much about his Jain faith. Its founder, Mahavira, was a contemporary and a relatively close neighbor of the Buddha. He too transformed from prince to pauper by casting aside his fine clothes and his treasures and nearly starving himself to death. For twelve years Mahavira underwent castigation and endured bodily and spiritual injury to emerge a renowned preacher and founder of a new religion. The name "Jain" is derived from the word *jina* (victor or conqueror), implying final victory over bondage to life's misery. Jains see Mahavira as the last of twenty-four *tirthankaras*, or perfect souls. Over the centuries, these perfect souls have come to be worshiped as gods, but Jains don't really believe in a controlling creator that judges and directs retribution.

Like Buddhists and Hindus, they embrace karma and cosmic power. Jains aim to live an ethical life of exacting discipline, practicing *ahimsa*, or nonviolence, in thought and action toward all living creatures. Some Jains take this concept to an extreme degree—followers of one sect insist on nudity, wear a mouth mask to stop themselves breathing, eating or drinking microscopic animals and carry a broom to sweep away insects in their path. It's a long way from *jihad*.

Rita says *ahisma* is the only thing that makes sense to her now.

"If those men who flew the planes had felt no hatred, no anger, the world would be different today. If we appeal to barbarism, it will be unleashed. This war is starting another round of hatred. I can feel the dark forces strengthening over lifetimes to come."

Over the last three months Rita has attended some Jain prayer sessions and teachings about reducing violence in the mind. She sits up and preaches a sermon in the grass, urging me not to eat meat. I don't get the chance to tell her I've been vegetarian for nearly a year.

"Any connection to killing is violence, it's all the same path. Think about how many things you have killed in your life. We are all guilty on some level."

A year ago I would have told Rita to ease off but I've come a long way to understanding where she's coming from. When we first arrived in our new home in Vasant Vihar we had a mouse and I stood on chairs like the woman in the Tom and Jerry cartoons and screamed for its murder. I laughed when Lakan set a Hindu trap—a large box that slammed shut when the critter walked into it. But I grew infuriated watching Lakan catch the mouse every morning and set him free across the road, only to see the rodent back by lunchtime. Then we sealed up the cracks in the house, but the mouse kept finding more—one night it even jumped down the chimney. I again called for killing as the only solution. Lakan blocked the chimney. Now I am like my Hindu guard—unable to kill anything. I'm not only vegetarian; even cockroaches and mosquitoes are safe in our home.

Yet I'm aware that the Jain concept of abstinence can be taken to dangerous extremes. I recently read that in a Rajasthani village, Sassole, sages still give permission for the Jain ritual of *santhara*—starving oneself to death when all purposes in life have been served, or the body is useless. They most commonly give permission to old women seen as a burden to their families. Up to one thousand people take *santhara* a year in India—it's rarely investigated as a suicide because the act is public and sanctioned by sermons. To me, self-violence seems a desperate act that should never be condoned by religion. Suicide is now even more taboo to me since I've been living in India. I don't believe it's a horrendous sin, but in a country where life is so precious it seems wrong to waste what one is given.

Santhara aside, Rita insists India is the place to learn nonviolence.

"Gandhi ushered in political change peacefully with strikes, marches and hunger fasts. Nonviolence is written on India's soul, it will prevail."

Gandhi, who was greatly influenced by Jainism, knew dividing India on religious grounds and forming Pakistan would lead to bloodshed. The one million casualties of Partition in 1947 must have sat heavily on his soul and he would be devastated to see the hatred that's since developed between India and Pakistan. But while Gandhi is still much admired in India, perhaps it's now more as a nationalist than a peacemaker. During a recent screening of a movie set around the time of Partition, the audience laughed and cheered as Gandhi was gunned down by a hard-line Hindu. With the rise of Hindu nationalism, many Indians have come to view him as too pro-Muslim. Others see him as a funny little man all too willing to renounce creature comforts that they've worked so hard to gain. In the emerging consumerist India, even his grandson charges for interviews.

A few weeks later Rita rings distraught. She was just about to set out on a Jain pilgrimage to Gandhi's home state of Gujarat, but violence and hatred have flared again. Hindu fanatics are stepping up their campaign to build the Rama temple in the northern town of Ayodhya on the site of the mutilated Babri mosque. Hard-liners are descending on the town for mass *puja*s and threatening to start building work within weeks. India grows tense. A train of pilgrims returning from Ayodhya to Gujarat is torched by a Muslim mob. The state erupts in secular slaughter. In major towns and tiny villages Hindus turn on Muslim neighbors in an orgy of rape and murder. After four days of violence, around seven hundred people are killed—most of them Muslims burned alive while hiding in their homes, shops and mosques. The police stand by and do nothing; a curfew is imposed and Indian soldiers shoot at sight. The BJP Hindu nationalist government is accused of whipping up religious rivalry for its own political gains; of creating a monster it cannot control.

These hard-line Hindus are failing their faith of universal acceptance and earning themselves millions of more lives on earth. They are also breaking my heart, for it seems all religions, even the most inclusive of all, are ultimately perverted by humankind. The Jain desire for self-perfection, help for others and gradual abandonment of the material world, which to me once seemed an extreme reaction to violence, now makes more sense. The cycle of violence needs extreme love to break it. Indian Hinduism and Buddhism made me realize evil and good are not external forces; they exist within us all and we must take responsibility for our own cycles of violence. I push away from feeling fearful and angry with India. I step back from the spiral of regret and resentment within my relationship. These feelings must be replaced with gentle love that's free of fury—and the need for jewelry.

Rita stays in Delhi for a few weeks waiting for the violence to abate. It doesn't, so she leaves for the United States. She gives up on India as a spiritual land, but I still cling to optimism for a secular religious nation that gives equal rights to all. I have faith in this country of many cultures, many languages and many ways to God. I believe its greatest gift—its diversity and acceptance of difference—will not be lost. I don't want my journey to end with me biting the Hindu hands that have fed me so much. I don't want to reject religion as the cause of human hatred.

The Australian Broadcasting Company has found a new correspondent and now it's time to leave for Australia and let the tide of a billion lives ebb and flow without us. Aarzoo sets Jonathan free from his brotherly duties, for she has fallen in love on her own. She's secretly dating an extremely conservative bloke who wants her to take out her belly ring, tells her she has to stop smoking, won't let her wear Western clothes and says she'll have to stop working if they marry. Billie is still short of a suitable match but is set to fly to America for the birth of her nephew. She lets me hug her good-bye. My Bollywood-loving friend Jeni is staying in India to be with her boyfriend Vinal. I heartily approve—he is a sweetheart and the only Indian man I've met who knows how to scrub a bathroom floor; he and Jonathan have become fast friends. Ruth and her husband, Indre, are about to move to Mumbai—he to manage Preity Zinta, and she to have their baby.

It's a traumatic good-bye to our Indian staff family. Mary tries to touch my feet and when I stop her she falls into my arms weeping. Peter is loyally stoic as we pack up, while Moolchand moans as he drops off our last laundry. Rachel proudly pronounces that she is the architect of my new flabby stomach and thighs, and then holds me close for ten minutes while we sob softly. Lakan and Aamar stand in an honor guard at the door. Aamar cannot talk; Lakan bites his lip and says to Jonathan, "Sir, I am having such strong feelings I cannot say."

Jonathan's face falls and he hides his distress by hugging them both hard; Lakan and Aamar cling to their sahib, leaving a large wet patch of tears on his chest. As we climb into the car and look back at the people who have become our friends and family, our bravery falters and bursts. We both lose it in the backseat, clutching each other and sobbing uncontrollably all the way to the airport. Abraham drives like he is commandeering a hearse.

I hiccup tears as we pass a horrendous wedding band and a groom stiff on a horse bathed in neon. I start to laugh when we see a service station stacked with staff sitting and chatting, deaf to the blast of horns from an impatient queue of cars. At the airport turnoff, three camels stand knock-kneed urinating; a wise man atop one of them salutes my wave. Outside the terminal, Abraham unpacks our bags and clutches Jonathan before falling into the car and crying inconsolably on the front seat.

Over the last few years, I've imagined bounding through the airport doors ecstatic and excited to be escaping this country, but now my legs feel heavy and painful and reluctant. We drag ourselves into the terminal feeling older, wiser and more Indian than when we arrived. The soldiers clap and yell in delight when we speak in Hindi. I pinch a few baby cheeks and patiently queue for a check-in that ignores my excess baggage. I belch as the security woman pats my crotch behind a curtain, and I compare my *mehindi* with the newly married toilet beggar's, thankful she cannot read my palm through the henna stains. She shakes my hand and strokes my face.

"Good-bye, are you coming back to India?"

I wobble my head in the Indian way: yes, no, maybe.

We order champagne as we cross the Australian coast. I feel my soul swell at the sight of my land so red raw and bumped like an ancient crocodile back or stretching with blue salt pan veins on the palm of an ancient hand. These mountains of worn rock, these silver blue seas and white sands all seem so empty; scoured by millennia but not humans, they have an energy and vitality that swells my heart. The words of the guru Krishnamurti come back to me.

"When one loses the deep intimate relationship with nature then temples, mosques and churches become important."

In Sydney I rediscover my relationship with nature. The ocean becomes my temple and my Ganges. I bathe with an inner joy; floating in clean water, my body is buoyant with the love of life. I lie on my back and enjoy the pain of a strong sun striking my eyes. My feet kick the water into a cascade of diamonds that splash my face. Salt sticks to my skin. There are silent mornings and days of doing nothing but gulping lungs full of fresh air and staring up at high endless bright blue. I walk through the pristine quiet of the suburban bush of my childhood as fluorescent orange streaks across the sky. There are kookaburras and boat sheds and picnics and sand and so much water so silver bright and the light I love. Gleaming cars zoom fast on empty, wide, clean roads. A couple bent double laughs with hysterical abandon at a café table. I delight to see such open joy and such easy lives, yet at times the luxury and space sit uneasily. My country and I want it all—to be part of a war but not to face its consequences, to be part of the global community but not a port for its refugees. The city rants religiously of real estate and fashion, of "in" restaurants and the latest stupid styles. I read about obsessions with Brazilian bikini waxes and Botox injections and throw away papers full of articles about fulfilling desires for sexual adventure. The worship of land ownership, the body beautiful, self-help and self-obsession for beings blinded by option overload is strangely unfamiliar.

I went to India for love and the country tested that love to a large degree. Now, as Jonathan and I finally spend time together, I realize my relationship has been strengthened and scarred by the shared hardship and solitude. Recovering intimacy takes time and we are less starry-eyed but more realistic about life. Our souls share a shadow cast by India. We now both have a new view of our so lucky lives, yet our innocent optimism about humanity has been sucked from our hearts. The overall feeling about our adventure is positive, though. Jonathan's career has taken off and I've gained much in my karma chameleon journey. I'm reborn as a better person, less reliant on others for my happiness and full of a desire to replace anger with love. Plus, I've gained another home. For I have two spiritual homelands now—the quiet empty lands of my birth and the cataclysmic crowded land of my rebirth.

When I remember India I think of its ability to find beauty in small things—the tattoo of circles on a camel's rump, a bright silk sari in a dark slum, a peacock feather in a plastic jar, a delicate earring glinting by a worn face and a lotus painted on a truck. I miss the sheer exuberance of a billion individuals and their pantomime of festivals.

Of all the wild, mad, hair-raising stops in my spiritual journey through the subcontinent, the most holy Hindu city of them all has branded itself on me most boldly: Varanasi on the Ganges. Downstream from the Kumbh Mela and upstream from hell, it's a city that attracts the faithful and the freaks and those dying or being bid farewell. Souls sent from this place on earth go straight to heaven. A few weeks ago, on a hotel roof above India's holiest city, Jonathan and I inhaled clouds of hash spiced with wafts of singed hair and burning bodies. We walked among Varanasi's rats, dogs and street urchins as they competed for garbage in a maze of twisting dark alleyways and stained palaces that rot into the black mud. At dawn we floated in a wooden boat past candles, flowers and human ashes in holy waters littered with bobbing bloated bodies.

In Varanasi my final *puja* was to Kali—the fearsome goddess of black skin, many arms, a red tongue and a necklace of bloody heads who destroys egos and sin. At five on a pitch-black morning, I sat in a tiny Kali shrine. A sacred fire burned deep within a dark pit, throwing shadows and light upon the hovering face of a *pundit* smeared with sacred ash. He offered Kali divine gifts by sprinkling sandalwood, milk and rose petals into the flames. He rang a small bell bringing our senses into momentary oneness with the deity and burned camphor to encourage us to let our small egos merge into the infinite. The small semicircle of souls started chanting Sanskrit prayers. Blissed and blessed, I floated on faith. Suddenly the explosion of a massive fart ripped the air and an unholy stench arose. The woman beside me lifted her butt cheeks, blurted out another fart and then burped boldly in time with the chants of "om."

I remember this because I love what it shows about India. India is the land of the profound and the profane; a place where spirituality and sanctimoniousness sit miles apart. I've learned much from the land of many gods and many ways to worship. From Buddhism the power to begin to manage my mind, from Jainism the desire to make peace in all aspects of life, while Islam has taught me to desire goodness and to let go of that which cannot be controlled. I thank Judaism for teaching me the power of transcendence in rituals and the Sufis for affirming my ability to find answers within and reconnecting me to the power of music. Here's to the Parsis for teaching me that nature must be touched lightly, and the Sikhs for the importance of spiritual strength. I thank the gurus for trying to pierce my ego armor and my girlfriends for making me laugh. And most of all, I thank Hinduism for showing me that there are millions of paths to the divine.

Yet, I have brought back something even more important than sacred knowledge. A baby is growing inside me. A baby conceived during our last weekend in the country. This child will forever remind me of the land I lived in and what it took and what it gave. And this baby, made in India, will always remind me that India, to some extent, made me.

ACKNOWLEDGMENTS

Thank you so much to the people who encouraged and assisted me to write my rants into a book. In particular, admiration and adoration to my agent Fiona Inglis, my editors Kim Swivel and Nadine Davidoff, and the ever exuberant Fiona Henderson from Random House.

Lastly and most important, I thank Jonathan and the people of India for taking me on this journey. I've attempted not to take too many liberties with the people who gave me so much. Names have been changed and some characters merged or divided to protect the privacy of certain individuals.

Big love to all the Suzies, Ruth, Jeni, Poonam, the Australian Broadcasting Company India staff and to Prajna, my darling drama queen.

JONATHAN HARLEY

A NOTE ABOUT THE AUTHOR

SARAH MACDONALD grew up in Sydney and studied psychology in college. Rejecting the idea of ever practicing as a shrink, she traveled for a year hoping that a few months in India at the end of the journey would give her a vision of her destiny. It didn't, bar a soothsayer's prediction that she would return. After completing a cadetship at Australian Broadcasting Company Radio News, she worked as a political correspondent called Triple J. Sarah at the highly influential Australian Youth Radio Network, then presented the Youth Network's *Arts Show* and worked on television productions such as *Recovery, Race Around the World* and *Two Shot.* She presented the *Morning Show* until the end of the century, when she left to join her partner, Jonathan Harley, in India. And then the true adventure began. Sarah now presents *Bush Telegraph* on Radio National.